Yesterday's Tomorrows

The Golden Age
of Science Fiction Movie Posters,
1950-1964

Bruce Lanier Wright
Foreword by Ray Harryhausen

Taylor Publishing Company
Dallas, Texas

For My Parents

Designed by Deborah Jackson-Jones

Published by
    Taylor Publishing Company
    1550 West Mockingbird Lane
    Dallas, Texas 75235

Library of Congress Cataloging-in-Publication Data
Wright, Bruce Lanier.
    Yesterday's tomorrows: the golden age of the science fiction movie poster, 1950-1964
    /by Bruce Lanier Wright
    p.   cm.
    ISBN 0-87833-818-7 (hc)   ISBN 0-87833-824-1 (sc)
    1. Film posters. 2. Science fiction films — History and criticism.
    I. Title.
    PN1995.9.P5W75
    791.43'615—dc20   92-34613
                            CIP
Printed in the United States of America
10 9 8 7 6 5 4 3 2 1

Table of Contents

Acknowledgments

Yesterday's Tomorrows benefited from the support of many good people. Dan Orwoll, film collector, scholar, and real sport, made enormous contributions to the preparation of this book. It quite literally would not have been possible without his help. Vaughn Ritchie and Don Regelin also were most gracious in their assistance. Mike Benton, author and *raconteur*, was extremely encouraging and helpful in the early stages of this project, and I am grateful for his support. Jeff Rowe, of Austin Prints For Publication, did a wonderful job with the photography; I have fond memories of chatting conspiracy theories with him as the work progressed.

The astonishing video archives of Mark and Laura Shaw provided me with much research material. The equally humongous movie horde of Parker Riggs also came into play. Special thanks to Jim Aschbacher for helping me track down some rarities. Thanks also to Ron Moore, who rendered valuable assistance in the preparation of the appendix. Melissa Honeycutt helped me with a difficult transition between two computer environments during the course of this book, and I thank her as well.

Extra-special thanks to Parker Riggs, Lavon Dunaway (where *are* you, man?), Ray Files, deceased, and the cast and crew of Mystery Science Theater 3000 for providing Lifetime Bad Influences. Ray, I wish you could have seen this. Eternal thanks to my father, Jack Wright, whose own love of science fiction infected me at a young and impressionable age. And finally, I owe more than I can say to Laura Perkins, who shoved me into this, and whose patience and faith in me has never wavered.

Foreword

The images in this book take me time travelling, to a marvelous age I remember well.

In earlier days, movie posters were magic gateways promising new worlds of adventure and fantasy. The theater owner, with the help of these highly coloured and imaginative posters, brought these strange visions into each community, giving young and malleable minds their first taste of worlds beyond their own.

H.G. Wells stretched his mind far into the future to conceive the wonders his time traveller encountered. Today, the cinema and video are the 20th century's Time Machines. With the

thousands upon thousands of movie subjects available on video and laser disc, we are able to witness the parting of the Red Sea, the tribulations of Cleopatra, and prophecies of what the future may be like — all in the comfort of our own homes.

Wells' grand vision has now come true in more ways than one. Yesterday and Tomorrow are at our fingertips, and all we have to do to range at will throughout history is to visit our local video store. I must admit, though, I eagerly await the perfection of the moving hologram to make it a complete personal fantasy experience. ☾

RAY HARRYHAUSEN

Introduction

As that noted philosopher Scrooge McDuck remarked, no man is poor who can do what he likes, and I like to spend a good deal of time watching the old science fiction movies of the 1950s. My affection for the genre extends to the brightest souvenirs of this peculiar corner of cinema history: the classic science fiction movie posters of 1950 through 1964. These gaudy depictions of robots, rockets, monsters, and time travellers are simply a part of my environment, like faithful childhood friends. I couldn't imagine living any other way, and I know I'm not alone, because 1950s science fiction posters are among the hottest collectors' items today.

My main subject isn't grubby commerce, however, although I discuss the basics of poster collecting elsewhere in this volume. I suppose *Yesterday's Tomorrows* is mostly about love, a quality difficult to communicate through cold print. If these images make your heart beat a little faster, you already understand.

This book features science fiction movie posters, of course, but it's primarily about the films themselves. This is not to say that these posters don't have an intrinsic merit. Most are the products of accomplished illustrators, and can and should be discussed as such. Also, I would be the first to admit that in many, perhaps *most* cases documented here, the posters are better works of art than the films. Moreover, they are often cheats, calculated to lure unwary viewers to movies that had little or nothing to do with the lurid and exciting images depicted in the poster.

Nonetheless, a poster is a tangible expression of a movie, and I cannot separate my affection for these posters from what I feel for the films behind them,

"*F*or those who like this sort of thing, this is the sort of thing they like."

—Max Beerbohm

no matter how cheap-looking or lamely acted. The best 1950s SF movies, such as *Forbidden Planet*, easily outclass the cookie-cutter Schwarz-explosion epics that now haunt our multiplexes each summer. What they lack in shattering glass and exploding heads, they make up with intelligence, wit, and a sense of innocent wonder.

Most of the era's films, of course, don't even approach the rarified heights of the classics. They were made cheaply and quickly, for a fast buck. The actors were obscure players, either on their way up or down; no self-respecting "star" would jeopardize his or her career with such trash. Also, and I think importantly, most 1950s filmmakers knew little and cared less about the rich and imaginative concepts of written science fiction, which at the time—save for a few "breakthrough" authors like Ray Bradbury—was largely a despised and ignored ghetto literature. As John Baxter pointed out in his seminal 1970 work, *Science Fiction in the Cinema*, SF film developed entirely apart from written SF, and for better or worse, they're still separate today. (For what it's worth, I think there are perhaps a dozen films, give or take a few, that qualify as good science fiction in the thoughtful, literary sense.)

However, while the pleasures of the lesser SF films are usually unrelated to their artistic merits, nearly all of these movies possess a certain anarchic charm that transcends their papier-maché production values and often-shoddy scripting and direction. Part of this is nostalgia, of course; these films have a poignant appeal for many of the former kids of that era. But nostalgia isn't the only factor. In fact, I'd venture to say that in some ways, 1950s SF is more popular *now* than when it was made.

Movies like *The Day the Earth Stood Still* seem as timeless and relevant today as when they were made, and, thanks to the video revolution, they're finding new audiences at your local video store, as well as on cable. It's gratifying—for me, at least—to notice how many fans of these films weren't even born when they were released. This isn't true of all "fan" genres; B-Western conventions, for instance, are beginning to look like meetings of the Veterans of the Spanish-American War. With fresh blood, I have reason to hope that interest in 1950s SF movies will live on.

The discussions of individual movies in this book are of necessity brief. Nonetheless, I've tried to go beyond the two-sentences-and-a-critical-assessment approach employed by most surveys of SF film. Call them mini-essays, or "mega-captions." I take these movies seriously, and I try to give them serious attention— when they merit it.

It's worth noting that there are several approaches to discussing '50s science fiction film. The traditional way to critique these films has been simply to treat them like any other movies; for instance, Howard Hawks' *The Thing* has an excellent script, good production values, and competent acting, and therefore it's a good film. The trouble with holding '50s SF to conventional standards is that it can lead you to miss much of what's interesting about these films.

What is one to make of *Attack of the Crab Monsters*, for instance, a zero-budget quickie that's flatly directed and indifferently acted—but has an intriguing, inventive and idea-packed script? Often, you find the best bargains in the basement, and that's

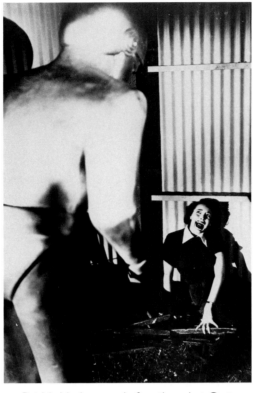

Patricia Neal cowers before the robot Gort, one of science fiction's most memorable icons, in the 1951 classic, *The Day the Earth Stood Still*.

nowhere truer than in these movies. In the last few years, increased awareness of the special qualities of '50s genre film has led to quite a lot of interesting, respectful criticism in publications like *Filmfax* and *Psychotronic*, and I can only applaud this development.

Yet another approach is what might be called the *badfilm* movement (a term coined by the cheerful subversives of the "Church of the Sub-genius"). Badfilm began attracting attention about a decade ago, with books such as *The Golden Turkey Awards*, *The 50 Worst Films of All Time* and *The Psychotronic Encyclopedia of Film*, Joe Bob Briggs' newspaper columns and, not least, the critical rediscovery of the cult classic *Plan Nine From Outer* Space, a "worst-movie-ever" contender that's considerably more entertaining than 90 percent of Hollywood's current output. A central tenet of badfilm theory is that a *truly* bad movie is a *boring* movie. A good badfilm is anything but boring; the question of whether its entertainment value was *intended* by its makers is irrelevant.

Yesterday's Tomorrows falls between these schools, I think. True *badfilm* connoisseurs resent books like *Golden Turkey*, which takes cheap and uninformed shots at low-budget filmmaking. I hope it's clear that I really do have affection for even the worst of these films. However, I don't see any sin in having a little fun with some of the more prominent no-hopers. And, when I believe a film really, really stinks, I say so.

A third approach to film criticism is the academic style, and I do not indulge in this vice. The diploma mills of this great nation belch forth an unending flood of doctoral candidates who must find something—

anything—to deconstruct in suitably impenetrable prose. With the coming of the *auteur* movement in film criticism, and the subsequent discovery by auteurists of directors like Roger Corman and Jack Arnold, '50s SF has been subjected to some of the most incredible pseudo-profound argle-bargle you've ever read. It does little to advance our knowledge of the genre, I think, to read (as I have recently) that the alien vampire in Roger Corman's *Not of This Earth* is actually "a metaphor for the toppling of the personality from within."

I do not mean to imply that academics are incapable of genuine insight into genre film; or perhaps I do. I'll get back to you on that. You will note that I do in fact occasionally use the term *auteur*; in those instances—and I think they are far rarer than academics would have you believe—in which the judgment of a single individual, not necessarily the director, has clearly determined the shape of a movie.

Final notes. First, the images of this book were selected to provide an overview of the best 1950s SF poster art. The films themselves make up a useful survey of the era's films, both good and bad, but the selection is *not* comprehensive, and fans will notice some prominent omissions. Often these are due to the fact that, while the movie itself is a classic, its poster art is either drab and uninteresting or extremely rare. This is the case with two particularly important 1950s SF films, *The War of the Worlds* and *Invasion of the Body Snatchers*, as well as with one of my favorite monster movies, *20 Million Miles To Earth*.

Secondly, I have stretched my definition of the "1950s" all the way to 1964. This is justifiable, I believe, because eras in American history rarely end neatly. The last wisps of what we now remember as the 1950s were still dissipating for some months after the impromptu presidential election of November 1963. Besides, both the films and posters of the early 1960s represent the tail end of the '50s SF boom, and are clearly linked with earlier works. In retrospect, the gap between 1964's *The Time Travellers* and 1968's *2001* seems like much more than a matter of four years—it was a generational leap into a new and entirely different sort of film. ☪

YESTERDAY'S TOMORROWS

It was an Age of Innocence with turquoise tailfins, a land of neon starbursts, atomic-symbol clocks, test-ban treaties, boomerang coffee tables; of New Frontiers, pushbuttons, duck-and-cover drills, and hamburger stands with soaring arches. The words "new and improved" seized the public imagination; toothpaste contained secret ingredients that sounded like rocket fuel, vacuum cleaners looked like Sputniks, and cars sprouted wings.

Postwar America had come home and, to its surprise, had found itself inheritor of a wealth and power unprecedented in human history. Europe and Japan lay in ruins, but in the USA, under the protective mantle of the atom bomb and a global empire, the luckiest one-twentieth of mankind began consuming half the world's bounty. The time dreamed of for so long, so often summed up simply as "After the War," had arrived at last. And the luckiest ones reacted to their good fortune like good Americans. They went shopping for the future.

Yet it was a future that America faced with both joy and trepidation. Despite the soaring prosperity of the times—not shared by everyone, of course, but by

Rod Taylor, as the time traveller George, tests the controls of his elegantly Victorian time machine in George Pal's 1960 film of the same name.

more people than ever before—a quiet, insistent *fear* lurked at the edges of the public consciousness, a Golden Age of Paranoia, an unease symbolized by those civil defense spots on radio and TV: "This is *only* a test," they promised, but would the day come when the warning was in earnest? Children taught to hide beneath their school desks in case of nuclear attack learned to question the apparent permanence of the American Century.

And what of the Other? What about those strange lights in the sky, seen by so many people? And what of that menace, that Bear, bottled up in its frigid, disagreeable territories across the sea? It, too, possessed the ultimate power; stolen from us, of course, but the Atom serves anyone who holds its secrets. Were there agents among us, seeking to subvert from within? In their ranch-style homes, in half-finished subdivisions across the nation, Americans wondered: *Could we lose all this?*

They were rich, nervous, improbable times, in an America that had reached its zenith, in an age that today seems as dead and distant as the pharaohs. It was a science fiction kind of place. ☪

The 1950s Space Program

Shortly after World War II, in a lonely stretch of the New Mexican desert called White Sands, America began tinkering with the German missiles and scientists it had "liberated" from Hitler. (Master survivor Wernher von Braun made it easy for us, thoughtfully loading a truck convoy with interesting bits of equipment and driving for the American lines; he had no wish to end his days as a "guest worker" for Papa Joe Stalin.) Soon, creditable copies of the V-2 rockets that had so recently smashed into London's docklands were soaring through the deep blue New Mexico skies. The military's interest was clear. Missiles promised to be ideal delivery vehicles for the A-bomb.

Others aimed higher. The first films taken from American V-2 clones showed the ground dwindling away impossibly fast, until the earth's curvature was clearly visible. These newsreel images were enormously impressive to audiences of the late 1940s and later, as stock footage, found their way into a number of 1950s science fiction films. Suddenly, the dreams of lonely visionaries like Robert Goddard, who had imagined manned rocket flights in the 1920s, didn't seem quite so fantastic.

American publishers also played an important role in preparing the public for the coming leap into space. A series of coffee-table books by our dependable Teutonic rocketeers, von Braun and Willy Ley, helped to stimulate America's interest in the possibilities of space travel. Perhaps most influential of all was Ley's 1949 work, *The Conquest of Space.*

The Conquest of Space is a popular scientific account of the problems and possibilities of space travel. By today's standards, it's not a particularly difficult work, but one suspects that it was the *A Brief History of Time* of its day, much purchased and admired but little read. However, the book's real attractions were its astonishing illustrations by renowned astronomical painter Chesley Bonestell. Bonestell's painting was characterized by razor-sharp,

> ## "Who controls the Moon controls the Earth!"
> —"General Thayer" in *Destination Moon*

photo-realistic rendering and rigorous mathematical and scientific accuracy. The Moon missions and our unmanned exploration of the solar system have invalidated many of the assumptions on which Bonestell based his art, but such was his talent that even today, his work has the curious quality of appearing *more* real than the reality we've since discovered.

One can imagine the effect these paintings had on the audiences of the day. Bonestell showed us the Future. All that remained was for us to reach out and claim it. Naturally, when Hollywood decided to make the trip first, Chesley Bonestell was enlisted immediately.

In 1948, a meeting between Hungarian-born filmmaker George Pal and Robert Heinlein, America's greatest science fiction writer, led to the production of the screen's first serious story concerning space travel. By today's standards, *Destination Moon* (1950) is a plodding account of the first Moon mission marred by insipid comedy relief; it's currently fashionable to dismiss the film as hopelessly dull. (*Rocketship X-M*, a cheapie cranked out a few months before *Destination Moon*'s premiere to cash in on the latter's advance publicity, seems to have more fans at present.)

However, there's much to respect in *Destination Moon*'s painfully earnest, documentary approach to space travel. Gorgeous background paintings by Chesley Bonestell typify the film's admirable insistence on technical accuracy. *Destination Moon* was a major financial success in its day, and its graceful, Bonestell-designed spaceship *Luna* became the prototype for all respectable spacecraft until superceded by the humdrum reality of the Mercury Redstone rocket. Similarly, many of the movie's features—such as the voyagers' comical reactions to weightlessness and their near-miss encounter with a meteor shower—are repeated in later films as if by rote.

But while *Destination Moon* spurred the entire 1950s science fiction wave, it had relatively little

The cracked-mud lunar surface—an inaccuracy that appalled production artist Chesley Bonestell—of George Pal's groundbreaking *Destination Moon*.

influence on the films that followed it. Scientific accuracy and convincing visual effects were expensive and time-consuming, and producers quickly found they could dispense with them and still turn a profit. Furthermore, most 1950s SF films involve either earthly menaces or aliens that come to *us*, for fair or foul purposes. The idea that *we* might go to *them* was relatively rare. This might seem to indicate a certain pessimism about manned space flight on the part of writers and producers, but it probably has a lot more to do with the fact that earthly props and sets are more congenial to limited budgets.

In 1951, schlock specialists Monogram Pictures released their own *Destination Moon* clone, *Flight to Mars*. The picture begins with much the same pseudo-documentary air as *Destination Moon*, but soon betrays everything the earlier film tried to accomplish; the spaceship's crew encounters a perfectly human, English-speaking Martian civilization, complete with scantily clad Mars maids and a Ruritanian plot to conquer the earth, which our heroes naturally foil. Two years later, with *Cat-Women of the Moon*, Hollywood in effect answered the question "How low can you go with these space sagas?" with a succinct "Got a shovel?" *Cat-Women* is, nonetheless, a fan favorite today, if only because it staggers the imagination that *anyone* could have intended this movie to be taken seriously.

Another 1953 effort, *Project Moonbase*, shares *Cat-Women*'s spit-and-cardboard look—in fact, the spaceship interiors in both films are so similar I suspect that they're the same set—but at least it deserves points for a more adult approach, possibly due to Robert Heinlein's involvement in the script, his second and last such effort. Heinlein's work was substantially altered, however, and *Moonbase* is no *Destination Moon*. A "battle of the sexes" subplot, involving a will-they-won't-they relationship between male and female astronauts, may have seemed cute forty years ago but plays like pure lead today.

George Pal returned to the space-travel theme in his film *Conquest of Space*, one of the saddest misfires in science fiction history. The film bears no direct connection with Ley's 1949 book, although Chesley Bonestell returned to provide more of his always-wonderful visuals. Despite his involvement, however, and minor contributions by Wernher von Braun as a "technical advisor," the film is a turgid disaster due to a rotten script that peoples the Mars mission with offensive racial stereotypes and —crowning inanity!—arbitrarily forces the expedition's commander to become a homicidal religious fanatic!

With a single exception, the films of the 1950s Space Program deal with near-future expeditions —maiden voyages to Earth's immediate neighbors. This may reflect the excitement and anticipation felt over our imminent step into space, or, more likely, the filmmakers' lack of imagination. However, we can be grateful the era gave us at least one

Astronauts prepare for a shuttle ride to "the Wheel" in George Pal's pretty but disappointing *The Conquest of Space.*

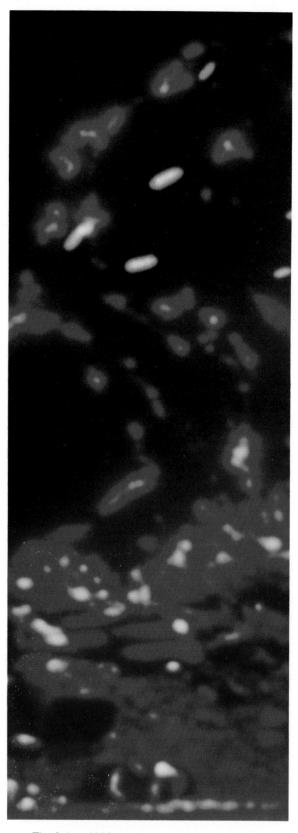

The furious Id Monster rages against a force field, in a colorful effect created by Disney animators for the 1956 stunning space opera, *Forbidden Planet*.

space-exploration movie that achieved something different: *Forbidden Planet*.

Although its themes were common enough in the era's science fiction magazines, *Forbidden Planet* is the *only* SF film made in the 1950s that postulates a more distant future in which man has moved out into the galaxy, exploring and colonizing new star systems. (*Star Trek*, a perfect distillation of mediocre 1940s space opera, owes quite a lot to this ground-breaking movie.) Blessed with a sizeable budget, superb special effects—many of which haven't been bettered, even today—and, more importantly, thought-provoking and literate concepts, *Forbidden Planet* is one of the very few SF movies ever made that reflects something of the fertile imagination of the best literary science fiction.

Unfortunately, *Forbidden Planet* was, for its day, a very expensive gamble, and one that didn't pay off. Its disappointing box-office receipts squelched what might have been a significant movement toward upscale, intelligent science fiction. As if to prove that *Forbidden Planet* was indeed a fluke, the same year also brought us the ghastly *Fire Maidens of Outer Space*, a *Cat-Women of the Moon* without the unintentional humor.

Meanwhile, the real-life exploration of space, so confidently predicted by Ley, von Braun, and others, was beginning at last. On October 4, 1957, America was shaken by news of the launch of the first orbital satellite, Sputnik I. The Soviet satellite, circling the earth every ninety minutes at an altitude of about 600 miles, was a direct and personal affront to western notions of technical superiority.

From a blasé 1990s perspective, it's hard to imagine the impact this event had on the public. Senator Henry "Scoop" Jackson called the launches a "devastating blow" to American pride. President Eisenhower made a hurried television appearance to reassure Americans that our own space program, Project Vanguard, was making progress. Shortly afterward, on December 6, 1957, when a Vanguard rocket exploded on the ground during takeoff from Cape Canaveral, Florida, America's humiliation seemed complete. The U.S. finally succeeded in lifting a small Explorer satellite into orbit on January 31, 1958, but Russia's lead in rocketry lasted for several more years, and talk of a "missile gap" provided lively political fodder for the 1960 presidential campaign.

Zsa Zsa Gabor is under the gun while a befuddled Earthman looks on in the bizarre semi-comedy, *Queen of Outer Space*.

As to what effect these events had on the science fiction films of the day, the astonishing answer was: almost none. There was a brief vogue for (illogically) calling spacecraft and UFOs "satellites," but films concerning manned space exploration remained stuck in their post-*Destination Moon* rut. In film after film—in *Queen of Outer Space, Twelve to the Moon, Angry Red Planet, Journey to the Seventh Planet,* and others—the same sorts of wearily intrepid crews face similar menaces (nearly always including those damned meteor showers), fight rubber monsters, and sample the charms of leggy space women.

The cycle played itself out, probably killed by an overdose of reality. When real space travel becomes mundane—and I will *never* cease to be amazed at how quickly America became bored with its Moon missions—it may be that there is no room left for fictional treatments of the same thing.

Ironically, in recent years the pattern of the 1950s Space Program has been almost totally reversed. The American public seems to have lost its taste for exploring space, probably dreading the tax bill. There hasn't been a decent realistic treatment of near-future space travel since 1968's *2001*. But at our theaters, space opera is a big seller. We still enjoy travel to the stars, it seems, but only if it's a long, long time ago, in galaxies far, far away. ☾

Worlds Enough, and Time

Despite the relentlessly sunny good cheer of America's media-dominated culture, many Americans found life in the 1950s to be a complicated affair. The '50s saw the large-scale introduction of many modern plagues—urban sprawl, and the often sterile life of the suburbs; limited, frustratingly inconclusive warfare in hot and cold varieties—and beneath the headlines, at a nagging, pre-conscious level, a constant pressure for uniformity in public and private life.

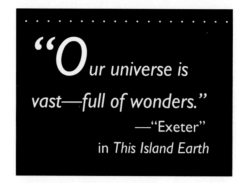

"*Our universe is vast—full of wonders.*"
—"Exeter"
in *This Island Earth*

In business, the grey-suited Organization Man came into his own, while home life, the proper domain for "well-adjusted" women, was measured against the Nelsons, Cleavers, and other television fantasies. During the commercial breaks, Madison Avenue cheerfully helped to tighten the screws, cultivating an increasingly frantic cult of consumerism. George Walker, Ford Motors' chief designer, beautifully summarized the era's attitude toward consumption: "We design a car to make a man unhappy with his 1957 Ford 'long about the end of 1958," he proudly announced.

It's not surprising that so much of 1950s popular culture expresses a wistful longing for simpler worlds. It seems no accident, for instance, that Americans of the period went absolutely gaga over westerns, which expressed such crisp moral certainties, and delivered simple and final solutions to life's problems. For the same reasons, I suspect, the '50s also marked the apogee of America's interest in ancient historical epics, a genre virtually dead today.

Science fiction, of course, was by definition ideally suited to deliver a wide variety of other worlds to those weary of mundane, mid-twentieth-century civilization. One of the era's most brilliant SF films, *The Incredible Shrinking Man*, explored the notion of worlds *within* worlds. In the movie's harrowing finale, the hero, shrunk to insect size by a mysterious encounter with a radioactive cloud, becomes a latter-day frontiersman forced to fight for survival in the vast, hostile wilderness of his own basement. Another excellent film, special effects master Ray Harry-hausen's adaptation of H.G. Wells' *First Men in the Moon*, looks simultaneously backwards and forwards by chronicling the adventures of the first lunar expedition—in the year 1899. Few period SF works have been filmed so faithfully or successfully.

A few films revived romantic, Edwardian notions of lost worlds hidden in isolated regions here on earth. Universal's odd 1956 film *The Mole People* concerns a lost pocket of Sumerian civilization living deep below the Earth's surface; the next year, the sporadically interesting *The Land Unknown* gave us a dinosaur-haunted Mesozoic world tucked away in a hidden Antarctic valley. George Pal's garish *Atlantis, The Lost Continent*, attempts to evoke the splendors of the mythic past, but trips over its own velour robes in the attempt, combining half-baked science fiction elements with the vulgarism of the era's worst sword-and-sandal mock-epics. (A few years later, a bizarre Japanese SF movie marketed in America as *Atragon* would revive the more obscure lost continent of Lemuria, whose inhabitants threaten the world from their sunken home beneath the Pacific.)

Still more Other Worlds lay in outer space. 1962's awesomely wretched *The Phantom Planet* is a moronic *Lost Horizon* involving a castaway astronaut who finds love and adventure, of a sort, among the six-inch-tall inhabitants of a wandering asteroid, only to lose his miniscule space beauty when duty forces him to return to the realm of full-sized men. To the extent that the film is about *anything*, it's oddly reminiscent of a South Seas adventure; the simple natives even dine on synthetic breadfruit.

A significantly better film, *This Island Earth*, interestingly inverts the prevalent '50s desire for a simpler world by thrusting humans into the midst of galactic war between faceless aggressors—the Zahgons—and an advanced but largely unsympathetic

One of the warty, bug-eyed principals of *The Mole People* puts the squeeze
on veteran Universal character actor Nestor Paiva.

Pee Wee's Playhouse? No, it's the comically fierce elasmosaur,
in an unconvincing still from Virgil Vogel's lost-world yarn, *The Land Unknown*.

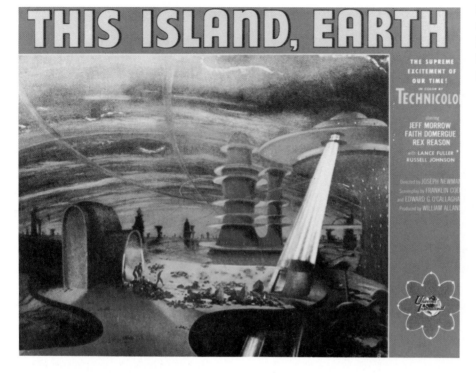

THE SUPREME
EXCITEMENT OF
OUR TIME!
IN COLOR BY
TECHNICOLO

starring
JEFF MORROW
FAITH DOMERGUE
REX REASON
with LANCE FULLER
RUSSELL JOHNSON

Directed by JOSEPH NEWMAN
Screenplay by FRANKLIN COE
and EDWARD G. O'CALLAGHA
Produced by WILLIAM ALLAND

Earthlings flee the crumbling underworld refuge of Metalunan civilization, in a much-wanted lobby card poster from *This Island Earth.*

civilization, the Metalunans, who regard Earth as a sort of third-world nation to be plundered for its resources (in this case, nuclear scientists). In *This Island Earth,* Earth is the primitive backwater, and *humans* are the simple natives, ripe for exploitation. Even so, the scientist hero invokes the implicit claim of Noble Savages everywhere to moral superiority, twitting the Metalunans' leader about the humans' closer relationship to God.

Finally, a quartet of 1950s SF movies explored a similar theme while taking a different route to other worlds: time travel. By far the best of these was George Pal's 1960 adaptation of H.G. Wells' *The Time Machine.* While mostly faithful to the book, Pal's movie replaces Wells' didactic socialism with a more red-blooded, American-style faith in action and

physical courage. The far-future Eloi have fallen into a lassitude so profound that they're literally cattle to the subterranean Morlocks, but Pal's time traveller, a heroic man of action, is able to shock them out of their torpor and teach them to fight again.

The same idea is present in the highly similar *World Without End, Beyond the Time Barrier,* and *The Time Travellers,* each of which places variations of *The Time Machine*'s Eloi in a devastated, post-nuclear world. In all three films, intrepid time travellers from the present day prove themselves morally and physically superior to the super-scientific but effete and bloodless survivors of tomorrow.

It was a message any harried account executive of the era might well have taken to heart. Clearly, civilization can become too much of a good thing. ☾

Big Trouble!

According to pulp writer H.P. Lovecraft, "The most merciful thing in the world...is the inability of the human mind to correlate all its contents." That forboding phrase, written in 1926, neatly captures America's attitude toward the atomic age it ushered in at Hiroshima—an attitude characterized above all by *denial*.

The development of atomic power received a curiously muted and ambivalent treatment in the American mass media of the 1950s. Throughout the era, official propaganda concerning the atom was endlessly upbeat. The messages ranged from the 1953 "atoms for peace" campaign, which promised a paradise of cheap energy, nuclear-powered Chevys and the like, to the can-do optimism of civil defense programs that assured us a few more inches of topsoil on the root cellar would be more than enough to fend off pesky Russian gamma rays.

> *"The release of atom power has changed everything except our way of thinking."*
> —Albert Einstein

The harsher realities of the nuclear age remained hidden—the Japanese fishing boat fatally contaminated during the U.S.'s Pacific "Bravo" bomb test in 1954; the 1957 Russian nuclear accident in the Urals, which irradiated hundreds of square miles; the forty pounds of plutonium scattered across the Australian outback by the British government in the early 1960s—and the fatal persistence of radioactivity received little attention in the mainstream discourse of the era.

At times, nuclear holocaust seemed to be virtually walled off from conscious thought and public debate, as a topic too terrible to be considered, a problem with no solution. As author Mick Broderick has pointed out, it was a fear that debilitated and led to resignation rather than anger or outrage. Even so, despite mass denial and the government's best public-relations efforts, the image of the mushroom

Makeup man Paul Blaisdell, wearing his own costume as the three-eyed, radioactive mutant menace in Roger Corman's *Day the World Ended.*

cloud had wormed its way too firmly into America's psyche to be dispelled.

Only a handful of the era's films, such as Roger Corman's *Day the World Ended*, looked at atomic war directly, and even these movies ended with a hint that "normalcy" might someday be restored. Another end-of-the-world opus, George Pal's *When Worlds Collide*, was actually based on a pre-atomic novel of the early 1930s, but its relevance for the nervous years of the 1950s was clear. That film too ends with the requisite note of hope, as a tiny fragment of mankind escapes to begin life anew on an idyllic garden planet.

Despite the scarcity of direct treatments, however, atom-fear bubbles to the surface repeatedly in 1950s science fiction cinema. It's been said that the modern horror tale is "a rehearsal for death," a way of becoming accustomed to the idea of personal mortality. But these films cover a larger canvas, as rehearsals for the death of the race. And amazingly often, the atomic threat comes in the guise of an enormous monster, what author John Brosnan has aptly dubbed "the metaphor that ate Tokyo."

This symbolism is explicit in the era's seminal Big Trouble movie, Ray Harryhausen's *The Beast From 20,000 Fathoms* (1953). The film concerns a primordial dinosaur, freed from an icy tomb in the Arctic by a nuclear test, which eventually comes ashore at New York. The army wounds the creature only to find that its blood spreads a virulent disease—a suitable analogue for radiation. The atom, which brought the dinosaur to life, becomes the vehicle of its destruction when the beast is slain by a rifle grenade loaded with a radioactive isotope.

The Beast's impressive box-office success spurred another excellent movie in the following year. *Them!* is a tense and effective story of giant ants,

Top: Big Trouble arrives: Ray Harryhausen's "rhedosaurus" sees New York, stomps same, in the seminal monster tale, *The Beast From 20,000 Fathoms*.
Middle: Dr. Pat Medford (Joan Weldon), plucky entomologist and love interest, encounters a giant ant in the much-imitated 1954 bug epic, *Them!*
Bottom: One of the molecularly altered, heat-projecting, brain-absorbing giant crabs of Roger Corman's intriguing *Attack of the Crab Monsters*.

born in the nuclear fires of the first bomb test at Alamagordo, New Mexico, that ravage the American Southwest. *Them!* was one of the first movies to deal with the threat of radiation-induced mutation, the era's most common method for creating monsters.

Them! led to numerous imitators, most prominently Jack Arnold's *Tarantula*, which places an enormous, hostile spider in the same lonely South-western desert as the earlier film. The nuclear theme is more muted in *Tarantula*, but it's worth noting that the artificial nutrient that spawns the monstrous bug is "atomically stabilized."

After a brief pause, the Big Trouble school of film *exploded* in 1957. In Roger Corman's weirdly inventive *Attack of the Crab Monsters*, the jumbo crustaceans of the title are the inadvertent offspring of South Pacific nuclear testing, while the giant grasshoppers of Bert I. Gordon's silly *Beginning of the End* grow as a result of eating radioactive foodstuffs at an experimental government laboratory. Before a scientist-hero devises a way to end the menace, the military is seen rather casually contemplating the atomic "sterilization" of Chicago as a means of wiping out the voracious bugs.

In Gordon's follow-up movie, *The Amazing Colossal Man*, a man exposed to the full force of an atomic blast mutates into a deranged giant that ultimately threatens Las Vegas. The movie is a mediocre affair at best and obviously derivative of the *The Incredible Shrinking Man*, but it was successful enough to generate both a sequel (*War of the Colossal Beast*) and an imitation (*Attack of the 50 Foot Woman*, which is significantly more entertaining, though not necessarily better).

In 1959, Eugene Lourié, director of *The Beast From 20,000 Fathoms*, released a semi-remake of the earlier picture called *The Giant Behemoth*. *Behemoth* features a seagoing monster generated by atomic radiation, but this time, the huge lizard is itself lethally radioactive. *Behemoth* is a fairly lackluster outing, but it's interesting for its explicitly antinuclear stance, a rarity in those days. The movie's scientist-protagonist delivers an impassioned and interestingly prescient

Giant grasshoppers wander the streets of the Windy City in Bert I. Gordon's bargain-basement bug romp, *The Beginning of the End*.

warning against the hazards of radioactive waste.

A clutch of films flowing from earlier Big Trouble outings lack overt atomic themes, but, with their scientific bells and whistles and their predilection for destroying metropolitan areas, they still resonate as metaphors for the Big One. Such films include the horrendous *The Deadly Mantis* and *The Giant Claw*, which unleash a giant praying mantis and a supersonic space-bird with an antimatter shield; the critters pay deadly visits to Washington and New York, respectively. The far more interesting *Monolith Monsters* concerned a mysterious crystalline meteor from outer space. The crystal induces a gradual petrifica-tion in its victims—like the *Beast*'s pestilent blood, the effect is suggestive of radiation poisoning—and grows until it threatens to wipe out a nearby town.

The Big Trouble trend in movies faded out ignominiously in the early 1960s. The real Big Trouble is still out there, of course, despite our best efforts to ignore it. ☪

Invaders From Elsewhere

According to a joint Air Force and Naval Intelligence report declassified in 1985, these were the last words transmitted by Captain Mantell, whose P-51 Mustang crashed as he investigated a UFO sighting near Godman Air Force Base in Kentucky. Mantell's death was officially attributed to pilot error due to oxygen starvation; the UFO sighting was variously "explained" by the military as the planet Venus and the ever-popular weather balloon.

The unfortunate Captain Mantell may indeed have perished due to anoxia, or he may be an early martyr to a continuing mystery. Strange Things were sighted in the night skies of the 1950s. A new and disquieting acronym, UFO, entered the American consciousness, and visitors from outer space became the single most common theme in the ensuing science fiction movie boom.

Science fiction fans and writers alike tend to be nineteenth-century rationalists at heart, and by and large they're utterly dismissive of all paranormal claims—possibly because, in their hearts, they feel that this skepticism helps them atone for the peculiarly un-American sin of imagination. At any rate, most surveys of science fiction include a *pro forma* statement of derision concerning the great 1950s UFO craze.

Note that I'm not following suit.

I'm not a "believer" in any dogma, and I'm quite aware that the UFO world has a loud and lively lunatic fringe. There's very little we can say with any certainty about the saucer phenomenon. But one thing we *can* feel sure about, thanks to the federal Freedom of Information Act (FOIA), is this: *During the 1950s, our government lied its collective buns off concerning UFOs.*

As late as 1973, then-FBI director Clarence Kelley blandly stated that "the investigation of Unidentified Flying Objects is not and never has been...within the investigative jurisdiction of the FBI." Three years later, an FOIA request yielded some 1,100 pages of agency reports on the subject. The Air Force, meanwhile, spent much of the 1950s reinforcing myths such as "UFOs have never been tracked on radar"; a detailed Air Force intelligence report declassified in 1985 describes a series of radar sightings, involving up to twelve unidentified "targets" at a time, made at Washington National Airport during the celebrated UFO flap of July 1952.

So what? So nothing, I guess. If our rulers know much more about UFOs than we do, they're not talking. And the press, which performed yeoman service in perforating the Air Force's "swamp gas" explanations of the 1960s, seems to have returned the subject permanently to its nut files. The mechanics of our informal national policy of censorship by ridicule haven't changed much since they were detailed in 1953's *It Came From Outer Space.*

Writers by the dozen have attributed the popularity of alien invasion stories in the 1950s to Cold-War tensions, and I also believe this is largely true. But perhaps we should pause briefly and remember that, as Freud said, sometimes a cigar is just a cigar. At least some of the alien hordes that whizzed across America's theater screens in the 1950s weren't metaphors for *anything*, but a genuine reflection of the nation's fear and wonder at an inexplicable phenomenon.

This said, it's not hard to understand why so many see the Invaders From Elsewhere cycle as an elaborate sublimation for the collective Red Mania that gripped America in the early and mid-1950s. It was a mistrustful and sometimes frightening time. There were perils aplenty right here on earth without dragging other worlds into the picture.

> "*I*t appears to be a metallic object... tremendous in size...directly ahead and slightly above...I am trying to close for a better look."
> —National Guard Captain Thomas Mantell, January 7, 1948

Paul Blaisdell's endearingly absurd Saucer-Men strike a belligerent pose in this rare lobby card from *Invasion of the Saucer-Men*. What *is* that can-opener thing?

CREEPING HORROR...
From the depths of time and space!

INVASION OF THE SAUCER-MEN

STEVE TERRELL • GLORIA CASTILLO • FRANK GORSHIN • Executive Producer SAMUEL Z. ARKOFF
Produced by JAMES H. NICHOLSON and ROBERT GURNEY Jr. • Directed by EDWARD L. CAHN • Screenplay by AL MARTIN
Additional Dialogue by ROBERT GURNEY Jr. • A MALIBU PRODUCTION • AN AMERICAN INTERNATIONAL PICTURE

Before we vent our fashionably liberal disapproval of the era's excesses, it's salutary to recall that Americans of the 1950s had reason to feel threatened by international events. Particularly troublesome were 1949's twin blows to our complacency—the "fall" of China to Mao Tse Tung's not-so-tender mercies, which put most of the vast Eurasian landmass under communist control, and the detonation of the U.S.S.R.'s first atomic bomb, along with the subsequent discovery that Russian espionage had played a part in its development. Red scares are a perennial theme of twentieth-century U.S. politics, but the loss of America's nuclear monopoly made the communist threat a vivid and personal one. (I recall asking my mother, during the Cuban missile crisis of 1962, whether we were going to die. I was six years old at the time.)

Even so, many events in the America of the 1950s seem marked by a kind of madness difficult to understand in our more jaded era. It was a Cold War in a much more real sense than the pallid and cynical confrontations of the 1970s, a kind of jihad—a time in which Revlon's "Russian Sable" face powder was withdrawn and retitled; in which Monogram Pictures cancelled a film concerning Hiawatha because the Indian leader's peace-making efforts among warring tribes might be interpreted as "communistic"; in which Las Vegas casino owners forced their employees, including B-girls and strippers, to sign loyalty oaths.

Battle lines were being drawn in America. Preparedness was everything, and pleas for peace, understanding and cooperation were automatically suspect. This divide between opposing mindsets spilled over into science fiction cinema. In 1951, two excellent films, Howard Hawks' *The Thing From Another World* and Robert Wise's *The Day the Earth Stood Still*, marked the opposite poles.

In *The Thing*, hard-headed Average Joes of the Air Force successfully battle an inimical alien at an isolated Arctic scientific base. The scientists' leader, goateed and vaguely Russian-looking, betrays the military's efforts due to his misguided belief that a creature capable of space travel must be susceptible to sweet reason. His motives may be pure, but his ivory-tower ideals very nearly get everyone else killed.

The Day the Earth Stood Still, by contrast, argues the opposite case with a conviction and forcefulness that today seem downright astonishing, considering the nation's mood at the time. The movie's alien emissary refuses to take sides in Earth's Cold-War shenanigans—refuses to take *our* side, the side of Right and Light!—and warns us that our own aggression may lead to our extinction. The film's military men seem like misguided children compared with the kindly, rational scientist who becomes the alien's ally.

The philosophies expressed in *The Thing* and *The Day the Earth Stood Still* can be found at war throughout the era's Invaders From Elsewhere movies. Sometimes the viewpoints are embodied in opposing characters, often, as in 1959's *The Cosmic Man*, a scientist and a military officer. In terms of sheer volume, though, 1950s science fiction movies came down firmly on the side of paranoia. In film after film—*Target Earth, Earth Versus the Flying Saucers, It Conquered the World* (a giveaway, that), *The Crawling Eye*, and many more—other worldly life is simply a menace, to be battled and stamped out (an attitude rarely expressed in written SF then or since, by the way).

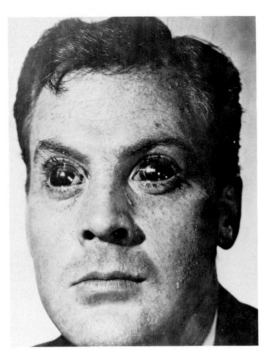

Science fiction stalwart John Agar, possessed by an evil space brain, makes Spooky Eyes in the energetic *The Brain From Planet Arous*.

Sometimes the aliens arrive in force, like the flying-saucer fleet in *Earth Versus the Flying Saucers;* just as often, though, they infiltrate quietly as fifth-columnists and saboteurs, as in Gene Fowler's excellent *I Married a Monster From Outer Space* and the ludicrous *Satan's Satellites*. In either case, though, aliens are just No Damned Good. Interestingly, these malevolent ETs were nearly always portrayed as aloof, logical, and unemotional, qualities we often imputed to our chess-playing communist enemies as well; offhand, only the gleefully sadistic *Brain From Planet Arous* comes to mind as an exception to this rule. (Another decade would elapse before *Star Trek*'s Mr. Spock could make a virtue of alien stoicism.)

Sometimes subversion took a particularly ugly form. One trend in bad-alien movies of the 1950s may owe something to a disturbing event of the Korean War. After a dramatic opening year, the conflict settled into an inconclusive series of retreats and advances that led some to dub it the "concertina war." One of the inevitable outcomes of such warfare was the taking of about 7,000 American prisoners. Approximately a third of them died under harsh and brutal conditions; even more disturbing, though, was the revelation that as many as one in three American P.O.W.s had collaborated with their captors in signing confessions, denouncing the U.S. for "war crimes."

This depressing spectacle was attributed to techniques of indoctrination, interrogation, and systematic terror developed by Mao's Red Chinese, with KGB aid, which came to be called *brainwashing*. In retrospect, the fact that prisoners succumbed to torture, drugging, and starvation seems understandable enough, but at the time, this ability to turn men against their own kind seemed almost like a terrifyingly supernatural power. This theme—the loss of will or identity—emerges again and again in 1950s SF cinema.

In Roger Corman's *It Conquered the World*, a cone-shaped Venusian neutralizes a small town by establishing hypnotic control over key authority figures. Furry entities from beneath the Earth's surface execute a similar scheme in 1958's *The Brain Eaters*. In the same year, *The Brain From Planet Arous* controlled the mind and will of a scientist in a way reminiscent of demonic possession, while the squidlike aliens of *The Crawling Eye* make zombieish slaves of dead men. Perhaps most terrifying of all are

Peter Graves grapples with Beulah, the unforgettable Venusian cucumber menace in Roger Corman's *It Conquered the World*.

the eerie, sky-spawned children of *Village of the Damned*, who can force their victims to do anything—even commit suicide—with a glance from their silvery eyes.

It seems telling that movies weighing in on the side of *The Day the Earth Stood Still* were far rarer during the 1950s. It just wasn't a trusting era; fear of the Other was too great. The mistreated alien in Edgar G. Ulmer's minor classic of 1951, *The Man From Planet X*, the interplanetary castaways of *It Came From Outer Space*, and the benign visitor of *The Cosmic Man* were, at best, exceptions that proved the rule of *de facto* antagonism between Us and Them. ☪

Gloria Talbott learns just how little she knows about her husband in the surprisingly adult and effective *I Married a Monster From Outer Space*.

Bogey Persons

Science fiction and horror have enjoyed successive waves of popularity and eclipse throughout the history of the movies, and sometimes a period of decline for one genre has been a boom time for the other. The two genres often seem like opposite faces of the same coin, the Rational and Irrational, ego and id battling for dominance of America's collective subconscious.

To say this, of course, is to imply we can draw a definite line between science fiction and horror movies. The closer we examine that line, however, the more indefinite it seems.

For instance, it's not enough to say, as some writers have, that horror is fundamentally pessimistic while science fiction is fundamentally optimistic. This might be largely true of literary horror and SF, but as John Baxter has noted, science fiction film is often *profoundly* pessimistic—really closer to "anti-science" fiction in spirit. As we have seen, this was particularly true in the 1950s.

Mood also plays an important part. Many film scholars have commented on the stark contrast between the atmospheric trappings of the horror films of the 1930s and 1940s—those fog-shrouded graveyards in moonlight—and the flat, grey, matter-of-fact appearance of most 1950s SF. Of course, that flat look was more often dictated by budget than by choice. And what about *The Thing*, which is at once more frightening and more atmospheric than most horror films, but still (at least to me) pretty clearly a science fiction story?

A more formal definition might run as follows: The extraordinary elements in science fiction must turn on either accepted science or reasonably plausible pseudo-science (hello, *Star Trek*), while horror contains elements of pure fantasy presented *without* reference to technology. Of course, by this definition both *Frankenstein* and *Dr. Jekyll and Mr. Hyde* are

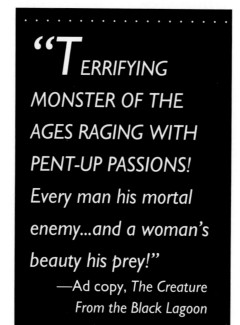

"*T*ERRIFYING MONSTER OF THE AGES RAGING WITH PENT-UP PASSIONS! *Every man his mortal enemy...and a woman's beauty his prey!*"
—Ad copy, *The Creature From the Black Lagoon*

science fiction movies, even though few people think of them that way. (And, for that matter, this definition of horror excludes all those tedious butcher-knife sagas of the 1980s, which is perfectly all right with me.)

At any rate, while these definitions may fall short, they at least help us make our own decisions in separating the two genres. Science fiction and horror are characterized by their own unique conventions—and, as film scholar Bill Warren has said, it's a difference more of approach than content—but there's enough blending at the edges to ensure that everyone has to draw the line for themselves.

For instance, a friend of mine recently took semi-serious umbrage at my calling *I Was a Teenage Werewolf* a science fiction movie. However, while its makeup and transformation-attack-remorse plot structure are obviously modeled on Universal's *The Wolf Man, Teenage Werewolf* is entirely devoid of the earlier movie's supernatural trappings. Michael Landon becomes the Teenage Werewolf through a combination of drugs and hypnotic therapy. There's no curse involved, no wolfbane or full moons, and no suggestion that only a silver bullet can slay him; conventional police ammunition eventually proves quite satisfactory.

And that, I think, is the real significance of 1950s Bogey Persons—the transliteration of traditional horror and supernatural themes into science fiction.

The 1930s and 1940s are now regarded as the Golden Age of horror movies, largely due to the popularity and continuing reputation of Universal's horror cycle (*Frankenstein, The Mummy,* and the rest, as well as their legions of sequels). Science fiction film was much less popular during the 1930s, limited to a few forms—Buck Rogers space opera, like, well, *Buck Rogers*; ponderous social commentary, such as H.G. Wells' interesting but cold *Things to Come,* and gothic,

The Last Classic Monster: a publicity shot of Jack Arnold's *Creature of the Black Lagoon*.
His ruby-red lipstick isn't apparent in the black-and-white film.

is-it-horror-or-is it-SF films like *The Invisible Man*. By the 1940s, SF film had virtually vanished. Perhaps the Allies were too busy waging war on a very real band of mad scientists to take much comfort in seeing them on the screen.

However, by 1950, the tables had turned. The horror cycle that began in the early 1930s sputtered out with increasingly wretched mad-doctor movies and—worse insult—the low-brow slapstick of the Abbot and Costello horror comedies. Compared with the technological horrors unleashed at the end of World War II, caped vampires with quaint accents seemed pathetically old-fashioned. *Science* was now the force to be reckoned with, the primary source of America's hopes and fears, and the movies soon reflected this new interior landscape.

But the Irrational never really goes away, after all. It just moves with the times, transmuting itself to match our subconscious expectations. A number of 1950s science fiction movies put a shiny veneer of science on the traditional Bogey Persons (for some

are women, after all) and revived them to new popularity. We've already seen how the Wolf Man was re-introduced; Dracula showed up again as well, in various guises—an alien seeking blood for his dying civilization, in Roger Corman's *Not of This Earth*, and a wraithlike vampire who feeds on his victims' life force, in the interesting *4D Man*. The Invisible Man, arguably a SF character already, was dusted off and updated as an interstellar visitor in *Phantom From Space*.

And what were the *Devil Girl From Mars* and *The Astounding She Monster* but witches? Both have witchy sorts of frightening, inexplicable powers, and sour dispositions to match. The Devil Girl, in particular, is such an archetypal witchwoman in costume and mannerism that you almost expect her to blight the crops and sour the cows' milk. Another feminine Bogey Person, Roger Corman's silly *The Wasp Woman*, borrows heavily from *Dr. Jekyll and Mr. Hyde* in telling the story of a fading beauty who monsterizes after ingesting "royal wasp jelly."

Beverly Garland prepares a transfusion for Paul Birch as an alien vampire from Davanna, in Roger Corman's micro-budgeted but imaginative *Not of This Earth*.

Frankenstein's monster can be seen faintly in the era's clanking robots, such as Robby (star of *The Invisible Boy*) and *Tobor the Great*. These false-men are entirely sympathetic, even chummy, but then Karloff's character was only misunderstood, not evil. By the more tolerant 1950s, a boy could be *pals* with a man-made monster. The decade's most original Bogey Person, *The Creature from the Black Lagoon*, is a "living fossil" from the Devonian period, but he goes about his deadly business in a very Frankensteinian way, crushing and strangling, and he, too, has a weakness for the fairer sex. The *Creature*, in turn, was sufficiently popular to generate two sequels as well as various imitators including *The She-Creature* and *The Phantom From 10,000 Leagues*—both aquatic and both favoring the Grab-and-Squeeze approach to killing, although the Phantom has the added advantage of being radioactive.

Ironically, though, as the great 1950s science fiction boom began to wither at the decade's end, the Irrational came creeping back into the light. This second horror wave was triggered primarily by two events. One was the sale to television, beginning in 1957, of the Universal horror classics, which introduced a new generation of movie-goers to the old standbys. The other factor was an energetic new interpretation of those classics introduced by Britain's legendary Hammer studios.

In a string of movies beginning with 1957's *The Curse of Frankenstein* and 1958's *Horror of Dracula*, Hammer revitalized the old forms with a heavy dose of heaving bosoms and (by contemporary standards) shocking and bloody violence, all filmed in lurid color. Christopher Lee's suave and ruthless Dracula was sexy in a way never dreamed of by Lugosi's stagy Count. Soon Roger Corman, never slow to smell a trend, weighed in with his equally colorful and ornate Edgar Allan Poe films. Suddenly it was flat, grey

Look fast: the "diving-suited" invisible alien eludes capture again in W. Lee Wilder's plodding *Phantom From Space*.

Nyah, the *Devil Girl From Mars*, summons the terrifying robot Chani, here looking like some sort of major household appliance.

The gorgeous hypnotist's assistant, Andrea (Marla English), and her monstrous "past-life" incarnation, *The She Creature*. Note the monster's voluptuous figure.

science fiction movies that looked stodgy and out-moded. By the time that most Irrational of decades, the 1960s, was well under way, horror films were the pop culture of choice at America's movie theaters once again.

But that's another story. ☾

The 1950s
Space Program

*"Do we go to lunch or
do we go to the Moon?"*

—"General Thayer"
in *Destination Moon*

The Robot For All Seasons:
Forbidden Planet's much-loved
Robbie the Robot, the only special
effect to have his own film career.

Destination Moon

➤ 1950

This movie gave birth to the 1950s science fiction cycle by proving that fantastic subjects could be big box office (it made $5 million, no small piece of change in 1950). Unfortunately, it had little influence on the nature of the films that followed. *Destination Moon* combines a visionary optimism about man's future with a rigid insistence on scientific accuracy—sentiments not often echoed in the subsequent SF craze.

Destination Moon was the brainchild of revered science fiction writer Robert A. Heinlein. Heinlein went to Hollywood in 1948 with the intention of writing the first intelligent, adult space-travel movie—this in an era when "Buck Rogers" still summed up what little most Americans knew about science fiction. He teamed up with a seasoned scriptwriter, Alford "Rip" Van Ronkel, and then met one of the most remarkable filmmakers of the era, George Pal. Hungarian-born Pal was at this time just breaking into independent producing; intrigued by Heinlein and Van Ronkel's script, he signed a deal, beginning the most fruitful career in the history of SF film.

It's impossible to imagine the shape of 1950s science fiction without George Pal, whose films include *Destination Moon, When Worlds Collide, War of the Worlds,* and *The Time Machine*. The quality of his movies varies wildly. He had an unfortunate fondness for sophomoric comedy relief—especially bad in this film—and was not always able to fend off ignorant studio interference. But Pal's saving grace was that he really *loved* science fiction, and fought hard to bring it to the screen with the respect and production values it deserved. I was fortunate enough to meet Pal some years before his death in 1980, and can attest to his warmth and enthusiasm for the genre.

Destination Moon has a simple and single-minded plot. Retired General Thayer (Tom Powers) leads a personal crusade to put Americans on the Moon. The Cold War rears its head; the general is convinced that "the first country that can use the Moon for the launching of missiles will control the Earth." He recruits brilliant scientist Dr. Cargraves (Warner Anderson) and a maverick, Howard Hughes-style industrialist, Jim Barnes (John Archer) to his cause. Barnes, in turn, raises backing for a Moon mission among patriotic tycoons.

They build a graceful, prototypical 1950s rocketship, the *Luna*. Opposition from short-sighted pinko dupes, who are probably friendly with a Foreign Power, almost halts the voyage, but the *Luna* blasts off in defiance of a court order. The space travellers encounter various dangers, land on the Moon and return—and that's it. No love interest, no miniskirted Moonmaids.

Some of *Destination Moon*'s special effects predictably show their age, but much of the film is still surprisingly beautiful and convincing, thanks largely to the contributions of Chesley Bonestell, the century's greatest astronomical artist. Bonestell provided paintings and designs for the Moon settings and the rocket and, with Heinlein, oversaw matters of technical accuracy. The Moon missions superseded some of Bonestell's visual concepts, but I've always preferred his harshly lit, steeply-mountained Moon to the dull grey beach we actually found.

The poster is suitably archetypal for this groundbreaking film—a clean, uncluttered image featuring the *Luna*, the swollen needle that became the model for all others during the decade. Some collectors find it dull. They are Philistines. ☪

Destination Moon. © 1950 Eagle-Lion. One-sheet, 27 x 41 inches.

Flight to Mars

➤ 1951

Flight to Mars is one of a handful of films whose current notoriety rests almost entirely on the merits of their posters. Even so, the movie deserves a historical footnote as the first Martian mission of the 1950s Space Program.

Flight to Mars was Monogram Pictures' entry in the flurry of post-*Destination Moon* science fiction projects. Monogram was one of Hollywood's lowest-echelon studios, remembered now mainly for a series of tedious, micro-budgeted horror films starring Bela Lugosi and other faded actors. The studio was an unlikely candidate for a science fiction epic; in view of their previous products, even their decision to film *Flight to Mars* in color (albeit the primitive "Cinecolor" process, which renders almost everything in blurry oranges and greens) comes as a faint shock. Shortly afterward, Monogram was no more, but the studio re-emerged as Allied Artists and became a major force in 1950s SF movies, both good and bad.

Flight to Mars begins with a certain matter-of-fact realism, although in slavish imitation of *Destination Moon*, right down to the requisite narrow escape from a meteor shower. Even the astronauts' Mars-walk apparel—aviator-style oxygen masks and flight jackets—makes a dopey kind of sense, although their ensembles look a bit light for the planet's sub-zero temperatures. Soon, however, they meet the Martians, who're wearing pressure suits left over from *Destination Moon*, but without the faceplates, and the movie rapidly degenerates into Buck Rogers shenanigans.

It emerges that the Martians' underground civilization depends on a rare element, "Corium," supplies of which are nearly depleted. The Martians are longing for a change of scene, so they resolve to steal the Earthmen's ship, build a duplicate fleet of them, and conquer Earth. (They're centuries ahead of us, but apparently a simple rocket is beyond their capabilities.) However, some dissident, pacifist Martians oppose this plan and tip off the rocketeers, who manage to escape.

Oh yes, and there's also an interplanetary romance between the brainiest human scientist and a comely Mars maiden—not the last time such a biologically implausible coupling would take place in 1950s science fiction films. The female Martians are all fetching, by the way, and display fabulous legs in micro-miniskirted costumes that feature epaulets. The men wear tunics decorated with large shields bearing crossed swords.

The cast is notable mainly for an early appearance by an extremely young Cameron Mitchell as a wisecracking reporter who becomes the romantic lead. Mitchell later became one of the busiest character actors around, and seemingly made at least one appearance in every television series produced during the 1960s and '70s. Also making a creditable early appearance, as the evil Martian leader Ikron, is Morris Ankrum, a veteran character actor who soon became a fixture in '50s SF movies.

But, gosh, even if the movie bites, isn't the poster nice? Space flight themes are relatively rare among the science fiction posters of this period, and *Flight to Mars* features the ultimate in silvery, graceful rockets, well integrated in a bold graphic. Many collectors prefer this spaceship even to *Destination Moon*'s. All pieces from the film are highly desirable; this half-sheet is probably the best of the various posters. ☾

Flight to Mars. © 1951 Monogram Pictures. Half-sheet, 22 x 28 inches.

Cat-Women of the Moon

➤ 1953

"You've never seen anything like it" proves to be no idle boast in this case. There are good movies, bad movies, and then there's the peculiar genre dubbed *badfilm*—movies so amusingly and astonishingly inept that they achieve a kind of greatness. True badfilm is in the details, and I almost despair at the task of conveying *Cat-Women of the Moon*'s sublime stupidity in so brief a space.

Part of the joy of *Cat-Women* is the incredibly perverse casting of the two male leads. Playing the part of Commander Laird Grainger, the inflexible, by-the-book leader of the first Moon expedition, is Sonny Tufts—a pudgy and befuddled lout with one or both thumbs perpetually hooked in his belt, who looks quite a bit like *Married With Children*'s Al Bundy. Victor Jory, one of Hollywood's most dependable villains, who was apparently *born* looking like evil incarnate, plays Kip, the romantic hero who gets the girl. (Marie Windsor, who later rose above this sort of thing, plays the love interest, Helen.)

Laird is the first to set foot on the lunar surface; his first words for posterity are: "It works!" While wearing spacesuits, the actors all shout their lines at the top of their lungs, probably because they're deaf as posts inside their helmets. They enter a large cave. Kip surmises that because it's hard for them to walk, the cave must have gravity and, therefore, air. (What?) He lights a match and it burns, so everyone immediately takes off their helmets and spacesuits. Kip whips out a pistol. "Where there's oxygen, there can be life. And where there's life—there's death," he says genially, patting his roscoe. Seconds later they're attacked by a large spider puppet. It screams loudly while the explorers bludgeon it to death. Descending deeper into the cave, they find a painting of a distant city (with fleecy clouds drifting by overhead)—the Cat-Women's lair.

The Cat-Women (the name is never explained) wear black leotards and heavy mascara. The three with speaking parts are named after Greek letters—Beta, Lambda, and their big cheese, Alpha. They speak English, of course, and all other earthly languages. "Our generation predates yours by centuries," Beta smugly informs Helen. The Cat-Women control Helen through telepathy. Lambda falls in love with Doug Smith (Bill Phipps), the ship's radio operator, and muses about going to the beach with him: "Stretching out on the sand, just a boy and girl together, and maybe, what you call—a Coke."

Conniving Beta tricks oily crewman Walt (Douglas Fowley) into explaining the ship's operation. She picks it up immediately. "You're too smart for me, baby...I like 'em stupid," Walt says, admiringly. Meanwhile, the other Cat-Women do an interpretive dance to an electric-piano rumba. Beta takes Walt to see a "cave of gold," but treacherously stabs him. (She calls him Doug just before doing so.) Then, Alpha tells Lambda that the four of them—Alpha, Beta, Lambda, and Helen—will return to Earth, place all the women under their control and conquer the world! There's more, but I trust you get the idea.

Posters on this title are rather clumsily executed, but at least they offer a fine view of the Cat-Women. Note that they're played by the Hollywood Cover Girls. Only in America. ☪

Cat-Women of the Moon. © 1953 Astor Pictures Corporation.
Title card, 11 x 14 inches.

Project Moonbase

➤ 1953

Project Moonbase begins with a vintage Cold War premise. America is attempting to establish a moonbase, despite the subversion of Evil Spies who've smuggled an agent aboard the flight, disguised as a scientist named Wernher (Larry Johns).

The moonship is piloted by an irksomely perky woman, Colonel Breiteis (Donna Martell)—"Bright Eyes," get it?—and co-piloted by Major Moore (Ross Ford). They're obviously interested in each other, but Breiteis has a Gibralter-sized chip on her shoulder, and Moore is in high macho dudgeon over Breiteis' command of the mission. Enroute to the Moon, Moore discovers that Wernher is a spy; the clincher is that Wernher's supposed to be from Brooklyn, but this guy's never heard of the Dodgers(!). The spy sabotages the ship, and they're forced to crash-land on the Moon. Moore treks across the lunar surface and erects a television antenna to contact their space-station headquarters. The spy, forced to accompany him, accidentally dies, but Moore completes the job.

The reluctant lovebirds are ordered to consider *themselves* the first moonbase, and to wait for supply ships. Moreover, their commanding general (Hayden Rorke, Doctor Bellows on TV's *I Dream of Jeannie* and the only real actor in the film) informs them that public opinion on Earth demands that they marry(!!). Breiteis, of course, was secretly *pining* for hunk Major Moore. They're married via television and personally congratulated by the president, who turns out to be a woman also. (The sentiment of the scene is marred by the fact that the "viewscreen" on which the president appears is clearly a hole in the set wall, behind which the actress sits at a desk.) Oh, yes, and the president also promotes Moore to general—apparently he has to outrank Brighteyes to feel frisky, if you get my drift.

Project Moonbase. © 1953 Lippert Pictures Inc. Insert, 14 x 36 inches.

Project Moonbase was assembled from pilot episodes of an unsold television series that evidently was intended to be a more cerebral *Rocky Jones, Space Ranger*. The special effects are actually better than in most 1950s science fiction television, not that that's saying much; the rocket models still spurt Zippo-lighter flames. On the other hand, sequences set in the zero-gravity space station are rather nice. The magnetic-booted personnel sit or stand on whatever wall they please, like in an M.C. Escher etching, neatly anticipating similar scenes in *2001*.

Project Moonbase was also, after *Destination Moon*, the second and last movie on which Robert A. Heinlein worked. Reportedly, his initial draft was substantially "improved" by producer Jack Seaman. It's possible to recognize a few Heinleinian touches, such as the female president; his fiction is filled with smart, tough females. But the movie's cornball tone bears little resemblance to Heinlein's literary work.

Nonetheless, *Project Moonbase* is a must-have for collectors of space imagery. Its posters are among the very best of the era, each bearing a cleanly rendered, archetypal spaceship, gleaming against a gorgeous (if absurd) lapis-blue starfield. The vibrant colors in this insert rival the best stone lithography. ☪

Conquest of Space

➤ 1955

When George Pal's science fiction movies are good, they are very good indeed, and when they're bad, they are *Conquest of Space*.

Having canonized Pal for *Destination Moon*, it's now my duty to discuss his worst genre effort ever. This frustrating movie is utterly defeated by a hackneyed and improbable script. Pal subsequently claimed that the film's problems were due to "improvements" imposed by Paramount executives, which certainly could be true. But many of the film's flaws—poor writing, cornball humor, bathos, and pompous religiosity—are traits that pop up in greater or lesser degrees in much of his work.

SEE HOW IT WILL HAPPEN...IN YOUR LIFETIME!

CONQUEST OF SPACE

COLOR BY **TECHNICOLOR**

PRODUCED BY GEORGE PAL   DIRECTED BY BYRON HASKIN   SCREENPLAY BY JAMES O'HANLON
ADAPTATION BY PHILIP YORDAN, BARRE LYNDON AND GEORGE WORTHINGTON YATES   BASED ON THE BOOK BY CHESLEY BONESTELL AND WILLY LEY   A PARAMOUNT PICTURE

Conquest of Space. ©1955 Paramount Pictures.
Half-sheet, 22 x 28 inches.

In the near future, the first interplanetary spaceship has just been built in orbit, near a wheel-shaped space station. The Wheel's builder and commander is starchy Colonel Samuel Merritt (Walter Brooke), who is slated to command the spaceship as well. Also on board is his estranged son, Captain Barney Merritt (Eric Fleming). The ship's announced destination is the Moon, although no one has wondered why a moonship would need enormous wings; the answer comes when their goal is changed at the last minute to Mars.

The expedition's crew consists of the Merritts and some poorly drawn ethnic stereotypes. These include an obnoxious Brooklynite named Siegle (Phil Foster), who's a living anti-semitic joke; a Japanese crew member, Imoto (Benson Fong), who apologizes for World War II(!) and refers to his race as "little men living in paper houses," and a beefy, stubborn Irishman, Mahoney (Mickey Shaughnessy), who idolizes the colonel and stows away on the Mars mission to be near him.

So far this would be tolerable, but soon after the departure for Mars, Colonel Merritt becomes a religious fanatic. This plot twist comes from so far out in left field as to induce whiplash in the unwary viewer. Suddenly, the colonel's worried that they're "invaders of the sacred domain of God," and spends a lot of time muttering about "abominations." He tries to crash the ship on landing and has to be subdued. Later, he sabotages their water supplies and is accidentally killed by his son while wrestling for a gun. Mahoney swears he'll see the son hang from the highest yardarm on their return, or words to that effect.

Now the unhappy crew has to wait a year for Earth to move into favorable position for their return flight. They replenish their water supplies with some *highly* unlikely Mars-snow, and are almost marooned by a marsquake. After a narrow escape to orbit, Mahoney forgives Captain Merritt for his father's death, but by this time our interest has long since waned.

The only things of interest in *Conquest of Space* are its uneven but often wonderful special effects. Chesley Bonestell returned for his last Pal film with more exquisite astronomical art. Sets and models are usually excellent, although some matte work is surprisingly poor. Some of the space scenes—particularly one involving a "space funeral" for an astronaut accidentally killed on the outward voyage—are among the best ever filmed. It's a pity they couldn't have graced a more competent script.

The posters from *Conquest* are bold and colorful, with interesting 3-D typography; all show the Mars ship departing the Wheel for its rendezvous with Destiny, or whatever you'd care to call it. ☾

Forbidden Planet

➤ 1956

Here it is, the Jewel in the Crown, the stunning poster for the finest science fiction film of the 1950s. That last sentiment is debatable, of course, but for me, no other film of the era evokes quite as much shiny-bright wonder as *Forbidden Planet*.

Forbidden Planet's story was devised by Irving Block and Allen Adler. (Block was better-known as a technician who produced cheap and cheap-looking special effects for a number of 1950s science fiction projects; the alien in *The Atomic Submarine*, for instance, was played by his arm in a monster-sock.) Their concept for *Forbidden Planet* was imaginative and literate, deliberately paralleling Shakespeare's *The Tempest*, and most of it survives in the finished film. Then-MGM head Dore Schary saw its possibilities, and decided to make *Forbidden Planet* the studio's first foray into science fiction.

As *Forbidden Planet* opens, the United Planets cruiser C-57D has been dispatched to a lonely planet circling the star Altair to search for survivors of a colonists' ship long presumed lost. The ship's crew, commanded by J.J. Adams (an achingly young Leslie Nielsen), finds the lost ship's only survivors, Dr. Morbius (Walter Pidgeon) and his daughter Altaira (Anne Francis, at her most toothsome). Adams learns the other colonists died years before, killed by some mysterious, malevolent force.

The castaways haven't merely survived, however. Morbius and Altaira live in a futurist mansion-fortress, attended by Robby, science fiction's all-time favorite robot, and obviously possess technology superior even to that of the United Planets. For Morbius has discovered some of the secrets of a godlike race, the Krell, who inhabited the planet millennia ago. As Adams begins to unlock Morbius' secret, the force returns, unleashing its fury on the hapless men of the C-57D.... And maybe I'll just leave it at that. If you've never seen *Forbidden Planet*, it would be pretty lousy of me to go any further.

Most of the science fiction films made during the 1950s were *very* low-budget and profitable. With Forbidden Planet, MGM gambled on a full-color, "A" production, which, unfortunately, did unspectacular business. The film features the best special effects of any science fiction film prior to *2001*. In a previously unheard-of arrangement, MGM hired Disney studios to create astonishing visual sequences set inside the twenty-cubic-mile underground Krell laboratory, as well as the "Id monster," the mostly invisible creature stalking Adams' crew. The production design is equally superb; *Forbidden Planet*'s future is a beautiful extrapolation of '50s style, from the Noguchi-like furniture to Robbie himself, who looks more than a little like a vacuum tube.

The film isn't perfect. Pidgeon's performance is oddly stilted and windy; reportedly he didn't care for the film or the role. Earl Holliman's "Cooky" character, the comedy relief, misfires badly. And the primitive electronic score of "tonalities" by Louis and Bebe Barron sounds pretty much like a Mr. Coffee on overload today. But these are quibbles. *Forbidden Planet* is a unique landmark in the history of science fiction, a colorful, exciting and thoughtful movie that still entertains today.

Forbidden Planet's continuing popularity has driven demand for its posters sky-high. Prices for this title have risen tenfold since the mid-1980s. All posters from the film are gorgeous, but this one-sheet is by far the most desirable. Today the poster ranks alongside *The Day the Earth Stood Still* and *Creature From the Black Lagoon* as the number-one science fiction film collectible. ☾

Forbidden Planet. © 1956 Loew's Inc. One-sheet, 27 x 41 inches.

Fire Maidens of Outer Space

➤ 1956

This truly *wretched* film was graced with a memorable poster. This was, however, the only luck the movie had.

The makers of *Fire Maidens of Outer Space* obviously held us in contempt, so I see no reason why we shouldn't return the favor. While *Fire Maidens* is similar in theme and plot development to both *Queen of Outer Space* and *Cat-Women of the Moon*, it lacks any trace of those films' goofy charm, and achieves the amazing feat of making them seem like good movies in comparison. With *Fire Maidens*, the 1950s Space Program hits rock bottom. Nevertheless, your hard-bitten reporter has exposed himself to the thing so that you won't have to.

Astronomers discover that the thirteenth moon of Jupiter is an Earthlike world that may be capable of supporting life. An expedition blasts off in a stock-footage V-2 rocket to determine what's what. Upon arrival, a mysterious voice gives them landing instructions. The coordinates don't seem right, but "perhaps their gravitational laws and magnetic poles are contrary to ours!"—a fascinating interpretation of physics. Upon disembarking, the explorers see a blonde in a mini-toga, or, as one of the astronauts puts it, "A woman! With all the necessary ingredients!" They follow her into a borrowed-looking castle set, which turns out to be New Atlantis. Yes, Jupiter's moon is inhabited by the descendants of lost Atlantis. How do they explain this? Ha ha! They don't!

The woman is actually Hestia, one of the many daughters of Prasus, the "lone male survivor of Atlantis." Prasus is an old duffer given to shouting things like "New Atlantis must not die!" in a shrill voice. Prasus enlists the Earthmen's aid in killing the local monster, who wears a black leotard and an ugly mask. Hestia falls in love with the most heroic of the astronauts, Luther. This apparently displeases her sisters, who attempt to sacrifice Hestia on the firey altar of their sun god—the only reason I can find, by the way, for calling these ladies "Fire Maidens." Hestia lives. Hestia gets Luther. The monster is killed. Prasus dies. The other astronauts promise to return and marry as many Fire Maidens as they can.

There's little point in discussing cast and crew on an atrocity as thorough-going as this. Note, however, that Luther was played by Anthony Dexter, who also appeared in *The Phantom Planet* and *Twelve to the Moon*. This must be one of the worst batting averages in science fiction history.

While the movie itself is a stinker, the poster is a typically riveting image by one of the few "names" in the field, designer extraordinaire Albert Kallis. Kallis, who began his career in the studio of master designer Saul Bass, served as primary art director for American International Pictures for seventeen years, and illustrated or supervised the poster artwork for many of Roger Corman's best-known science fiction films, as well as his Edgar Allan Poe cycle. Kallis' importance to AIP's success can hardly be overstated. AIP's ad campaigns were designed well before their films' actual production; Kallis' bold artwork helped sell unseen works to exhibitors who knew that the right poster could fill a drive-in. His titles include some of the most valuable and sought-after posters of the 1950s. ☪

Fire Maidens of Outer Space. © 1956 Topaz Films. One-sheet, 27 x 41 inches.

Queen of Outer Space

➤ 1958

If you happen to be a woman, or if you just *like* women, say, this movie may well give you pause. *Queen of Outer Space* must have seemed weird even in 1958, but today, it's downright surreal.

As *Queen* opens, it seems like a typically dull science fiction film. Early attempts at comedy relief are pretty awful, but that's not unusual in pictures of this kind. As the movie grinds on, however, the "comedy" comes thicker and faster, and you begin to suspect that it's *supposed* to be funny. It's hard to be sure about this, though, since long stretches of pure wood separate the alleged jokes.

Earth rocketeers have been assigned to ferry a Professor Conrad to his brainchild, an orbiting space station. Before they can reach it, however, the station is destroyed by a mysterious ray, which also strikes the rocket, and somehow carries it all the way to the ray's point of origin, the planet Venus. We know it's Venus because the Professor tells us so after examining a leaf from a shrub. We never learn the reasoning behind this rather impressive surmise.

Venus turns out to be inhabited by lightly clad showgirls. A crewman leers at his Amazonian captor and says to his buddy, "Hey Mike, how'd you like to drag *that* to the senior prom?" As usual, they've learned English by tapping our broadcasts (how come they never speak French?); they explain that, after a destructive war with another planet, the Venusian women revolted against their male leaders, and exiled all men to an orbiting satellite.

Naturally, though, these "gals" are panting to get to know some red-blooded Earth males—all except their masked queen, who's got a permanent mad on against the hairy-chested set because (as we learn) she was disfigured by "men and their wars." And even the queen is attracted to the stalwart ship's captain; she just has, you know, *personality problems*. Finally, the pro-men women, led by a scientist with a thick Hungarian accent (the ineffable Zsa Zsa Gabor), stage a revolt against the man-haters, and male dominance is quickly re-established. This plays just as silly as it sounds.

Queen's odd shifts of tone, from feeble drama to feeble comedy, are apparently due to a mid-course correction in the production. Director Edward Bernds has stated that *Queen* originally was intended to be played straight, but was altered when its makers decided the film might have a better chance as a "spoof." According to Bernds, Zsa Zsa was such a joy to work with that producer Ben Schwalb required ulcer surgery halfway through the production.

Interestingly, this appalling movie has some prestigious names in its credits, including that of Ben Hecht—writer or co-writer of *Gone With the Wind*, *Spellbound*, and *Notorious*—who received credit, if that's the proper word, for the film's story. (Apparently this was just an outline, and one assumes the check cleared.) Furthermore, the script was by Charles Beaumont, a talented writer who produced many fine fantasy short stories before his untimely death in 1967.

The poster itself represents a high-water mark in the annals of camp—as does its star, now that I think of it. It's long been prized by discerning collectors, but its value has *skyrocketed* since Zsa Zsa socked that cop. ☾

Queen of Outer Space. © 1958 Allied Artists. One-sheet, 27 x 41 inches.

Twelve to the Moon

➤ 1960

As this interesting poster indicates, *Twelve to the Moon* stars an entire *boxcar* full of astronauts, in one of the lamest, most contemptible films of the 1950s Space Program.

In *Twelve*, an international space agency mounts man's first Moon expedition, apparently deciding to send enough astronauts to get the whole fool thing explored all at once. The plucky, multinational crew strap themselves into reclining lawnchairs and blast off in a stock-footage Atlas rocket; it becomes a completely different ship in space, with the stars clearly visible through it.

In space, they have the obligatory close shave with a meteor shower, a standard feature of nearly every space movie after *Destination Moon*. That finished, the astronauts are free to indulge in some particularly vacuous political and ethnic stereotyping. It's the kind of movie in which the blustery Russian scientist, Dr. Orloff (Tom Conway), endlessly brags about the superiority of Soviet technology. At one point, he refers to Poland as "liberated," to which feisty Polish-Jewish David Ruskin (Richard Weber) snaps "Don't get any ideas about liberating *my* country—Israel!"

Upon landing, this mob explores the Moon just as pictured here, in tight single file, like a conga line. In an inspired bit of cheesy ingenuity, the fact that their helmets have no visors is explained by a reference to "invisible electromagnetic ray screens." Meteors constantly fall all around them, like a Kansas hailstorm. A female crew member and her lover stray into a cave and are kidnapped by mysterious, shadowy moon-things who wish to study this thing called love.

Meanwhile, the others find a big, glowing jewel; an excitable African crewman says "It's beautiful—but evil! Evil and sharp, like the jewel of Medea!" Next, molten metal starts spouting from a rock, and Dr. Orloff sticks his plump Communist fingers in the flow, burning the dickens out of himself. Then, another astronaut dies in lunar "quicksand," but he's had zero character development and the cast needed thinning out anyway.

Back on the ship, the survivors receive mysterious printed signals on some sort of tape display. It looks vaguely like Chinese, and an oriental crew member, Hideko (Michi Kobi), can read it fluently. It's a long-winded warning from the local superior intelligence, "the Grand Coordinator of the Moon." The Chinese Moon people order the Earthlings to leave the Moon, and also demand their two cats(!), which "have a special interest for us." Shortly after takeoff, that "Jewel of Medea," now stored on board, bursts into flames! Next, they pass through *another* meteor shower (this may be the most meteor-happy movie ever made).

While approaching Earth, the astronauts are discomfited to see the Moon people freeze *the entire North American continent* before their eyes, as a warning of sorts. Unimpressive paintings show various cities covered with glaciers. One scientist surmises that it's "the principle of the hydrogen bomb in reverse...implosion bombs!" Thinking quickly, and you must believe I am *not* making this up, the astronauts unfreeze the continent by dropping a homemade atomic bomb down the Mexican volcano, Popocatepetl.

Astonishingly, *Twelve*'s director, David Bradley, and its writer, DeWitt Bodeen, both became prominent and well-respected film historians. This effort of theirs will remain a distinctly minor footnote in cinema. ☾

Twelve to the Moon. © 1960 Columbia Pictures Corporation. Half-sheet, 22 × 28 inches.

The Angry Red Planet

➤ 1960

This imaginative poster is probably the best thing about *The Angry Red Planet*, a tedious failure of a movie with some redeeming points of interest.

Angry Red Planet's story concerns the first Mars expedition, a four-member crew of stereotypes. There's tough guy Tom O'Banion (Bogart look-alike Gerald Mohr), who leads the expedition; he's got an unnerving habit of gesturing and pointing with his Army .45. Then there's thoughtful, beard-stroking Professor Gettell (veteran SF player Les Tremayne); wisecracking Brooklynite noncom Sam Jacobs (Jack Kruschen), who's along for comedy relief, and female scientist Dr. Iris Ryan (Nora Hayden), who's all woman despite being every bit as good as a man, you bet. Tom is patronizingly attracted to Iris, who he insists on calling "Irish"; two guesses as to whether she falls for the big lug.

For some time, this crowd ambles about, saving one another from various menaces. Iris walks into a carnivorous plant, and has to be freed with a blast from Sam's "freeze gun," of which he is inordinately fond. (He strokes it and talks to it a lot. Not the sort of person with whom you'd care to share a duck blind.) Best of all, though, is the monster depicted in this poster. Usually called the "Bat-Rat-Spider," because it seems to be a cross between all three, it's such an amusingly unlikely critter that it's acquired a considerable fan following over the years. At present, there's even a limited-edition Bat-Rat-Spider model kit available.

Finally, the expedition is chased back to their ship by a "giant amoeba"—that's what they call it, anyway; it's a Manhattan-sized hump with a central eye that rotates like a police siren, which absorbs the doomed comedy relief and threatens to eat the ship until it's chased away by electrical shocks. Lurking in the background, there's a "controlling intelligence" that looks like a three-eyed lobster. The surviving expedition members (the professor dies of a heart attack) are eventually sent packing, with the standard Superior Civilization Kiss-off lines you may recall from a dozen other films and several *Star Treks*: they've been monitoring our broadcasts, our technological advancement has far outstripped our spiritual progress, we're dangerous savages, emotional infants, so we'd better keep our noses clean, beat it, etc. The usual. Cheeky bastards.

The most unusual thing about the film is the bizarre film process used for the Martian sequences: dubbed "Cinemagic" by its inventor, co-producer Norman Maurer, it basically resembles a red-tinted negative image. Dark areas appear light, and vice versa. Its intent was to lend a cartoony unreality to the live-action sequences, so that they would blend in with line-drawing backgrounds substituted for more-expensive sets or matte paintings. Unfortunately, it doesn't work as intended. The drawings still look like drawings (although they're nice enough), and the live-action sequences are so blurred and watery-looking that they're downright unpleasant to watch.

There are some interesting names connected with this flop. Besides Norman Maurer, who was also a talented comic artist (he personally designed the Bat-Rat-Spider), the film was co-produced by Sid Pink, who ignited the 1950s 3D craze with *Bwana Devil*, and directed by Ib Melchior. The Melchior-Pink team co-wrote the script and also wrote other fine entertainments together, including *Journey to the Seventh Planet* and *Reptilicus*. ☾⋆

The Angry Red Planet. © 1960 American International Pictures. One-sheet, 27 x 41 inches.

Journey to the Seventh Planet

> ➤ 1961

This exciting image, reminiscent of the era's best SF comics covers, marks another film by shoestring filmmaker Sid Pink. Unfortunately, as with *The Angry Red Planet*, the poster is far better than the movie, and, alas, these intriguing space bugs play no part in the proceedings.

This nano-budgeted production ($78,000 for a full-length color feature!) was filmed in Denmark with a mostly Danish cast. The script, written by Pink and Danish-born Ib Melchior, has a few good ideas that I'm inclined to attribute to Melchior. He's not a good writer, but he did often use imaginative concepts from written SF that are relatively rare in movies. Nonetheless, terrible acting and sub-zero production values largely short-circuit the movie's good intentions.

Seventh Planet concerns a manned mission to Uranus, part of a search for life throughout the solar system. (In his memoirs, Pink implies that the idea for *Star Trek* was stolen from *Seventh Planet*, which seems whimsical at best.) The expedition lands on Uranus—a scientific absurdity, since gas-giant planets such as Uranus have no definite surface; the idea wouldn't have passed muster in the lowliest 1960 SF magazine—and finds the planet inhabited by a cave-dwelling giant brain with tremendous mental powers.

The brain creates a synthetic terrestrial environment around the explorers' ship, complete with forests and farms and even people copied from the astronauts' memories. (This idea is almost certainly lifted from a famous Ray Bradbury short story, "Mars is Heaven.") In one rather nice scene, the astronauts find a force-field barrier surrounding the Earthlike "bubble"; one who thrusts a bare arm through the barrier nearly loses it to the 200-below temperature of Uranus' actual surface. The brain-thing fights a war of nerves with the astronauts, creating monsters based on their deepest fears, and using beautiful women dredged up from their memories to spy on them, until the earthers finally track the thing down in its cave and destroy it.

Seventh Planet's physical production can only be called amateurish. "Uranus" was built on an 18 × 44-foot(!) soundstage by theatrical set designers, and it's pretty but utterly unconvincing. American International Pictures tossed out most of Pink's Danish-made special effects and replaced them with new scenes that are none too good themselves; the Uranian brain looks like papier maché. A fairly decent one-eyed monster, animated by Jim Danforth and Wah Chang, puts in a brief appearance. Pink claims his discarded Danish effects were gorgeous, but too "subtle" for AIP's money boys—but then, he says the same sort of things about his *Reptilicus*, for God's sake.

The acting in *Seventh Planet* is generally terrible, although it's difficult to pass judgment on dubbed actors (Pink dubbed one role personally). Even so, the Danish actors play their roles as if heavily sedated; none of them seem capable of an emotional reaction. SF stalwart John Agar, the "name" for American audiences, is a little better, but completely unpersuasive as a lady's man. Greta Thyssen, a Danish actress who had a brief success in America, is insipidly beautiful in a curiously reptilian way. In his memoirs, Sid Pink memorably likens her sex appeal to that of "a three-eyed sloth." ☾

Journey to the Seventh Planet. © 1961 American International Pictures. One-sheet, 27 x 41 inches.

First Spaceship on Venus

➤ 1962

This gorgeous one-sheet gets my vote as one of the major sleepers. It's a subdued, beautifully rendered image that captures the wonder and mystery of space exploration as well as any other genre piece of the period. Collector frenzy hasn't discovered this one yet, but it probably will.

As a film, First Spaceship on Venus is problematic at best. It doesn't seem proper to cast judgment, though, since the American version represents little more than half of the original film. First Spaceship is a joint East German-Polish production that, according to some sources, originally was well over two hours long. Crown International, the movie's American distributor, cut it down to seventy-eight minutes for its U.S. release. The film that remains is frequently puzzling and incoherent in places, and a poor dubbing job doesn't help matters.

In the distant future of 1985, a mysterious "spool" is discovered in the Gobi desert, in debris from the enormous 1908 explosion in Tunguska, Siberia. (This really happened, by the way. Explanations have ranged from a meteor strike to a collision with a comet to a UFO crash, as in this film.) The spool is clearly extraterrestrial and a message-recording device of some kind. Scientists studying the spool determine that it's from Venus and mount an exploratory mission.

A multinational crew is chosen to man the *Cosmostrator I*, the elegant if aerodynamically absurd spaceship portrayed in the poster. (Actually, the artist has improved the ship considerably by lengthening its main hull; on the model used in the movie, the engine nacelles are nearly as tall as the main body of the ship, making the craft look like a medieval castle.) The ground launch personnel wear colorful jumpsuits with foot-tall capital letters "A" or "M" on their chests, and for years I've wondered what that's all about.

Enroute to Venus, scientists aboard the *Cosmostrator* succeed in translating the spool, which turns out to be a Venusian scout's report discussing ongoing plans for conquering Earth! This adds a sense of urgency to their mission, although the report does date from 1908, so the Venusians aren't exactly cracking the whip on this project. Upon landing, the explorers discovered the ruined remains of a civilization that evidently destroyed itself just as it was preparing to attack our planet. There's a "vitrified forest," actually a weapon the Venusians planned to use against Earth; a giant glowing sphere that can transform matter into energy; radioactive mud that chases the explorers around—and, I am sorry to report, none of this makes a great deal of sense, probably due to the movie's missing chunks.

God only knows whether the full version is better; I suspect most Americans would find it dull. Even Crown's chainsaw edit conveys the "feel" of East European science fiction—it's glacially paced, with a heavy, didactic quality. Still, it says something that the Red Terror was making movies with multiracial protagonists, including a Black, two orientals, and an Indian, in 1960—who'd have starred in the U.S. version? Rex Reason? Richard Carlson? Two characters are even identified as Americans, at least in the dubbed version, but they sport the heavy eyebrows and ship's-prow pompadours favored only by the Russian Politburo and certain television evangelists. ☾★

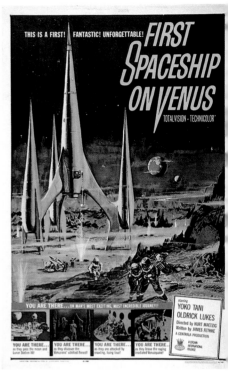

First Spaceship on Venus. © 1962 Crown-International Pictures, Inc. One-sheet, 27 x 41 inches.

Worlds Enough, and Time

"The Universe. Worlds without number, God's silver tapestry spread across the night..."

—"Scott Carey"
in *The Incredible Shrinking Man*

This homely yet laughable Solarite menace is the primary heavy in 1961's appalling *The Phantom Planet*, a strong candidate for Most Hopeless SF Film Ever.

This Island Earth

➤ 1955

This astonishing Reynold Brown piece is one of the finest examples of science fiction art ever produced. Few other posters succeed so well in evoking the mystery and romance of the best SF.

This Island Earth opens with a mystery. Nuclear scientist Cal Meacham (Rex Reason) receives a catalogue for electronic devices that are far more advanced than anything produced by current science. Intrigued, Meacham orders components to build an "interociter," a communications device. A man called Exeter (Jeff Morrow), who has white hair and an extremely high forehead, appears on the interociter screen and tells Cal that his construction of the device was a competency test; having successfully done so, Cal is now worthy to join a secret research project. Cal is curious enough to accept the stranger's offer.

He's flown to an isolated laboratory in Georgia, run by Exeter and manned by a group of prominent scientists, including Cal's old flame and nuclear expert Ruth Adams (Faith Domergue). Also around are more white-haired men resembling Exeter. Cal and Ruth soon learn that Exeter's people are Metalunans, a race whose planet faces destruction in a genocidal war with a planet called Zahgon.

The Metalunans need earth's scientific prowess to create synthetic uranium, because they need massive amounts of atomic power to keep their planet's defensive shields operating. (Most of Metaluna's scientists have died in the war.) Cal and Ruth are shanghaied to Metaluna, where they find a super-civilization in its death throes.

Against Exeter's wishes, the humans are slated for brainwashing, to make them more tractable to Metalunan orders. They attempt to escape, and a conscience-stricken Exeter comes to their aid. Their escape features some extended, superfluous business with the "Mutants," insectlike slaves of the Metalunans who seem included only to provide a monster for the publicity campaign. These sequences are colorful and exciting, but ultimately it's monster-movie fluff that betrays the promise of the film's atmospheric opening.

This Island Earth's acting is generally mediocre. Douglas Spencer, excellent as "Scotty" in *The Thing*, is surprisingly stiff as the "Monitor," Metaluna's leader. Faith Domergue's performance is shrill when danger threatens and otherwise forgettable. Rex Reason is one-dimensional throughout, stalwart and nothing more. His lines don't help; his retort to the Monitor in defense of humanity—"Our size is the size of our God!"—sounds downright *strange*. By contrast, Jeff Morrow makes the most of his role, turning in the film's best performance. Morrow's Exeter is noble, but weak and self-divided, which makes him by far the most interesting and likeable character.

The primary joys of *This Island Earth* are visual. Filmed in the old three-strip Technicolor process —infinitely superior to any film stock used today—the movie's effects are generally top-notch throughout. Scenes of Metaluna's destruction, with Zahgonite meteors smashing through the planet's crust and impacting amid the ruins of graceful subterranean cities, are among the most exciting SF images yet put on film.

Even if it's not a classic, *This Island Earth* is an enjoyable movie, certainly one of the best second-stringers of the era. ☾⋆

This Island Earth.
© 1955 Universal-International Pictures.
Insert, 14 x 36 inches.

World Without End

➤ 1956

World Without End. © 1956 Allied Artists.
Half-sheet, 22 x 28 inches.

World Without End is an interesting change from the general run of 1950s SF posters; understated, semi-abstract—hell, it's downright *tasteful*.

World Without End was indeed, as the copy says, the first wide-screen color science fiction film. For Allied Artists, it looks fairly expensive (which is not saying all that much). The higher production values might lead you to expect something a little better than the general run of 1950s SF. Alas, this is not the case, but the film is still a lot of fun if approached in a frivolous spirit.

A near-future Mars reconnaissance mission—it's the same model rocket used in *Flight to Mars*, incidentally—enters a standard-issue time warp while returning to Earth. The ship accelerates at incredible speed and the crew blacks out, awakening without injuries after crash-landing in a snowy mountain setting. The crew explores, discovering from grave markers that they're back on Earth, but at some time far in the future. They're also set upon by giant spider puppets and great big cavemen who have unusual numbers of eyes. Clearly, something is amiss.

Soon, the astronauts find the remnants of civilization in an underground city. Fortunately, the natives all speak colloquial twentieth-century English, so the crew can learn that it's now the year 2508. Atomic war in the late twenty-second-century caused mutations in the surface world and drove the civilized survivors underground. Now the men are all pale, apathetic, and scrawny (and wear really silly skullcaps). Their women, by contrast, are tall, gorgeous and very attracted *indeed* to the virile twentieth-century astronauts; the boss-man's beautiful daughter (natch) instantly falls in love with one of them. Her jealous suitor turns the Council of Elders, or Chamber of Commerce, or whatever, against the time-travellers, and temporarily frames them for a murder, but he's found out and flees the city, only to be killed by the variably-eyed mutants.

Our heroes decide that, since they've no hope of returning home, they'll help the effete undergrounders reconquer the surface world. They set the city dwellers to building bazookas—which would not be my personal choice for close-quarters fighting—and begin blasting the mutated cave-types out of the area, so that decent, binocular folks can breathe fresh air once again.

Interestingly, H.G. Wells' estate sued the makers of *World Without End*, claiming the story was a thinly disguised version of *The Time Machine*. A few years later, when the authorized version of *The Time Machine* was made, one of the *WWE* astronauts, Rod Taylor, was tapped for the lead role. As to the question of plagiarism, *World Without End* is a virtual catalogue of science fiction clichés, both filmic and literary—the light-speed-equals-time-travel bit; the giant spiders (why is it *always* spiders?); the post-nuke world, divided between mutated savages and decadent civilization; the beautiful daughter of the ruler, the insanely jealous rival—there's not so much as a *hint* of an original concept.

If Wells' estate had a beef, so did the creators of *Buck Rogers* and about half of the pulp writers working in the '30s and '40s. Still, you have to admire the straight-faced way in which the film presents these creaky devices, as if they were fresh ideas instead of the hoary chestnuts they were, even in 1956. ☪

The Mole People

➤ 1956

Either you hate *The Mole People* or you, well, *don't* hate it. Certainly it's a somewhat drab and often silly movie. Even its own director has cheerfully described the film as "piss-poor." However, it's mostly entertaining, in an undemanding way, and one of relatively few 1950s forays into a mainstay of earlier years—the lost-race adventure. It's hokum with a historical flavor, in the mode of *King Solomon's Mines*.

Mole People's star is John Agar as Dr. Roger Bentley, an archaeologist specializing in Sumerian antiquities. Bentley's expedition discovers a temple on an isolated mountain. An expedition member falls through an ancient pavement into a crevasse, and the others climb after him for quite some time *indeed*. According to director Virgil Vogel, the film was five or six minutes short, so they kept adding climbing-down footage, until we begin to think they're not going to stop until they hit magma.

An earthquake cuts off the explorers' escape route, leaving them no choice but to continue into the underworld, as it were, where they find a huge, oddly well-lit cave containing a lost city populated by albino Sumerians and their Mole People slaves. The albinos speak English, of course, but it's passed off as Sumerian; apparently Dr. Bentley has a working knowledge of spoken Sumerian, circa 3000 B.C. (It's not much of a rationale, but it's more than *Star Trek* ever had.) The Mole People were created by Jack Kevan, co-architect of *Creature From the Black Lagoon*. They're a warty, bug-eyed bunch, with powerful clawlike hands and hunched backs.

The underworld is dominated by a crafty priest of Ishtar, Elinu, played with oily overstatement by Alan Napier (Batman's TV butler). Elinu wants Bentley and his surviving buddy Jud Bellamin (Hugh Beaumont) dead, but they overawe the albinos with a flashlight, which hurts their "hypersensitive" eyes and fills them with religious dread. Bentley sets about reforming the Sumerians' culture, in his can-do, American way, forbidding them to beat their Molemen slaves. He also falls for a pretty girl, Adad (Cynthia Patrick), with normal coloration—a "marked one," who is treated with scorn by the albinos.

Elinu eventually convinces the weak king to have Bentley and Bellamin sacrificed to the "Eye of Ishtar," a mysterious chamber in which sacrificees are burnt crispy. At about this time, the put-upon Molemen revolt, apparently killing everyone, and the scientists and Adad wake up unharmed in the "Eye" chamber—it's a direct shaft leading to the surface, illuminated by sunlight. The cave-dwelling Sumerians have mutated to the point where simple sunlight is fatal to them. Which is absurd, of course. Still, it's a quaintly moving resolution, faithful to the spirit of Victorian romance—as is Adad's death in another earthquake, upon their return to the surface.

The gaudily colorful poster is the work of Philadelphia native Joseph Smith, who began working in Hollywood in the late 1930s as an artist and layout man for Disney studios. After further animation-related work for MGM and Harmon-Ising, Smith joined Universal's publicity department in 1949, later becoming a freelancer; his most famous assignment was probably his poster for *Ben Hur*. Horror fans remember his work for a number of classic Hammer films, including *Horror of Dracula*. ☾

The Mole People. © 1956 Universal-International Pictures. Half-sheet, 22 x 28 inches.

The Incredible Shrinking Man

➤ 1957

The Incredible Shrinking Man is quite simply one of the best science fiction movies ever made.

Shrinking Man is the story of Scott Carey (Grant Williams), a likeable Everyguy who is vacationing with his wife, Louise (Randy Stuart), when their boat passes through a radioactive mist. Months later, Carey notices that he's losing weight and, more disturbingly, *height*. Understandably, his wife and doctor refuse to believe him at first, but the process soon accelerates. Medical specialists theorize that the mist has triggered an "anti-cancer" in his body, causing his cellular structure to dwindle. By the time Scott reaches three feet, he's lost his job and become a tabloid sensation, unable to leave his house due to crowds of curious onlookers. A new medical treatment seems to stabilize him at child size, and he finds some peace in the company of Clarice (April Kent), a beautiful circus midget; there's an understated suggestion of an affair. Soon, though, Scott realizes he's begun shrinking again.

We next see Scott at eight inches or so, living in a doll's house. He's miserable, and taking his own torments out on long-suffering Louise. When she leaves the house briefly, the family cat tries to make a snack of Scott, who barely escapes into the cellar, falling into a sewing basket. Louise finds a bloody scrap of Scott's shirt, sees the cat licking its chops and leaps to the wrong conclusion. Meanwhile, Scott is still shrinking, and is marooned in his own basement, now an alien, hostile, and dangerous place.

The remaining half of the film is a moody and effective survival story, in which Scott adapts to his antlike existence and struggles to stay alive, finally fighting a spider for mastery of his new environment. As Scott dwindles entirely out of our world, he experiences a kind of religious epiphany. In an extraordinary soliloquy, Scott states: "My fears melted away, and in their place came acceptance. All this vast majesty of creation—it had to mean something. And then I meant something too....To God, there is no zero. I still exist." Some find this irritatingly indefinite—is he dead?—or too pompously pious. Personally, it works for me, although it's marred by swelling Hallelujah-chorus-type music.

With the exception of Roger Corman, no genre director of the 1950s has received as much retroactive praise as Jack Arnold, and in *Shrinking Man* his talents are displayed to their best advantage. He wasn't a stylist—there's no distinctive Jack Arnold "stamp" on his works, which ranged from SF to westerns to thrillers. He was, however, a careful craftsman with the keen eye of a graphic artist. The basement-world sequences, which Arnold storyboarded personally, are simultaneously surreal and powerfully convincing.

Shrinking Man was Richard Matheson's first screenplay, adapted from his own novel. Matheson is one of the better modern fantasy writers, with a long and successful career in movies and TV, but his *Shrinking Man* script was substantially altered by another writer, Richard Alan Simmons. The experience so offended Matheson that he largely disowned the picture for years. In more recent interviews, however, he seems to have warmed up to it considerably.

The poster for *Shrinking Man* is a suitably moody and understated Reynold Brown painting, with a nice 3-D feel. ☾⋆

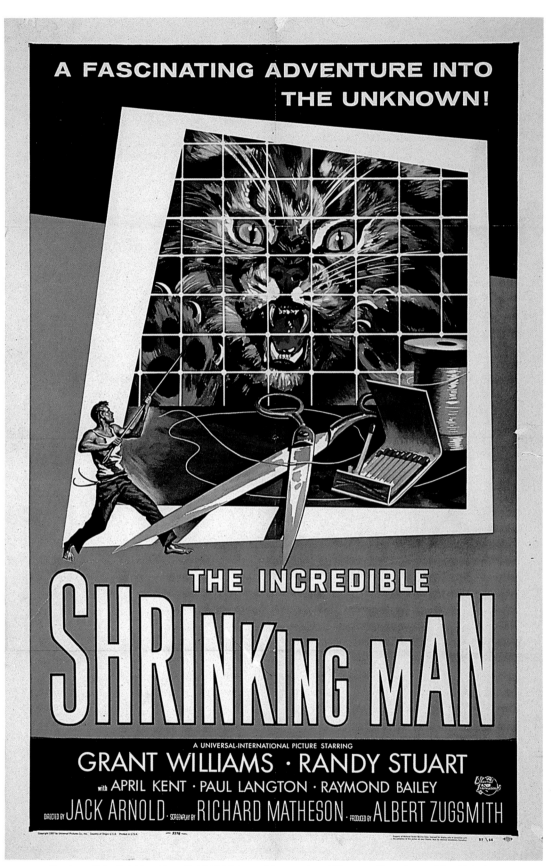

The Incredible Shrinking Man. © 1957 Universal-International Pictures. One-sheet, 27 x 41 inches.

The Land Unknown

➤ 1957

The Land Unknown.
© 1957 Universal International Pictures.
Title card, 11 x 14 inches.

The Land Unknown is a modest little lost-world film with some interesting touches, although it doesn't really deliver the thrills promised in the excellent poster by Reynold Brown and Ken Sawyer. Occult-kookery buffs should note that *The Land Unknown*'s premise is inspired by one of the twentieth century's great Weird Trip rumors: that Admiral Richard Byrd, in his famous polar expeditions, discovered mysterious *warm* regions that, according to some versions, are entrances to vast, unsuspected lands *inside the Earth.*

In *Land Unknown*, members of an Antarctic expedition crack up their helicopter in a deep hidden valley. The valley is an intact chunk of the Mesozoic period, steam-heated by volcanic activity and rife with dinosaurs; a blanket of perpetual fog seals the valley from the outside world and prevents the downed crew from contacting their base by radio. The party, led by Commander Hal Roberts (Jock Mahoney), stumbles around the Land Unknown, dodging dinos, until female reporter and inevitable love-interest Maggie (Shawn Smith) disappears. She's been kidnapped by Hunter (Henry Brandon), half-crazed survivor of a previous Antarctic expedition, who lives in a nearby cave.

Our heroes, of course, come to the rescue, and learn that the wreck of Hunter's copter may have the parts they need to fix their own craft and escape—but Hunter won't reveal its location unless they give him Maggie. Hal nixes this trade; weirdly, though, no one suggests that they rescue Hunter as well, and he doesn't mention it either, although he doesn't seem especially happy living in the L.U.

Hal and his men fail to do the logical thing, namely to encourage Hunter with a little judicious torture. Instead they mark more time in the dinosaur-haunted fog. Maggie decides to save the others by submitting to the caveman's embraces, but one of the men decides (finally!) to beat the wrecked copter's location out of him. In the ensuing fracas, Hunter regains enough fellow-feeling to tell them where his ship went down. Their helicopter is fixed; Hunter, friendlier all the time, saves Maggie from a dinosaur, and Hal in turn saves Hunter. Everyone makes it back, and Maggie announces her plans to have Hal's baby ASAP.

The Land Unknown does have its moments. The fog-shrouded valley is atmospheric; there are some good background paintings and matte work, and actors are combined well with dinosaurs. Unfortunately, the dinos disappoint. According to director Virgil Vogel, the movie was intended to be a high-dollar color production directed by Jack Arnold, but the dinosaur effects cost so much money that Universal scaled back the budget considerably. Vogel is awfully proud of these dinos, by the way, and *Picturegoer* magazine astonishingly called them "spine-chillers." They include a man in a baggy tyrannosaurus suit and a badly sculpted mechanical elasmosaur, both of which look like regulars on *PeeWee's Playhouse.* It gives one pause to think that *these* creations blew the movie's budget. The remaining dinosaurs are played by the usual monitor lizards. One dino-fight seems to end in an actual lizard snuff scene that is genuinely unpleasant to watch. ☾★

Terror From the Year 5000

➤ 1958

Terror From the Year 5000 concerns a time machine constructed in a lonely Florida laboratory by Professor Erling (Frederick Downs) and his assistant, Victor (John Stratton). With their device, they're trading present-day objects for curious items from the future, swapped by the inhabitants of that era. One of these, a small statue, piques the interest of a former student of Erling's, archaeologist Robert Hedges (Ward Costello.) When Hedges subjects the statue to carbon-14 dating, he's astonished to get a *negative* reading, indicating it was made in the year 5000 A.D. (That's *not* how carbon dating works, but it's still a nice idea.) Curiosity lures him to Erling's lab; in the film's most evocative moment, Hedges places a Phi Beta Kappa key, engraved with Greek letters, in the chamber and in exchange receives a medallion marked with the Greek words for "Save us."

Hedges discovers that, unbeknownst to Erling, Victor has secretly been sending *living things* across the time barrier; Hedges discovers a mutated, four-eyed future-cat Victor had hidden. Soon, Victor accidentally conjures up a deadly, radioactive and homely Future Woman, who wears a spangled leotard and screeches like a cat. She wounds Victor and escapes into the swamps. Later, she assumes the identity of a nurse (Salome Jens) summoned for Victor, with the aid of a gadget that peels off the nurse's face(!). The now-attractive Future Woman hypnotizes Victor and explains that the people of 5000 A.D. are ravaged by radiation-induced mutation; they need undamaged genetic material from the past to breed the human race anew. A climactic battle in the time chamber leads to the deaths of both Victor and the Future Woman, and the surviving cast members resolve to work harder to prevent irradiated futures, or something like that.

Terror's production values are minimal. The time chamber looks like a still, complete with curled copper tubing. Special effects mainly consist of an odd optical of white bubbles that appears over the Future Woman, denoting her radioactivity. Worst of all is the film's score, canned library music that's usually insipid or wildly inappropriate. On the plus side, some reasonably atmospheric photography works to good effect, and Salome Jens is pleasing sinister as the emissary from the future.

This is another excellent piece by Reynold Brown, the dean of movie poster artists. Brown began his career in newspaper comics, and in the 1940s was a successful illustrator for slick magazines such as the *Saturday Evening Post*. In the early '50s, he shifted to movie posters; his inimitable style, characterized by exaggerated, dynamic action and detailed rendering, was much in demand at Universal, MGM and other studios. In addition to high-profile projects such as *Ben Hur* and *Spartacus*, Brown created a number of memorable science fiction posters, including many in this survey. ☾★

Terror From the Year 5000.
© 1958 American International Pictures.
Insert, 14 x 36 inches.

The Time Machine

➤ 1960

This poster is arguably Reynold Brown's best science fiction work, and reportedly was a personal favorite of the artist's; it is, however, somewhat marred by a lousy printing job. On close inspection, the image breaks up into extremely large printer's dots.

The Time Machine is mostly faithful to its source, although the story is simplified, sentimentalized and given an anti-war slant in place of the ponderous socialism of H.G. Wells' novel. In a nicely realized 1899, we meet an inventor, George (Rod Taylor), who's obsessed with the nature of time, and has constructed a machine to travel through this fourth dimension of reality. George's friends scoff when he tries to explain his discovery—all but his closest friend, a young Scot named Filby (Alan Young), who urges him not to test this mad device.

George does so, though, racing months and years ahead; the days and nights flicker across his laboratory like a strobe light. In 1917, he stops, only to learn a war is on. His house is in ruins, for Filby, who inherited it after George's "disappearance," had refused to sell it. Another leap ahead takes him to 1940—another war—and a third to 1966, ironically just in time to witness London's destruction in a nuclear bombardment.

Disheartened, George pushes on to the far future of 802,701 A.D. In a sylvan landscape, he meets the Eloi, a handsome but indolent people raised as cattle by a troll-like underground race, the Morlocks. In Wells' novel, these two races were the descendants of the ruling class and workers of his own day; in Pal's movie, they're descended from survivors of a long war between East and West. (The idea that the politics of our time would have any bearing on the world 8,000 centuries from now is undeniably silly, as is the fact that the Eloi speak English.) George falls in love with an Eloi woman, Weena (Yvette Mimieux), and eventually inspires the apathetic race to rise against the Morlocks.

The climax, in which George descends into the Morlock "underworld" to rescue Weena, is exciting but overdone, and a little too monster-movieish, as are the cartoony-evil Morlock makeups. The film recovers nicely, however, with a bittersweet ending in which George revisits his own time briefly, but departs again for his new life with Weena. Filby arrives just after his friend's departure, to deliver the coda. When asked whether George will return, a thoughtful Filby says "One cannot choose but wonder, for you see, he has all the time in the world."

Time Machine's special effects are a decidedly mixed bag, but were well-received enough to win the Academy Award. Pal's unimaginative direction is redeemed by fine performances from Taylor and Mimieux. And Alan Young's performance is winning, although his Scottish accent isn't. Filby's affection for his friend is warm and convincing—more so than the George-Weena romance—and although this description doesn't convey it, I've always felt that their friendship provides the film's emotional center.

The Time Machine may well be George Pal's best-loved movie, although I prefer his gentle 1964 fantasy *The Seven Faces of Doctor Lao*. Despite its flaws, *Time Machine* is easily one of the best science fiction films, a wistfully romantic story that has aged very gracefully indeed. ☪

The Time Machine. © 1960 Loew's Inc. One-sheet, 27 x 41 inches.

Beyond the Time Barrier

➤ 1960

Beyond the Time Barrier is a top-notch genre poster, but as is so often the case, the film doesn't live up to the exciting graphics depicted here. *Time Barrier* features the director and star of *The Man from Planet X*, Edgar G. Ulmer and Robert Clarke, with considerably less happy results. Arthur Pierce's convoluted screenplay deserves points for ambition, but the film's cheapness and the indifferent talents of its principals rob *Time Barrier* of any impact it might have had.

Robert Clarke plays Major Bill Allison, a research pilot testing a plane at near-space altitudes. Allison passes through that standard plot device, the rift in time and space, and lands in the year 2024. He's captured by the inhabitants of a vast underground citadel, who are led by an old man called the Supreme and a brawny, suspicious Captain, who speaks with a West Texas twang and has a Pappy Yokum beard. Except for these two, the citadel dwellers are deaf mutes, due to mutations springing from a "cosmic plague" in the 1970s caused by nuclear testing.

The citadel is under siege by even more mutated survivors, the bald gentlemen in the insert shown here. The Supreme's grand-daughter, Trirene, is the only fertile person left in the citadel, and naturally, she falls for Allison, providing our love interest. Meanwhile, Allison learns of other time-travellers present in the citadel, a sinister and vaguely Eastern-Europeanish trio. One, an icy woman named Markova, comes from the year 1973, when humans began escaping the plague-ridden Earth for colonies on Venus and Mars; the other two, General Kruse and Professor Bourman, are from 1994, when these colonies of "scapes" are well-established. These three are plotting against the Supreme and the Captain....As you can see, this film has a lot more plot than it needs.

The most interesting thing about *Time Barrier* is its production design, in that it *has* one, which is more than you can say of most zero-budgeted sci-fi films. The citadel sets were designed by Ernest Fegté, who also worked on *Destination Moon*, and consist of repeated motifs of triangles—triangular doorways, mirrors and view screens and massive inverted pyramidal wall supports. The citadel dwellers' triangle obsession is never explained, but it does have a pleasantly Deco look that enlivens the leadenness of the proceedings somewhat. But it takes more than production design to make an entertaining movie, as anyone who saw *Dick Tracy* knows.

A final note: according to Robert Clarke, much of *Time Barrier* was filmed in Dallas, Texas' State Fair Park(!); the fairground's huge pavilions, normally used to display prize-winning chickens and such, served as soundstages for the production. As a native Texan, I would *love* to know more about that. ☾★

Beyond the Time Barrier.
©1960 American International Pictures.
Insert, 14 x 36 inches.

The Phantom Planet

➤ 1961

A small confession: while I've been familiar with this poster for years, I'd never seen *The Phantom Planet* prior to researching this book. Now, having done so, I don't expect to repeat the experience. *Phantom Planet* is a drab and funereally paced film that's not funny enough to be camp and not good enough to be anything else.

The film's hero, granite-jawed Captain Frank Chapman (Dean Fredericks) is a space pilot marooned on an asteroid that looks sort of like a brain, or perhaps an apple fritter. When exposed to the asteroid's atmosphere(!), Chapman shrinks to about six inches high and meets the similarly-sized denizens of this worldlet, called Rehton. Rehton seems a distinctly underpopulated place, inhabited by about a dozen extras and four actors that have gosh-all to do.

The alien leader, Sesom (spell that backwards) explains that they don't speak English; they merely "translate it through voice tone waves." Oh. Chapman also learns that the Rehtonites controlled his landing on their planet by "releasing the pressure in our space warp." This, too, is enlightening. Predictably, Chapman is told he cannot leave Rehton. There are only two women of any plot significance: Liara (Coleen Gray), Sesom's perky blonde daughter, and Zetha (Dolores Faith), a mute brunette (the poster's "Girl from Outer Space!"). Both women, of course, instantly fall for Chapman.

More events occur. Chapman fights a duel over lethal gravity plates, winning the respect of the only man in the picture other than Sesom who has more than two lines of dialogue. There's a space war between the Rehtonites and the Solarites, a race of plug-uglies that hail from a firey "sun satellite" (isn't that what the Earth is?) and fight with "heat bombs," just as people from Minnesota, for instance, might be expected to arm themselves with "slush grenades." A Solarite prisoner escapes and aimlessly wanders Rehton's empty corridors for awhile, with an unconscious Zetha in his arms (as per the poster). Apparently he's overcome with lust for her, and isn't it strange how so many alien species seem to share our standards of beauty?

Just before Chapman finally gets to return to Earth (come on, you *knew* he would) Zetha presents him with a lucky rock as a token of her love. Later, when he's in a rescue ship, restored to full size, he begins to wonder if it was all a dream... but no, there in his pocket, is Zetha's rock, looking somewhat smaller than before—but still a *hell* of a lot bigger than the one she actually gave him, assuming they were both six inches tall at the time. The film ends with the words "The Beginning" flashing across the screen, for no reason whatever that I can see.

Actually, all this may make the movie seem more entertaining than it is. But mostly, *Phantom Planet* is a deadly dull series of medium shots filled with actors that talk, talk, talk (or, in Zetha's case, listen). The acting, for the most part, is no better than the script. Particularly sad is the fact that Sesom is played by Francis X. Bushman, Messala in the silent *Ben Hur*, and an actor once greatly respected. ☾

The Phantom Planet.
© 1961 American International Pictures.
Insert, 14 × 36 inches.

Atlantis, the Lost Continent

➤ 1961

This everything-but-the kitchen-sink painting is probably Joseph Smith's finest SF work; the original hung in producer George Pal's home until it was destroyed in a fire.

I've called *Conquest of Space* Pal's worst SF film. Others would nominate this movie. But *Conquest of Space* is offensively stupid, while *Atlantis* is pleasingly so. If you tune your I.Q. down by about forty points and approach this movie with the derision it invites, it's quite enjoyable. *Atlantis* is a distillation of every silly or vulgar '50s costume drama—all those late-RKO, Tony Curtis, Son-of-Ali-Baba, Anita Ekberg-in-silk-pajamas things—with science fiction elements laced in. It takes place in a never-neverland of ancient Greek and Roman architecture, with lots of funny hats.

In ancient times, a handsome Greek fisherman, Demetrios (Anthony Hall), finds a shipwrecked Atlantean princess, Antillia (Joyce Taylor), adrift in a small boat. She looks little the worse for wear despite having drifted 3,000 miles or so, and Demetrios falls in love. Antillia persuades Demetrios to sail her back to Atlantis, and while at sea *she* falls desperately and conveniently in love with him. Soon they're rescued by an Atlantean submarine(!) commanded by Zaren (John Dall). He's a villainous big shot who has the ear of the Atlantean king, Antillia's father, and wants her as well.

Antillia expects King Kronas (Edgar Stehli) to shower Demetrios with honors, but Zaren, sensing a rival, persuades the doddering king to have the Greek enslaved instead. (The Atlanteans have scads of high technology, but still need slaves to drag it around on wooden wheels.) Disobedient slaves go to the House of Fear, where they're transformed into animal-headed monsters—a blatant steal from H.G. Wells' *The Island of Doctor Moreau*.

For awhile Demetrios is slated to become pig-headed in a literal sense, but Zaren gives him a chance at freedom—the "ordeal of fire and water." Demetrios is tossed into a pit of burning coals and forced to fight an embarrassing gladiatorial combat with a great blubbery oaf. Demetrios gains the upper hand by setting fire to the wide-load's hair. Next the pit fills with water. He swims under the surface and pounds the fat fellow's toes with a rock, making him hop around like an extra in a Three Stooges short. Demetrios wins, and is granted his freedom.

He next meets the chief priest, Azor, who secretly worships the One True God, and has a syrupy Biblical soundtrack that follows him around. (Azor is played by Edward Platt, and the sight of Maxwell Smart's Chief wearing a floor-length chemise is pretty amusing in itself.) Azor brings Antillia and Demetrios together again, and explains Zaren's plan to build an enormous death ray(!) and conquer the world. Indeed. To foil this scheme, Demetrios pretends to help Zaren, proving his worth by accurately mapping the entire Mediterranean Sea. (As a fisherman, he was definitely overqualified.) Demetrios leads a slave revolt just as the death ray is finished, and then, while everyone rushes about, a volcano erupts and Atlantis sinks. Demetrios and Antillia watch the destruction from a boat that's about a hundred yards away.

I bow to no one in my affection for George Pal, who created some wonderful science fiction films. This wasn't one of them. ☪

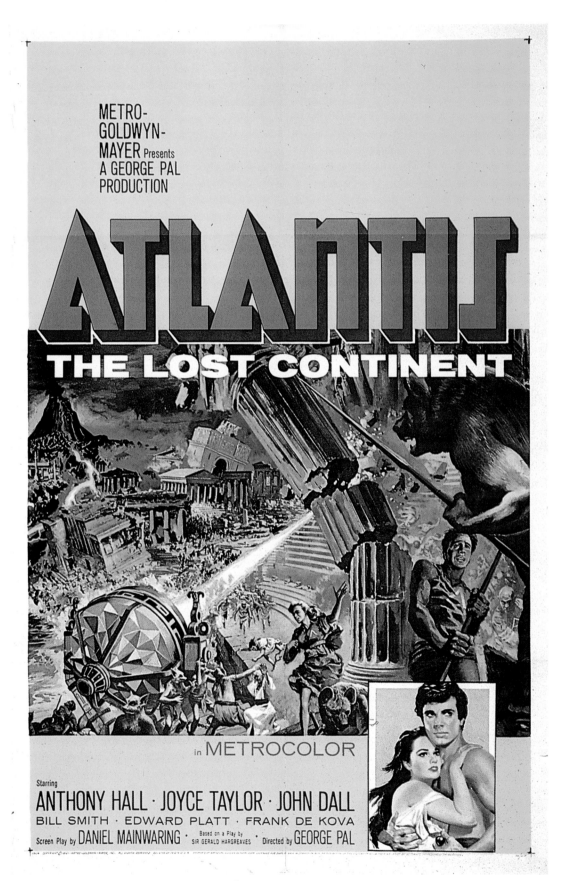

Atlantis, the Lost Continent. © 1961 Loew's Inc. One-sheet, 27 x 41 inches.

Atragon

➤ 1964

While there've been several movies based on Atlantis, I'm pretty sure *Atragon* is the *only* movie concerning Lemuria, the *other* lost continent. Some millennia ago, Lemuria—or Mu, as it's sometimes called—supposedly occupied a good deal of real estate at what is now the bottom of the Pacific Ocean. According to the Theosophists, it was the home of one of the "root races" that preceded man's dominance on Earth; in the earlier part of the twentieth century, a man named Churchward wrote a number of unreliable but entertaining books about Mu, its people and customs. (He believed that the Mayans were pretty much straight Muvian stock.)

Atragon is a Japanese movie originally entitled *Kaitei Gunkan*, made by Toho studios and directed by Inoshiro Honda, with special effects supervised by Eiji Tsuburaya—the same worthies who sparked the Japanese giant-monster craze with *Godzilla* in 1954. *Atragon* is a pleasant departure from Honda's usual fare, being more a straight SF project than a lizard romp. That is, of course, a relative assessment. By American standards, this is one *weird* movie.

In *Atragon*, the world is threatened by the resurgence of the "Mu Empire." As explained in a short film thoughtfully provided to the U.N. by the Muvians, Mu sank in the Pacific thousands of years ago, and built a subterranean civilization that eventually mastered a super-science based on geothermal power. The Mu Empire stakes out a pretty tough bargaining position with us topsiders, demanding nothing less than complete surrender and the abject enslavement of the human race. They don't sugarcoat things much. "We demand you become our colony!" says Agent 23, one of their representatives.

The Muvians are a colorful crowd who dress in modified Egyptian garb; they're all oriental in appearance, but many sport bright red and blonde wigs. They perform lengthy cast-of-dozens floor shows before their empress, in a throne room that looks vaguely like a Roman bath. Their submarines begin blasting the world's shipping indiscriminately with some sort of destructo-ray.

Fortunately, the world has a defender. Japan's greatest submarine commander from World War II has spent twenty years in hiding with his faithful crew, preparing to avenge Japan's defeat. The commander's hideout is an uncharted island that, judging from some amateurish matte paintings, is about the size of Scotland, and conveniently rich in raw materials. The submarine crew used these materials to build—all by themselves, mind you—an enormous underground sub pen, complete with cranes, and Atragon, a flying submarine the size of an ocean liner. (Make your own witticism about Japanese industriousness.) With its drill-bit nose, flaring tail fins and stubby, Vlasic-pickle body, Atragon is an *ultimate* bath toy.

Its captain is reluctant to throw in with the U.N.—Atragon was built for "Japan's prestige," not internationalist ends—but eventually Atragon takes the war home to Mu, bursting into their subterranean lair much as depicted in this snappy, high-voltage Reynold Brown poster.

Atragon is exciting, colorful and somewhat incoherent in its English edition, but even so, it's one of the better Japanese SF films. Judged on its own, non-Western merits—as a number of commentators have noted, Japanese cinema has never valued "realism" in the way that American audiences do—it's quite entertaining. ☪

Atragon. © 1964 American International Pictures. One-sheet, 27 x 41 inches.

First Men in the Moon

➤ 1964

First Men in the Moon is probably stop-motion animator Ray Harryhausen's most enjoyable film, rising well above most SF films by superior writing and acting.

Harryhausen's effects are always good, but his films sometimes suffer from mediocre scripts and performances. *First Men*, by contrast, was co-written by Nigel Kneale, the best fantasy screenwriter of the era, and features lively performances by Lionel Jeffries and Edward Judd. Harryhausen has called the film a "satire," which doesn't seem quite right. There's a lot of humor, some of it too broad; but at its best, *First Men* is that rarest of films, a successful blend of comedy and adventure.

While the movie is reasonably faithful to H.G. Wells' novel, Kneale updated the story with a framing device that adds to the film's charm. A near-future U.N. Moon mission finds, to its understandable surprise, a dusty Union Jack and a brief note claiming the Moon for Queen Victoria—dated 1899. (This scene never fails to send chills down my spine.) U.N. investigators trace the note to an elderly nursing home resident, Arnold Bedford (Judd). Bedford's story takes us to 1899 and the novel's basic framework.

Bedford, a likeable rascal, is in the country to avoid his creditors. He meets an eccentric neighbor, Cavor (Jeffries) who's developing a substance he calls "Cavorite." Cavorite blocks the force of gravity, just as lead blocks X-rays. Bedford sees millions in commercial possibilities, and schemes to become Cavor's partner. Cavor, on the other hand, plans to visit the Moon in a sphere covered with cavorite shutters. By opening and closing the proper shutters, Cavor can use the gravitational fields of the Sun, Earth, and Moon to navigate through space. Bedford is initially skeptical, but succumbs to Cavor's enthusiasm and decides to go along. At the last instant before takeoff, they're forced to bring along Bedford's fiancé, Kate (Martha Hyer). This introductory section is overlong and sometimes borders on slapstick, but in all it's quite enjoyable.

Once on the Moon, comedy takes a back seat for adventure, although there's inherent humor in the very notion of late-Victorian astronauts. Bedford and Cavor explore in diving suits, and, as indicated in the attractive if busy poster, discover an underground world inhabited by Selenites, insectlike creatures who use enormous prisms, mirrors, and crystals to generate an artificial atmosphere. Cavor wants to learn from the Selenites, but Bedford is interested only in escape.

In conversing with the Moon's ruler, the Grand Lunar, Cavor mentions war, which is unknown on the Moon. The Grand Lunar, upon learning of man's warlike nature, wisely decides to imprison the Earthmen. Bedford and Kate escape in the cavorite sphere, but Cavor stays behind to patch up Earth-Moon relations. Back in the "present," the U.N. team finds the crumbled remains of Selenite civilization; ironically, Cavor's terrestrial germs had wiped out the insect race.

First Men was Harryhausen's only Panavision film, and reportedly the wide-screen process posed a number of problems. Matte shots involving the Selenites' light-based technology are colorful and atmospheric. But rubber suits used to portray most Selenites are unconvincing, as is an animated giant caterpillar obviously intended to be the show-stopper. Despite these quibbles, *First Men in the Moon* is consistently entertaining, the best of the master's work during this period. ☪

First Men in the Moon. © 1964 Columbia Pictures Corporation. Half-sheet, 22 x 28 inches.

The Time Travelers

➤ 1964

Science fiction poster artists endured a great deal of meddling and "improvements" by studio art departments. As author Stephen Rebello has said, in this instance after-the-fact manipulation of an artist's image actually *did* improve a poster. The dramatic sapphire-blue starfield was added as a frame for Reynold Brown's original painting.

The Time Travelers was written and directed by Ib Melchior, who scripted several science fiction films including producer Sid Pink's *Reptilicus, The Angry Red Planet* (which Melchior also directed), and *Journey to the Seventh Planet.* Although it has some rough spots, *Time Travelers* is considerably better than these turkeys. It's probably Melchior's best SF film ever, largely because of a surprisingly original ending.

The movie's basic premise involves the same warmed-over Wellsian future as used in *World Without End* and *Beyond the Time Barrier.* Three scientists—Dr. Erik von Steiner (Preston Foster), Steve Conners (Phil Carey), and Carol White (Merry Anders)—have perfected a time monitor, a sort of TV for viewing the future. The scientists take a brief peak some 100,000 years in the future, and then look in on the bleak, post-nuclear world of 2071 A.D. At this point, they find that a mysterious malfunction has transformed the monitor into a portal, an actual doorway into the future. Technician Danny McKee (Steven Franken), impetuous and rather stupid, goes exploring in the blasted wasteland. The others reluctantly follow, only to be trapped when the portal collapses behind them.

The castaways are attacked by hordes of bald mutants, and rescued by members of an underground remnant of civilization led by Varno (John Hoyt). Varno's people, who're under constant siege by the vicious mutants, plan to flee Earth in a nearly completed starship. The cave-dwellers manufacture androids to serve as laborers and soldiers against the mutants. (Unfortunately, the androids serve mainly as low-grade comedy relief, complete with a slobbering circus-music score.) Evil Councilman Willard (Dennis Patrick) persuades Varno that the starship can't accommodate von Steiner and the others. This leaves them with no choice but to build *another* time portal, which they complete just as the mutants successfully break in and destroy the underground world. The time travelers and a handful of Varno's people escape through the portal.

At this point, *Time Travelers* takes an unexpected turn. The travelers return to a time just when they left, and find their past selves still in the lab. But their arrival has put them out of sync with normal time; they're living thousands of times faster than their past selves, who seem frozen, and aging rapidly in consequence. Their "normal-time" counterparts have just set the time monitor on the far future, so the travelers decide their only hope for survival is to enter the portal once again, this time for 100,000 A.D. Fortunately, the far future looks like a verdant paradise.

After they've gone, we see the same events played out in the lab as in the film's beginning. Increasingly rapid cuts reprise the movie's events, not once, but *twice*—suggesting the travelers have created a time loop that will repeat itself forever. It's an intriguing and disturbing finish, making *Time Travelers* one of the few films to explore some of the rich and paradoxical possibilities of time travel so often featured in written SF. ☾⋆

The Time Travelers. © 1964 American International Pictures. One-sheet, 27 x 41 inches.

Big Trouble!

*"When man entered
the atomic age he
opened a door
to a new world.
What we'll eventually
find in that new world
nobody can predict."*

—"Dr. Medford" in *Them!*

Philandering husband Harry Archer (William Hudson)
learns not to toy with the affections of his mutating wife
in *Attack of the 50 Foot Woman*.

When Worlds Collide

➤ 1951

George Pal's *When Worlds Collide* concerns the biggest Big Trouble of all, the end of the world. Many movies *threaten* to destroy the Earth, but this one actually *delivers*.

When Worlds Collide began as a best-selling novel of 1932 by Philip Wylie and Edwin Balmer; a sequel, *After Worlds Collide*, followed in 1933. I'm extremely fond of these books, possibly due to the fact that I haven't read them in twenty years; I'm almost afraid to now. Certainly they were creaky even then, both in terms of technology and sociology (I remember a lot of maundering about fascism and communism, hot topics of the day.) Even so, *When* and *After* together form an involving and densely textured work that couldn't possibly be accurately translated into a feature-length film—fans of *Dune* know what I mean. The movie, then, is no more than a rough sketch of the first book, but even so it's brisk and entertaining.

When Worlds Collide opens with the discovery by astronomers of two celestial bodies zooming toward the Earth. One is a star, Bellus, "a dozen times larger than our Earth" (which seems intended to sound impressively large, but, as any high-school astronomy grad knows, is actually an improbably small size for a normal star.) Linked with Bellus is an Earthlike world, Zyra. Bellus is on a collision course with Earth; Zyra will pass nearby and assume its orbit. A group of far-sighted astronomers and industrialists plan to save mankind by building a giant Space Ark to carry a handful of picked survivors to the new world, Zyra. After months of herculean efforts, the Ark blasts off just in time. Zyra, luckily, is an improbably beautiful, Maxfield Parrish sort of place.

The special effects are uneven but often impressive. Much of the production was designed by astronomical artist Chesley Bonestell, including the elegant Space Ark and the long "ski-jump" ramp along which the rocket travels during takeoff; these are among the most successful miniatures seen in SF films. The flooding of Times Square, one of the worldwide disruptions caused by Zyra's near-miss approach, is also spectacular and fairly convincing. Unfortunately, the actual destruction of the Earth is disappointing, seen only briefly on the Ark's viewing screen; and our only view of the new world is simply a pre-production painting by Bonestell. Pal had intended to create a detailed miniature of the Zyran landscape, but Paramount refused to spend an additional $5,000 on the scene.

Among the cast, Richard Derr is easily the standout as a dashing South African flyer who pilots the Ark and Gets the Girl. Derr, an accomplished stage actor who looks a bit like a more macho Danny Kaye, is several cuts above the usual stolid SF heroes of the Rex Reason mold. Here he invests his stock-heroic character with intelligence and a welcome, self-mocking humor. It's a pity he didn't do more genre films.

Despite its problems, *When Worlds Collide* is at least a minor classic, and the poster itself features an exquisite SF image. In today's market, these factors spell blue-chip. The poster seen here has become one of the most-wanted items among serious collectors of 1950s science fiction memorabilia. ☪

When Worlds Collide. © 1951 Paramount Pictures. One-sheet, 27 x 41 inches.

The Beast From 20,000 Fathoms

➤ 1953

This much sought-after poster commemorates the first and best of the big-lizard movies, a theme that eventually played itself out in dozens of increasingly hilarious Japanese films.

Beast is a historical landmark of some importance, as well as an entertaining little movie. The film is loosely based on a Ray Bradbury short story; its star is animator Ray Harryhausen's "rhedosaurus," a fierce if faintly comical giant dinosaur. The rhedosaurus, which had rested suspended in the Arctic ice for millions of years, is freed by a nuclear test. (This nuclear wake-up call figures in many subsequent giant-lizard movies.) The dinosaur destroys ships at sea and raids the coast, but the survivors are initially dismissed as crackpots. Eventually, however, the monster returns to its original spawning grounds, which happen to have been where present-day New York now stands.

A wonderful sequence ensues in which the rhedosaurus stomps Manhattan, nibbling on police and flattening cars. You've seen the same thing done a dozen times by actors strolling through train layouts in baggy lizard suits, but it's a real pleasure to see a city leveled *right*. Harryhausen's monster is animated smoothly and effectively; it really does seem alive. Ultimately, the dinosaur meets a firey death amid the burning ruins of a Coney Island amusement park, slain by a radioactive bullet.

Beast was directed by Eugene Lourié, an occasionally interesting director better known as a designer and art director for classics such as Jean Renoir's *Rules of the Game*. Lourié usually managed to squeeze a bit more than required from low-budget efforts of this type and, apparently, he liked the *Beast*, since he made two similar variations on the film (*Gorgo* and *The Giant Behemoth*). There's some effectively atmospheric photography, particularly in the Coney Island sequences, and a solid performance from character actor Cecil Kellaway as an amiable paleontologist.

Beast was Harryhausen's first solo effort, and the first fantasy film of the 1950s cycle to feature stop-motion animation—the painstaking frame-by-frame animation of mechanical puppets, rather than drawings. Stop motion was and still is the most effective way to create the illusion of alien life, but unfortunately, it's a time-consuming and expensive technique, which has limited its use ever since the fine work done by Willis O'Brien in the original *King Kong*.

A hugely successful 1952 re-release of *Kong* re-awakened public interest in stop motion, but Harryhausen realized that the painstaking techniques used in *Kong* would have to be streamlined to meet the tight budgets '50s fantasy films could muster. To replace the exquisite glass paintings and miniature sets used in earlier stop-motion films, Harryhausen devised the process he dubbed *Dynamation*—the combination of animation footage with live-action backgrounds and foregrounds, a "reality sandwich" that's convincing to the eye and far cheaper to film. *The Beast* lacks the uncanny sense of personality that Kong had, but like all of Harryhausen's critters, it's convincingly alive.

The Beast vindicated Dynamation. The film was produced for about $210,000 and brought in $5 million, an impressive sum in those days. Harryhausen had proved that the public was ripe for Big Trouble. But talents like his are rare, and stop motion remained largely a one-man show throughout the 1950s. ☾

The Beast From 20,000 Fathoms.
© 1953 Warner Brothers. Insert,
14 x 36 inches.

Them!

➤ 1954

Them! was quite possibly the most influential science fiction film of the 1950s. This taut thriller, inspired by the success of *The Beast From 20,000 Fathoms*, in turn fathered all the giant scorpions, grasshoppers, mantises, spiders, and gila monsters that skittered and slithered across the screen in its wake. It's also by far the best of the lot. None of its progeny deliver the same excitement.

Them! opens in the New Mexico desert. A police patrol finds a little girl (superbly played by Sandy Descher) wandering alone, obviously in shock. Her parent's trailer is found torn apart; there's blood, but no bodies, and an odd, unidentifiable track is found nearby. Soon the policemen find a local store similarly destroyed, with its owner mangled. One stays to await backup, and is killed by something we don't see, which makes an unnerving, high-pitched chittering sound. The surviving policeman, Ben Peterson (James Whitmore), is joined on the case by an FBI agent, Robert Graham (James Arness). Graham sends a cast of the mysterious track to Washington. To his surprise, the authorities send two entomologists—insect experts—to investigate.

Them! retains the kindly old scientist/beautiful female assistant team of *20,000 Fathoms*, with the added touch that Dr. Pat Medford (Joan Weldon) is the daughter of Dr. Harold Medford (Edmund Gwenn). (The scientist's-beautiful-daughter role subsequently became a standard element of '50s SF movies.) The Medfords study the scenes of destruction without discussing their conclusions, much to law enforcement's irritation, but all becomes clear when Pat's attacked by an elephant-sized ant. It's worth noting that *Them!*'s Big Bugs are just that, giant ants, going about ant business; they raided the trailer and store for sugar. There's none of the absurd fripperies of later films—they're not supersonic, bulletproof, or radioactive—although they were *produced* by radioactivity, specifically the first atom bomb test at Alamagordo.

After this atmospheric opening, the film becomes a war story of sorts. The Medfords, Graham, and Peterson become the core of an ant-hunting team that locates the giant insect's desert nest. The nest is bombed and gassed, killing most of the ants; a sequence in which Peterson, Graham and Pat descend into the poisoned nest to examine the queen's chamber is genuinely scary. Unfortunately, they learn that new queens have already hatched and flown away, setting up a cross-country chase that culminates in a tense search-and-destroy mission in the sewers of Los Angeles.

The giant ants of *Them!* are large mechanical props, and while they're not perfect—stop-motion animation would have greatly benefited some scenes—they're well used, usually seen only in dim light or smoke. One scene on an infested ship, in which an ant *erupts* through a wall to kill a radio operator, is startling and convincing.

As John Brosnan has pointed out, *Them!*'s matter-of-fact, "documentary" style owes more to the era's crime dramas than to previous SF movies. There are a few gratuitous "movie-style" shocks—one ant is seen adding a ribcage to a human boneyard near the mound entrance(!)—but for the most part, the film's understated approach greatly increases its effectiveness. *Them!* was both a critical and financial success for Warner Brothers, and other studios took notice. After *Them!*, the Big Trouble rush began in earnest. ☾

Them! © 1954 Warner Brothers. Window Card, 14 x 22 inches.

Tarantula

➤ 1955

This beautiful Reynold Brown poster (with cartoon insets by Ken Sawyer) is one of the most gloriously goofy of the era. Note the carefree grace displayed by our heroine as she rides perched in the spider's dripping fangs.

Director Jack Arnold denied that *Tarantula* was inspired by *Them!*, but no one ever seems to have believed him. Today, *Tarantula* is considered the best of the avalanche of *Them!*-clones that followed that movie's success. It's brisk and entertaining, but it never rises to the heights occupied by the original.

Tarantula opens with a hideously deformed man who staggers out of the Southwestern desert and dies. His body is discovered by Dr. Matt Hastings (John Agar), who establishes the cause of death as acromegaly, a disease that causes disfiguring growth in the head and extremities. The deformed man looks vaguely like an assistant of Dr. Deemer (Leo G. Carroll), a prominent scientist working at an isolated lab nearby. Deemer confirms this, much to Dr. Hastings' surprise—because acromegaly takes years to manifest its symptoms, and the dead man's condition apparently developed within a few days.

Back at Deemer's lab, we see cages with really *big* mice, rabbits and, yes, a spider. They've been fed a synthetic nutrient of Deemer's invention, which is "stabilized" with a radioactive isotope. There's a lot of talk about the impending population crisis and food shortages, so apparently Deemer's goal is enormous beefsteaks, titanic fryers, that sort of thing.

For some reason, however, Deemer and his assistants are anxious to test the nutrient on *a human subject*. (Why? To grow giant people to eat the giant food?) At any rate, Deemer's two assistants have tested the nutrient on themselves, only to contract lightning-fast acromegaly. One was the corpse at the opening; the other, maddened by the disease, bursts into the lab, smashes cages, wrecks equipment, and injects Deemer with the fatal nutrient. The spider, seeing its chance, walks out. (It's a six-footer at this point, but it's growing *real* fast.)

Meanwhile, Deemer carries on, with the help of a new (sigh) beautiful female assistant, "Steve" (Mara Corday). Dr. Hastings is suspicious, and sweet on Steve, which gives him two reasons to stay in the movie. Deemer's face begins to get all *weird*, and soon, this *humongous* tarantula starts snacking on local ranchers and their livestock. By the end, the tarantula towers over the film's little town like the Astrodome, and has to be killed with a napalm bombardment (from a jet squadron led by Clint Eastwood, incidentally).

Tarantula is graced with some first-rate matte work by Clifford Stine and David S. Horsley. Scenes of the giant spider clambering over hills are extremely convincing; the monster even has a realistic shadow that falls across victims and scenery alike. Best scene in the film: the spider's night raid on a corral of terrified horses.

However, *Tarantula* doesn't match up to *Them!* in the acting department. Although Leo G. Carroll turns in a typically urbane performance, the other principals are given little to do and fail to emerge as distinct characters. *Tarantula* is also weakened by unintentional humor. In one unfortunate scene, Corday prances about in a nightie while the giant spider watches her through a window; presumably he's consumed with arachnid lust. ☾★

Tarantula. © 1955 Universal-International Pictures. Half-sheet, 22 x 28

Day the World Ended

➤ 1956

Day the World Ended was Roger Corman's first directorial outing in science fiction, and his fourth film for American Releasing Corporation, soon to become the legendary American International Pictures, or AIP. The posters utilize one of Albert Kallis' earliest science fiction designs, and are graced with typically subtle, understated AIP-style copy (the half-sheets boast of "HUMAN EMOTIONS STRIPPED AWAY!").

The movie opens with the atomic devastation of the entire Earth. Despite all the stand-ins for the A-Bomb we've seen, films dealing with our real Big Trouble have always been rare; filmmakers are always reluctant to confront such uncomfortable realities directly. In a valley sheltered by hills containing lead-bearing ore, Jim Maddison (Paul Birch) has survived, along with his daughter Louise (Lori Nelson). Maddison, a former Navy captain, has expected nuclear war, and his carefully positioned house is stocked with provisions for himself, Louise, and her fiancé Tommy. Unfortunately, Tommy didn't reach safety in time.

Soon, a handful of survivors stumble into Maddison's valley, among them a gangster, Tony (Touch Connors, later Mike Connors); his girlfriend, Ruby (Adele Jergens); a heroic geologist, Rick (Richard Denning), and Radek (Paul Dubov), a horribly burned man in the first stages of atomic mutation. Maddison, mindful of his scarce supplies, wants to turn the refugees away, but Louise persuades him let them stay. Tony tries to strongarm his way to the top of this miniature society, but is checkmated by two-fisted Rick. Louise soon falls for Rick, but Tony wants her for himself.

Amidst this wrangling, the survivors find signs of strange creatures entering the valley from the irradiated wilderness beyond. Maddison knows what's happening; while on a naval vessel that participated in a Pacific H-Bomb test, he saw strange mutations in animals exposed to the blast. Meanwhile, Radek, who was expected to die, instead begins to *change*. He begins roaming at night, wandering in radioactive areas. He hunts down irradiated game, living on their raw flesh—and he *likes* it, see. Radek's evolving mutation is quietly chilling and provides the picture's best moments. "There's wonderful things happening out there," he says, with lunatic satisfaction, a post-nuclear version of *Dracula*'s Renfield.

Radek falls prey to a more advanced mutation—a three-eyed, horned man with a thick, scaly hide built and played by AIP monster-maker Paul Blaisdell. There's an interestingly indirect series of hints that this monster is actually Louise's lost fiance, Tommy. Ultimately, the monster comes for Louise, Maddison kills Tony as he prepares to ambush Rick, and a miraculous rainfall of unpolluted water kills the mutant, who cannot tolerate it. It's scientific nonsense, but poetically satisfying; God is giving mankind another chance. Rick and Louise link arms and face the future as the credits announce "The Beginning."

Day the World Ended is a crudely made but satisfying story that exemplifies the strengths and weaknesses of Corman's early work, and the vintage AIP style in general. Production values are minimal, as usual, and Corman's direction is no better than workmanlike. The plotline unfolds with the no-frills simplicity of a comic book, but the story is an interesting one, marked with Corman's signature pessimism and fondness for semi-ironic Biblical parallels, and the performances are a distinct cut above similarly budgeted efforts from other directors. ☪

Day the World Ended.
© 1956 American Releasing Corporation.
Insert, 14 x 36 inches.

Attack of the Crab Monsters

➤ 1957

This beautiful Woman in Peril is unhappily meeting some of the strangest Big Trouble ever—the mutated, intelligent shellfish of *Attack of the Crab Monsters*.

Crab Monsters has taken a certain amount of grief from filmic *ignorati* due to its colorful title, but it's a madly inventive film that is far better than one might expect. Like most of Roger Corman's movies, it has moments that redeem the poverty of the story's surroundings. And, as with many of his films, it's lively and entertaining, but has a premise that's *incredibly* grim if you stop to think about it.

Radioactive fallout from a South Pacific H-bomb test has blanketed an unnamed, downwind island, and a scientific party sent to investigate conditions on the island has disappeared. A followup expedition arrives; members of the new party soon hear the disembodied voices of the previous expedition, urging them to take long walks in the dark. Doing so leads to disaster. Furthermore, as more persons disappear, *their* voices join the ghostly chorus. The dwindling group slowly discovers what they're up against—not the supernatural, but two mutated giant crabs with an impressive array of powers.

These are no *ordinary* giant crabs. Radioactivity has altered their molecular structure so that they're virtually indestructible. Moreover, the crabs can project intense heat, and use it to tunnel beneath the island. Most fascinating, though, is scriptwriter Charles B. Griffith's ingenious way of giving the crabs intelligence. Due to their odd molecular makeup, human brains ingested by the crabs remain active within their bodies. In effect, each crab is now endowed with a committee of highly intelligent scientists' minds—and now they're *on the crabs' side*. Despite the often risable nature of the proceedings, there's something horrible in this idea.

The group-minded crabs outwit and devour the humans one by one, and taunt the survivors with speech they somehow broadcast through metal objects. Only three human survivors are left when one of them finds the crabs' weakness—electricity—and he dies in ending the menace.

Attack of the Crab Monsters. © 1957 Allied Artists. Insert, 14 x 36 inches.

Corman's direction is competent if flat; he was never an actors' director, and the performances here are mostly forgettable. Russell Johnson, the Professor from TV's *Gilligan's Island*, is fairly good as the movie's hero. The crabs are, to put it mildly, not terribly convincing, but endearing just the same. They've got lidded, human-looking eyes positioned on their shells, rather than on stalks, and buck-toothed mouths. These styrofoam-and-fiberglass creations were inhabited and pushed about by actor Ed Nelson, who also has a small part in the film. Griffith has also raised the interesting possibility that one of Corman's hangers-on of this period, Jack Nicholson, may have taken a turn huffing and puffing inside one of the crabs. ☪

The Deadly Mantis

➤ 1957

Another Reynold Brown poster, illustrating one of the least of the Big Trouble movies. A brisk three years of one-upmanship among bug-filmmakers brought us to this thoroughly contemptible picture, featuring a hundred-foot mantis that flies at 200 miles per hour and shrugs off rocket blasts without flinching. Putting aside the inherent impossibility of giant insects for a moment, at least the ants of *Them!* and the spider of *Tarantula* behave something like their natural counterparts; by the time *The Deadly Mantis* came along, mere gianthood was apparently no longer enough.

The film opens with stock footage and maps. As the Biblical-sounding narrator intones "For every action, there is an equal and opposite reaction," we see that a volcanic eruption in the southern hemisphere somehow precipitates a disturbance in the north polar icepack. I doubt this is the sort of thing to which Newton referred. An iceberg flips over, revealing a frozen, extra-extra-large praying mantis. You will probably not be surprised to learn that shortly thereafter, arctic weather stations, planes in flight, and a stock-footage Eskimo village all fall prey to the revived and now insatiable insect.

Deadly Mantis retains the mystery-opening of *Them!* to absolutely no purpose—what was that title again? We waste *way* too much time waiting for the government to find out what we knew before the opening credits rolled. The authorities bring in a paleontologist, who explains that prehistoric dragonflies had six-foot wingspans, and that therefore it could be a praying mantis that's eating these planes and villages. Meanwhile, the mantis begins working its way south, laughing at jet-fighter attacks and dining on a bus or two on the way. The bug briefly visits Washington, D.C., alighting on the Washington Monument. Then it heads to New York and is finally slain inside the "Manhattan Tunnel". Yawn.

Deadly Mantis really is fairly hopeless. The science isn't science. "Every known species of animal has a bony skeleton," the paleontologist sagely informs us, leaving us to wonder whether insects are, perhaps, vegetables. The mantis' complex proboscis is replaced with a 'gator mouth, and the thing roars like a lion.

The special effects aren't special. Brown has wisely chosen to portray the most effective sequence in the picture, the brief scene in which the giant mantis perches on the Washington monument. This scene uses a real mantis and is fairly convincing. Elsewhere the mantis is played by a poorly articulated mechanical bug whose head looks like a piñata. (In fairness, the filmmakers were at least conscientious enough to stage the mechanical mantis' appearances mostly at night or in fog, which hides its shortcomings somewhat.)

The actors seem embarrassed. Oddest is the fact that macho, beefy William Hopper gets the scientist role; Craig Stevens' military hero who Gets the Girl is colorless to the point of catatonia. It's as if each were playing the other's part by accident. (Stevens proved he really could act with his starring role in the *Peter Gunn* TV series.)

Director Nathan Juran sometimes had himself billed as "Nathan Hertz" on films he felt were not, shall we say, resumé material, such as *Attack of the 50 Foot Woman*. Why, then, did he use his real name on *Deadly Mantis*, which is significantly worse? ☾⋆

The Deadly Mantis. © 1957 Universal-International Pictures. Insert, 14 × 36 inches.

The Beginning of the End

➤ 1957

With this wonderful poster (scope the fangs on that 'hopper!) we come to the works of Bert I. Gordon, a founding father of the Big Trouble school of cinema. Gordon was a true, honest-to-God auteur if anyone ever was; he did it *his* way, producing, directing, and creating special effects for more than a dozen genre films. I must confess to a sneaking fondness for Gordon's work, which is no doubt related to my having seen them at the proper ages of six through ten.

Bert I. Gordon's unique *oeuvre* began in 1955 with *King Dinosaur*, a crude film that nevertheless demonstrates all the hallmarks of the B.I.G. style—cheap sets and cheaper actors, a ton of stock footage, and a poorly matted-in Really Big Thing, a lizard in this case. It's his fondness, nay, his fixation, for Really Big Things that makes his work charming; what seven-year-old *hasn't* dreamed of being big enough to squash his elementary school, with all hands aboard?

Over more than two decades, B.I.G. gave us a big spider, a variety of big insects, a big cyclops, a big man, a big skull-faced man and, most terrifying of all, big teenagers. Gordon's special effects are pretty terrible by conventional standards, to say the least, which is unsurprising considering he created many of them in his garage at home. But to young and impressionable minds, they're good enough to provide a vehicle for the imagination...Besides, I was just a kid. Gimme a break.

In *Beginning of the End*, the menace is grasshoppers the size of school buses. They've gotten big, shockingly enough, from radiation—in this case, from eating irradiated fruits and vegetables (something for Safeway to keep in mind.) The giant, voracious grasshoppers devour the residents of several isolated towns and begin marching, or hopping on Chicago. Chicago is evacuated, and the military prepares to drop an atomic bomb on the City of Big Shoulders to stem the threat. At the last minute, however, a heroic government entomologist played by Peter Graves devises an electronic signal that lures the giant grasshoppers to their deaths in Lake Michigan. Thought question: What would Lake Michigan smell like, on a warm summer's day, with thousands of dead school-bus-sized grasshoppers floating in it?

B.I.G. has been reviled for years by science-fiction fans, and while it's hard to disagree, it seems a little unfair in view of the demi-god status granted to his fellow schlockmeister, Roger Corman. Certainly Gordon couldn't have had any more contempt for his audiences than Corman, and both had a free-and-easy unconcern for plausible plotting, decent photography, and quality effects work. Moreover, if it matters, Gordon's rumored to be a very nice man, while Corman's reportedly shabby treatment of his actors and technicians is the stuff of legend. Still, overpraised though they may be, Corman's movies do have a quirky wit and intelligence that eludes Gordon.

In the case of *Beginning of the End*, the one-sheet depicting the slavering grasshopper is hands down the piece to get. The half-sheet and title card both feature a less exciting image, a sort of abstract, silhouetted 'hopper that looks vaguely like a giant spider, which is probably what the artist intended. ☪

Beginning of the End. © 1957 Republic Pictures Corporation. One-sheet, 27 x 41 inches.

The Giant Claw

➤ 1957

Here's a garish souvenir of an unforgettable movie. This Bizarro-World epic ranks with the immortal *Plan Nine From Outer Space* as one of the most consistently entertaining rotten movies ever made. Badfilm, like pornography, is hard to define, but you know it when you see it, and believe me, *The Giant Claw* is such a film.

The Giant Claw was produced by Sam Katzman, a name that's sort of a Good Housekeeping seal for wretched SF films. (To be fair, he was associated with a few interesting movies, in particular Ray Harryhausen's *Earth Versus the Flying Saucers* and *It Came From Beneath the Sea*.) *Claw* stars Jeff Morrow, Exeter from *This Island Earth*, a journeyman actor whose character here is just a little *too* damned bluff and hearty, a sort of Rod Taylor from hell. Also on hand for *Claw* was a raft of B science fiction regulars, including Morris Ankrum and the beautiful Mara Corday—the kind of people who can rise to the occasion with a decent script. No such luck here. *Claw* has the sort of screenplay which, when told he's the only surviving pilot to see the Giant Claw, requires Morrow to look downcast and mutter "That makes me chief cook and bottle washer in a one-man bird-watching society." Wow.

Like most other movies of its kind, *Claw* is patterned after *The Beast From 20,000 Fathoms*. There's the mysterious buildup, the opening attacks, the hero who sees the menace but isn't believed, the rampage, the hurried invention of the One Thing that will stop the beast, and so forth. As writer Bill Warren has said, until the monster comes aboard, *Claw* is trite but competent, more or less, and certainly no worse than a half-dozen other films of the same era.

This brings us, however, to the Claw herself—yes, she's a lady, and she's in a family way—who certainly must appear on any short list for most ludicrous special effect in cinematic history. The Giant Claw (never called that by the players, by the way) is a really, really *huge* space bird with an antimatter screen that makes it invisible to radar and impervious, oddly enough, to all earthly weapons, *plus* she's here to lay eggs. Warren tells an excruciating story: Jeff Morrow hadn't seen the finished product when he and his family attended the film in their own neighborhood theater. The gales of laughter that greeted the Claw's every appearance sent him slinking out of the theater, collar upturned, well before the end, telling his family he'd "meet them in the parking lot."

There's a good reason why this poster doesn't give a clear view of the Claw. As it happened, Sam Katzman had cut a few corners, farming the giant bird effect out to a thoroughly incompetent team who shot the footage for pennies in Mexico. I could say that the eye-rolling, neck-bobbing Claw resembles a demented Muppet, but I wouldn't want you to visualize anything that well-crafted. Imagine instead a folk-art hand puppet.

Today, *The Giant Claw* is pretty popular in video stores as an unintentional comedy classic. Personally, though, I can never see it without feeling sorry for Jeff Morrow. ☪

The Giant Claw. © 1957 Columbia Pictures Corporation. Title card, 11 x 14 inches.

The Amazing Colossal Man

➤ 1957

This big fella is probably Bert I. Gordon's most famous creation. *The Amazing Colossal Man* is also generally conceded to be B.I.G.'s best movie, though lord knows that's not saying much.

Beginning of the End was enough of a financial success to win Gordon a four-picture contract with his kindred spirits at American International Pictures. *The Amazing Colossal Man*, Gordon's first for AIP, is clearly an attempt to cash in on the success of *The Incredible Shrinking Man*. The idea of turning the previous story upside down by having the hero *grow* must have seemed like a natural to Gordon.

Colonel Glenn Manning (Glenn Langan) is caught in the full fury of a "plutonium bomb" [sic] test while attempting to save the pilot of a downed plane. As anyone who reads Marvel comics can tell you, such exposure inevitably produces strange effects, such as a desire to wear long underwear and fight crime. In Manning's case, though, the effect is rapid growth, and when I say rapid, I'm talking ten or so feet per day. The military covers up this startling development, as the military is wont to do, keeping Manning in a large circus tent on the grounds of a secret base. Manning is understandably grumpy and despondent over his condition, despite the presence of his fiancé Carol (Cathy Downs). In one amusing scene, Carol takes thirty-foot tall Glenn on a picnic in an effort to cheer him up, and there's a car parked nearby; *who drove?*, we wonder.

As if he didn't have enough troubles, Manning suffers from terrible chest pains. His heart is growing more slowly than the rest of his body, because the heart is basically *a single cell* (which is, of course, complete balderdash). This slower-growing heart will eventually kill Glenn if a cure isn't found. Working feverishly, a scientific team devises a formula—"sulfa hydrol"—to stop his growth, and another treatment to shrink him back to normal size through "high-frequency stimulation" of the pituitary gland. (Ah. Of course.)

By now, however, Glenn's mind has become unhinged. After a squabble with Carol he stumbles out into the desert. The army catches up to him and injects him with an eight-foot or so hypodermic filled with sulfa hydrol. Glenn takes this poorly, and skewers one of his tormentors with the hypo. He then tours the casino strip of Las Vegas, destroying a few local landmarks, and ends up holding Carol Kong-style while balancing atop the Hoover Dam. The army pleads with him to put her down. He does so, and gets blasted off the dam as a reward.

In spite of its many sins, this probably is B.I.G.'s most entertaining movie. The acting is generally quite good. In particular, Glenn Langan's Manning is interestingly un-heroic in his bitterness, although he does become a bit whiny before the show's over. The effects are, well, B.I.G. effects, unconvincing but fun. Gordon's matte work always seems underexposed, making the giant look fish-belly white; he really *should* get more sun.

The poster is one of Albert Kallis' most famous images from the 1950s, rendered with his customary dynamism. I am, however, curious as to just where the lower portion of the giant's left leg might be. ☪

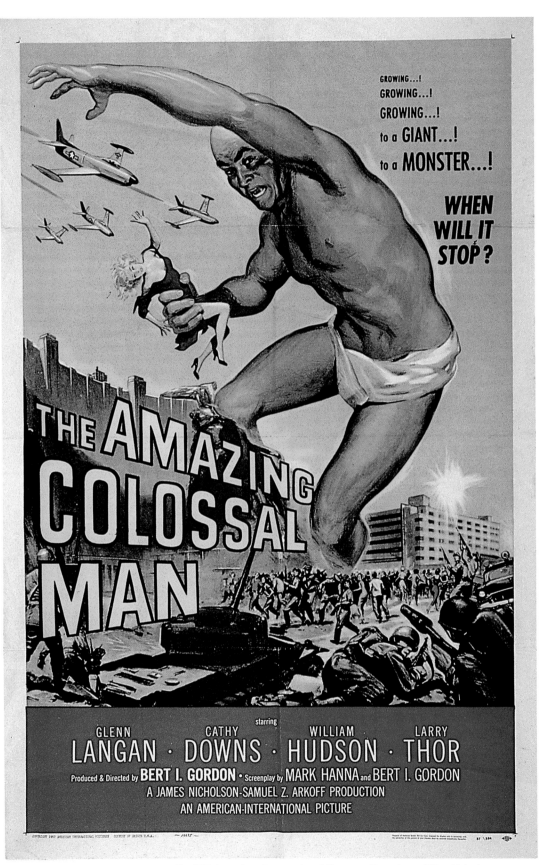

The Amazing Colossal Man. © 1957 American International Pictures. One-sheet, 27 x 41 inches.

The Monolith Monsters

➤ 1957

This classic comin'-at-ya image, employing his signature Antlike People Cowering theme, was one of Reynold Brown's last science fiction posters for Universal. *The Monolith Monsters* also proved to be one of the last relatively serious and adult science fiction films of the decade.

In *Monolith Monsters*, a meteor smashes into the California desert, near a sleepy town called San Angelo. Black, crystalline fragments of the meteor are scattered around the countryside; one is found by a geologist who takes it back to his lab. Water spilled on the rock makes it smoke in a sinister fashion. The next day, the man is found dead by his partner, geologist Dave Miller (Grant Williams). The dead man is literally *petrified*, and there are large chunks of the mysterious stone around the lab. Meanwhile, a little girl, Ginny (Linda Scheley), finds another meteor fragment and washes it in a basin. Her home is destroyed by more enormous pieces of black rock, her parents turn to stone, and the girl herself begins to stiffen.

By this time, we're pretty sure that these rocks shouldn't be immersed in water, but Miller and a colleague, Professor Flanders (Trevor Bardette), take a surprisingly long time to make the connection. Finally they do so with the aid of another helpfully accidental spill.

The scientists discover that, when wet, the black rock absorbs silicon from its surrounding environment and then *grows* at a fantastic rate. The rock can drain silicon from the human body as well, producing the mysterious petrification. Armed with this knowledge, a special solution is devised that saves Ginny (and the petrification subplot pretty much goes out the window). It's too early for congratulations, though. With a mutual look of horror, the scientists look outside and realize it's *raining*.

Soon the meteor fragments in the desert have become enormous, gleaming-black pillars, like a Manhattan from Hell, constantly growing, shattering, falling to earth, and growing again. The rains stop, but by this time the crystal monoliths are feeding off the water table, and their path of growth will, of course, flatten San Angelo in a matter of hours. Meanwhile, Miller and Flanders reason that the formula that cured Ginny might stop the rocks' growth as well, and discover that the active agent in the solution is actually its saline base—salt. The monoliths are halted by dynamiting a nearby dam, which sends a torrent across a local salt flat. The salty deluge stops the crystals' growth, leaving an impressive new tourist attraction just outside of town.

The story, based on a treatment written by Jack Arnold, turns on some too-obvious plot contrivances. In particular, the *looonng* time it takes the scientists to learn that *water* makes the rocks grow is irritating and serves only to pad out the film. Furthermore, there's an absolute *minimum* of character development, even for a 1950s SF movie; Miller is Brave, Flanders is Professorial—and that's about it. But if it's not a classic, *Monolith Monsters* is still an entertaining thriller. The monoliths are an offbeat and plausible-seeming menace, well-realized by some simple but effective special effects. The black towers have an unearthly beauty, and scenes of them looming near the town are among the most wonder-provoking in the genre. ☪

The Monolith Monsters. © 1957 Universal International Pictures. Title card, 11 x 14 inches.

Attack of the 50 Foot Woman

➤ 1958

And now for the distaff side of Amazing Colossaldom. Here's the ultimate *femme fatale*, in poundage at least. *Attack of the 50 Foot Woman* has become one of the most popular '50s schlock movies, and one of the most popular posters of the era.

50 Foot Woman was a $65,000 quickie shot in eight days, and one doubts that the participants knew they were making a classic. (Director Nathan Juran had himself billed on the film as "Nathan Hertz," which doesn't smell like pride.) As a work of science fiction, the film is, ah, inadequate. Fortunately, it has other things on its perverse little mind.

Nancy Archer (Allison Hayes), 50-Foot-Woman-to-be, is a wealthy woman living in the California desert, with $50 million, a drinking problem, and a philandering husband, Harry (William Hudson). Harry is keeping steady time with a tramp—there's no other word for it—named Honey Parker (Yvette Vickers), who French-kisses and wants both Harry and his wife's millions. On a late-night desert drive, Nancy encounters a "satellite"—the movie was made just a few months after Sputnik, and satellites were a hot topic—piloted by a bald giant wearing a tunic with a fleur-de-lis(!) on it. The next day, no one believes Nancy's story. One of those TV newscasters that exist *only* in these movies *specifically* ridicules her UFO report *and* makes fun of her marriage.

Nancy drags Harry back into the desert to prove her story. This time, she's kidnapped by the satellite jockey, while Harry beats it back to town. When Nancy is mysteriously returned to her home (*large* alien footprints are found in the garden) she begins growing. Her doctors keep her chained in her bedroom, which must be a mighty *big* room; Harry tries, unsuccessfully, to murder his expanding spouse; and finally, Nancy breaks her chains, bursts out of her house, tears apart the bar where Harry and Honey hang out, and kills them both before being slain by the gendarmerie.

The three principals all turn in considerably better performances than the script requires. William Hudson's two-timing Harry is interesting as a sort of ferret-faced Bill Holden. Allison Hayes projects a healthy, slightly bovine sensuality; usually, she provides plenty enough sex appeal for one feature. Here, though, she's overshadowed by Yvette Vickers, who is simply unforgettable. Vickers wasn't a classic beauty, but something in her pouty, Donna-Reed-gone-wrong features spells S-E-X in enormous, red neon letters. She was a fine Method actress who was sadly typecast by her genius for simulated sluttery; today she's enjoying new popularity, as fans rediscover her performances in this movie and *Attack of the Giant Leeches*.

The effects are rotten, even for the Bs. Backgrounds are clearly visible through process shots of "giant" figures, and the oversized hands used in several scenes are laughably crude. Who cares, though?

50 Foot Woman is another spectacular Reynold Brown painting; it's needless to say, perhaps, that this wonderful scene does not appear in the movie. Collector demand for *50 Foot Woman* began heading for the stratosphere in the mid-1980s, and the poster shown here is virtually unobtainable for less than four figures. Incidentally, it's hard not to read some significance into the fact that *50 Foot Woman* sells for nearly ten times as much as its male counterpart, *The Amazing Colossal Man*. ☪

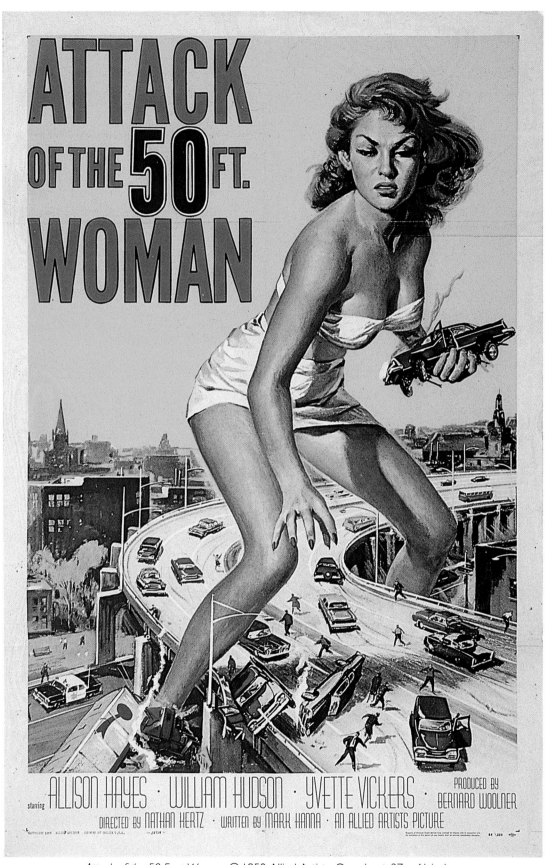

Attack of the 50 Foot Woman. © 1958 Allied Artists. One-sheet, 27 x 41 inches.

War of the Colossal Beast

➤ 1958

This sleazy, by-the-numbers sequel to *The Amazing Colossal Man* makes the original seem to shine by comparison, which is no mean feat. Even by the lowered standards one adopts in critiquing Bert I. Gordon's films, this is a *mess*.

Surprisingly enough, Colossal Man Glenn Manning didn't die when he did that triple-gainer from the top of Hoover Dam in *Colossal Man*. No, instead he drifted down the Colorado river (past some amazingly unobservant farmers, one assumes) and somehow found his way into the Mexican interior, where he's been eking out a living looting bread and dairy trucks and the like. His face, as seen in the poster, is grotesquely scarred from his fall from the dam; much of the skin is missing from the right side of his face, and an eye socket is horribly empty. It seems unlikely that a person, giant or not, could survive in the wild with such injuries, but it *does* allow Gordon to disguise the fact that Manning is now being played by a different actor (Dean Parkin).

Manning's fiancé is no longer around, so Gordon gives us a sister, Joyce (Sally Fraser). Joyce investigates the mysterious truck disappearances in Mexico, and eventually persuades the military, represented by the perfectly colorless Major Baird (Roger Pace), to help her search. Sure enough, the two find sixty-foot Glenn living in the mountains, surrounded by twelve-wheeled empties, as it were, and eventually capture him by slipping him a truck full of doped bread. B.I.G. then treats us to some feeble political satire as the problem of what to do with the giant is shunted from one government department to the next.

Finally, Glenn ends up living in a Los Angeles airplane hanger. The army keeps him tied down with heavy chains and shows him slides of his past in an attempt to reach his now deranged mind. To absolutely no one's surprise, the giant breaks loose. He briefly threatens a school bus full of kids (as per the poster, except that no one falls to their death), confronts Joyce but doesn't pick her up (which *is* a mild surprise), and then, apparently in a fit of remorse, electrocutes himself on some convenient high-power lines. Or at least one assumes he's electrocuted. Actually, he just disappears in a puff of smoke, like in one of those Georges Méliès fantasy shorts from 1898.

War of the Colossal Beast (what war?) feels tired and joyless throughout. The acting, a relatively bright spot in *Colossal Man*, here is perfunctory at best. The script doesn't even try to develop the characters, and worse, doesn't give our sixty-footer much of anything to *do*. Mostly Glenn sits around or lays in chains, growling. Even his final rampage is a weak-tea disappointment, with virtually none of the cardboard-set destruction that enlivened the first outing.

The poster is another Albert Kallis design. It's striking, but marred by its limited color scheme. Note that a blurb promises you'll see "a sixty-foot giant destroyed...IN COLOR!" This is true; the last minute of the film, featuring Glenn's self-immolation, is indeed in color. The remaining sixty-seven or so minutes of the movie are in glorious black and white. When it came to shucking its audiences, AIP had few equals. ☾

War of the Colossal Beast. © 1958 American International Pictures. One-sheet, 27 x 41 inches.

The Giant Behemoth

➤ 1959

The Giant Behemoth is an interesting piece of filmic *curiosa*, but it's easier to respect than to love.

Behemoth was directed by Eugene Lourié, who also helmed Ray Harryhausen's *The Beast From 20,000 Fathoms* as well as *Gorgo*. *Behemoth* is essentially a remake of the earlier two films; Lourié's third outing in the city-trampling dinosaur genre might be regarded more fondly if the first two weren't clearly superior.

Like *20,000 Fathoms*, *Behemoth* concerns a sea-going dinosaur, a prehistoric survival unleashed by A-bomb testing. Its first appearances are marked by massive fish kills. Soon fishermen and coastal dwellers are turning up dead from radiation burns, and talk of a sea monster spreads. A young, dedicated scientist faces ridicule, at first, for believing the monster exists, but ultimately is vindicated when the beast starts rearranging real estate (this time in London rather than New York). The movie's "paleosaurus" is 200 feet long, *and* electric, like an eel, *and* fiercely radioactive. Furthermore, he can't be killed with conventional artillery, as radioactive dino-bits would contaminate the ground. This is a fairly unpleasant lizard, all in all. As with the Beast, he's felled by a radioactive projectile—a torpedo, in this case—but a twist

The Giant Behemoth. © 1959 Allied Artists. One-sheet, 27 x 41 inches.

ending reveals that fish kills are occurring along the American coast. Apparently, more paleosaurs are on the way.

Behemoth is decidedly odd for its genre in that the acting and photography are really rather good. It's the *monster* that disappoints. It's doubly disappointing because *Behemoth* contains the final animation work of Willis O'Brien, creator of King Kong and the man who all but invented stop-motion animation. Special effects genius though he undoubtedly was, O'Brien seemed to lack the promotional skills that made Ray Harryhausen a success. His later career was marked by disappointments, failed productions, and underpaid, demeaning assignments. By 1959 O'Brien was an old man, and his long-time assistant, animator Pete Peterson, was suffering from multiple sclerosis. O'Brien and Peterson were given no more than a month and a half to complete *Behemoth*'s animation work; the film's total special effects budget was a paltry $20,000, and it shows.

Unfortunately, the creature is clumsily modeled and stiffly animated, lacking the smooth movement of Harryhausen's Beast. In what should be the film's climax—the monster's attack on London—the film's technical and financial shortcomings become especially apparent. Many animation shots are recycled repeatedly; the monster steps on the same car three times, and scares the same rather sparse London crowd (of twenty or so) up and down a number of different streets.

In spite of these problems, it's not a bad little movie. Gene Evans is fairly engaging as the scientist-hero, but outshined by Jack MacGowran as an eccentric paleontologist—a replay of the character played by Cecil Kellaway in *20,000 Fathoms*. Location filming in England helps, and the opening sequences set in Cornwall manage to generate an appropriately mysterious mood. The film's overtly antinuclear energy themes are also interesting, considering the period in which it was made. Evans' character delivers a warning against radiation that must have sounded pretty outlandish—in 1959.

As with the film, the one-sheet shown here is a nice example of the giant beastie theme, but no match for the vibrant *20,000 Fathoms* poster. ☾⋆

Konga

➤ 1961

In a field with many strong contenders, *Konga* may well be the most cynically misleading AIP poster ever. Still, it's a particularly fine example of Reynold Brown's talent for mass chaos and destruction.

Konga's poster promises a *King Kong* rip-off. That's a rip-off in itself, though, since *Konga* does not feature Big Trouble until its lackluster finish. For most of its length, it's a surprisingly mean-spirited rehashing of those gorilla-on-the-loose things that Monogram used to make back in the early '40s.

Botanist Charles Decker (Michael Gough) returns to England after a year in the African jungle. He brings with him strange plants, obtained from a witch doctor, and a baby chimpanzee named Konga. He's greeted by his live-in assistant and mistress, Margaret (Margo Johns), who obviously loves him. Decker however, is a heartless creep; we get his measure when he casually rips Margaret's flowers out of a greenhouse to make room for his carnivorous African plants.

These plants are the keys to Decker's experiments, which involve some gibberish about combining plant and animal cells. An extract from the plants makes Konga grow to maturity in seconds (courtesy of a simple lap-dissolve effect); another dose changes the adult chimpanzee into a gorilla suit—and not a particularly *good* gorilla suit, either. (It's the same one worn by the diving-helmeted alien in the infamous *Robot Monster*.)

What Decker ultimately plans to do with this formula isn't clear, although he obscurely promises to "dominate a corner of the Earth." At present, Decker *hypnotizes* Konga(!) and dispatches him to kill. The ape's first victim is the dean of Decker's college, who rightly thinks he has been acting oddly; next to die is a rival scientist. Margaret is troubled by these developments, but a marriage proposal shuts her up.

However, the wedding is not to be. Middle-aged Decker is interested in a shapely student, Sandra (Claire Gordon), and soon her boyfriend gets the Konga treatment. Incidentally, as murder weapons gorillas lack subtlety, as the animals are neither concealable nor easily portable. Decker's forced to cart Konga around in a large panel truck. Nonetheless, the police are conveniently baffled.

Ultimately, jealous Margaret releases Konga and gives him another dose of serum, which makes him...well, *really big*, although his size varies from scene to scene. Konga kills Margaret. Sandra is eaten by a carnivorous plant, just for the heck of it. Konga takes Decker on a walk through London, pausing, via poorly executed mattes, in front of prominent landmarks. Finally the army opens fire on Konga, who's still clutching Decker, and both tumble down to dusty death. In a chucklesome climax, the enormous gorilla dwindles down to a baby chimp once more.

Konga is one of a series of SF and horror films of wildly varying quality produced by Herman Cohen. Cohen was fortunate enough to work with a talented director, Gene Fowler, in making the surprising *I Was a Teenage Werewolf*. Most of Cohen's *oeuvre*, however, runs the gamut from mediocre (*Target Earth*) to dismal (this one, for instance.) ☾*

NOT SINCE "KING KONG" HAS THE SCREEN EXPLODED WITH SUCH MIGHTY FURY AND SPECTACLE!

KONGA

IN COLOR AND SPECTAMATION
starring
MICHAEL GOUGH · MARGO JOHNS
JESS CONRAD · CLAIRE GORDON
A HERMAN COHEN Production · An AMERICAN-INTERNATIONAL Picture
Screenplay by ABEN KANDEL and HERMAN COHEN · Directed by JOHN LEMONT

Konga. ©1961 American International Pictures. Insert, 14 x 36 inches.

Reptilicus

➤ 1962

Reptilicus is probably the finest big-lizard movie poster ever, dynamic yet graceful. The movie was produced and directed by Sid Pink, creator of *Angry Red Planet* and *Journey to the Seventh Planet*; and by this time you won't be shocked to hear that the film features *The Giant Claw*'s only serious rival for Silliest Menace in cinematic history.

Reptilicus was Pink's first Danish SF project, filmed before *Seventh Planet*, with many of the same cast and crew; lawsuits between Pink and AIP (concerning either the film's weaknesses, or the studio's "creative accounting," depending on who you believe) delayed the earlier picture's release. *Reptilicus* is far more leaden even than *Seventh Planet*. Virtually the only entertainment available is the sheer ineptitude of the monster effects, and that's a thin sort of amusement to carry you for an hour and a half.

The basic setup has a certain ingenuity, though. An oil-drilling rig in Denmark strikes *blood*. The drill bit is discovered to have bits of fresh-looking flesh clinging to it, which attracts the attention of local scientists. An excavation unearths a frozen tail that must have belonged to some gigantic reptile. The tail is taken to Copenhagen for study, and after it accidentally thaws out, it's found to be *alive*. The tail is placed in a nutrient solution, where it regenerates a new body like a starfish. A lightning storm wakes the newly formed giant dragon, which breaks loose from its vat and...can anyone tell me what happens next? Does the dweat big dwagon stomp on wocal metwopowitan aweas? Very good! Ultimately he's slain by a poisoned bazooka shell, in a virtual replay of the demise of *The Beast From 20,000 Fathoms*.

The dubbed Danish cast is utterly, completely forgettable. One and all, the actors display the stage presence of Formica countertops. That might be forgivable, if the monster were effective. It's not. The monster effects were done by a Dane named Bent Barfod, and consist almost entirely of marionette work on crude tabletop models (a few scenes look as though they might involve primitive stop-motion animation.) Strings often are clearly visible. The poorly made puppet closely resembles Fran Allison's Kukla—not exactly a sight to strike terror in your heart. Certainly it didn't seem to perturb the Danish crowds, who "flee from the monster" up and down streets with a cheerful, unconcerned air. Moreover, there doesn't seem to be a single matte shot of Reptilicus—that is to say, no attempt whatever to combine the monster with live actors. Encounters with the monster simply involve a shot of the happy panicking mob followed by a shot of the puppet cavorting on a card-table model of Copenhagen.

This said, and I take no particular pleasure in slamming a man's work, I would like to add that Sid Pink's autobiography is an entertaining and at times harrowing read. Zero-budget filmmaking is not for the meek, and Pink clearly did the best job he could under extremely trying circumstances. When one considers the amazing variety of things that can go wrong on a shoestring production of this kind, the wonder is not that so many of them are so bad, but that they actually get made at all. ☾⋆

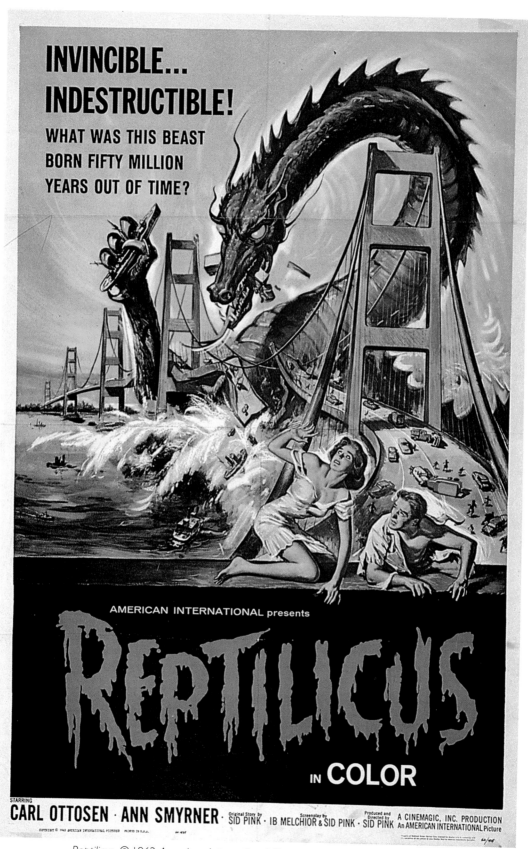

Reptilicus. © 1962 American International Pictures. One-sheet, 27 x 41 inches.

Invaders From Elsewhere

*"I bring you a warning...
To every one of you
listening to the sound
of my voice...
tell the world...
tell this to everyone,
wherever they are....
Watch the skies!
Watch everywhere!
Keep on looking!
Watch the skies!*

—"Scotty"
in *The Thing From Another World*

Bert I. Gordon's Colossal Man
(here played by Dean Parkin) takes
a stand on busing in the tedious
sequel *War of the Colossal Beast.*

The Thing From Another World

➤ 1951

This first and best of all Invaders From Elsewhere is one of the finest science fiction films ever made. It's also a *scary* film, far more intense than any of the alleged "horror" movies made during the 1950s.

The Thing is generally known by its shorter title; the words "From Another World" were hastily added to the title to avoid confusion when a Phil Harris novelty song, also called "The Thing," became a hit record just before the movie was scheduled to open. *The Thing* opens with the crash of a mysterious object in the Arctic. An Air Force team, led by Captain Pat Hendry (Kenneth Tobey), is sent to investigate. The team finds an enormous, circular vehicle trapped in the ice; they inadvertently destroy the flying saucer, but recover its alien pilot (James Arness) imbedded in a block of ice, and take it to a nearby scientific research station. A storm traps the military team at the base and makes radio communication impossible. Meanwhile, their unearthly prize thaws out and escapes into the frigid night. It's intelligent and *extremely* hostile.

The base's scientists are, of course, fascinated by this development, and their leader, Dr. Carrington (Robert Cornthwaite), assumes that a creature capable of interstellar flight can be persuaded to talk shop with fellow scientists. He's wrong. Hendry and his men are more awake to the threat, but ultimately, both scientists and military men battle for their lives, as the Thing lays siege to the base, picking off its inhabitants one by one.

The Thing is based on a classic SF novella, *Who Goes There?*, by John W. Campbell. Director Howard Hawks changed the nature of Campbell's alien—a shape-shifter that could absorb and assume the identity of its victims—probably because he felt the concept was either too difficult to film or too abstruse for 1951 audiences. (John Carpenter's interesting if gooey 1982 remake of *The Thing* returned to Campbell's original concept.) Hawks' alien, instead, is a vegetative lifeform, "an intellectual carrot," in the film's memorable phrase, that can reproduce itself via seedlings it nurtures with *blood*.

The Thing makeup is a disappointment; Arness's alien is just a powerful, rather Frankensteinian monster. However, it's well-used, mostly seen dimly, in explosive flashes of action. (In original release prints of the film, the monster's scenes were deliberately darkened to further obscure its appearance.) Most of the movie's terror comes from the claustrophobic intensity of its premise, a deadly cat-and-mouse game played out in the cramped, frigid quarters of the isolated arctic base. (The sets were built within a Los Angeles ice house; the actors' frosty breath and chilly discomfort are real.)

Hawks took a producer's credit on *The Thing*, while his favorite editor, Christian Nyby, was credited with directing. But the movie is so obviously done in Hawks' style that Nyby's role is usually downplayed by film writers. Most "Hawksian" is *The Thing*'s rapid-fire, naturalistic and overlapping dialogue, which increases the film's effectiveness enormously. While the cast of relative unknowns is uniformly fine, Ken Tobey in particular stands out; his Captain Hendry is a likeable mix of toughness, authority and self-deprecating humor. Hendry became the model for all subsequent military heros in 1950s SF, and Tobey himself played virtually the same character in two subsequent films.

In keeping with the film's highly successful "teaser" publicity campaign, posters for *The Thing* are deliberately uninformative. In view of the monster's unimpressive appearance, it's probably just as well. Nonetheless, *Thing* posters are sentimental favorites with many collectors, and priced and pursued accordingly. ☾

The Thing From Another World. © 1951 RKO Radio Pictures Inc. Half-sheet, 22 x 28 inches.

The Man From Planet X

➤ 1951

"Cult classic" is an overworked term that truly fits *The Man From Planet X*. This film is the most highly regarded genre effort by director Edgar G. Ulmer, who learned his craft in the heyday of German Expressionist cinema, working with Fritz Lang, F.W. Murnau, and Eric Von Stroheim. After directing a few "A" pictures in the 1930s, Ulmer descended permanently into Poverty Row, and helped found *film noir* with movies like *Detour*. The *auteur* movement in film criticism has since lifted Ulmer to heights occupied by only two other genre directors of the 1950s, Jack Arnold and Roger Corman, and some believe Ulmer to be the best of the three.

Planet X is set entirely on a lonely, fog-shrouded island in the north of Scotland, in what seems to be a perpetual night. Professor Elliot (Raymond Bond) has come to the island to study a mysterious Planet X, which is on a near-collision course with Earth. (The professor has chosen the island because it's "the nearest spot on Earth" to Planet X, which implies that the Earth doesn't rotate, but let it pass.) With him is his daughter, Enid (Margaret Field), a sinister colleague, Mears (William Schallert), and the hero, reporter John Lawrence (Robert Clarke), who falls for Enid and distrusts Mears.

An alien from Planet X arrives in a peculiar, lightbulb-shaped spaceship. The creature is friendly enough at first, but Mears soon tries to force scientific secrets from him. The alien retaliates with a raygun that enslaves the will; he then kidnaps Mears, Elliot and Enid, and recruits a zombie-like army among local villagers, who're put to work fortifying alien's landing site. Lawrence assumes the alien is the vanguard of an invasion fleet—a conclusion never verified by events, by the way. The reporter summons the military and rescues Enid, her father, and the villagers; an army unit destroys the alien and, in the process, the evil Mears. Planet X makes its closest approach to Earth, zips across the sky, seemingly makes a U-turn and heads back into the void.

One of the most interesting things about *Planet X* is the way Ulmer continually subverts the script's simplistic invasion scenario to build sympathy for the alien, who is never seen to act aggressively except in self-defense. Despite the ending, in which military might saves the day, the film's real villain is the greedy and ruthless Mears, not the rather sad alien.

This movie cost less than $50,000, and was filmed primarily on sets left over from *Joan of Arc*. Even so, *Planet X* is one of the best-looking science fiction films of the era. Ultimately, it's the visual elements that make *Planet X* seem like a minor classic; its look is comparable to the best of Universal's horror classics of twenty years before. The film's exquisite photography sets it far above the monotonous flat-grey look of most 1950s SF. While the film is cartoonlike in its simplicity, and at times badly paced, Ulmer's rich, Gothic mood disguises the flaws of both sets and script.

Posters of any kind from *The Man From Planet X* are extremely rare and priced accordingly. The one-sheet is beautiful and almost impossible to find; this insert, with its portrait of the alien, makes a nice consolation prize. ☾⋆

The Man From Planet X.
© 1951 United Artists. Insert, 14 x 36 inches.

The Day the Earth Stood Still

➤ 1951

The Day the Earth Stood Still figures on most "best-ever" lists of science fiction films. *TDTESS* was conceived and executed as a completely adult science fiction film; it's a great shame that it had so little influence on subsequent genre efforts. Producer Julian Blaustein, prime architect of the project, wanted to make a science fiction film with a "peace theme"—a done-to-death idea by now, perhaps, but refreshing in the darkest days of the Cold War. Hindsight tends to make any idealism look naive, but for the most part, *TDTESS* holds up nicely on its own terms, even today.

Klaatu, the film's alien ambassador, lands in Washington not to conquer but to bring a warning. Earth's "petty squabbles" are our own business, but man's technology is fast approaching a level that would enable us to extend our taste for violence beyond our own planet. And the worlds that Klaatu represents simply will not allow this, even if they must destroy the Earth. Klaatu's mission is to deliver this message to all the world's peoples.

After being imprisoned in a military hospital, Klaatu escapes and decides to see something of earthly life, to learn why humans seem so enslaved by fear and distrust. Posing as a man named "Carpenter," he becomes friends with a young widow, Helen Benson (Patricia Neal) and her son Bobby (Billy Gray), as well as a kindly Einstein surrogate, Dr. Barnhardt (Sam Jaffe). To impress the seriousness of his mission on the world's peoples, he uses his spaceship's technology to neutralize all electrical power everywhere for an hour (hence the film's title). The federal authorities close in on Klaatu, who is killed and then resurrected by his robot compatriot, Gort—a plot twist that upset Breen Office censors so much that they demanded the resurrection be made "temporary!"—but with the aid of the men and women of goodwill he's met, Klaatu is able to complete his mission after all.

TDTESS brought together a number of significant talents. Michael Rennie, as the somewhat saintly but thoroughly "human" Klaatu gives the best performance of a too-often mediocre career. Patricia Neal is equally fine as Helen Benson, Klaatu's primary ally. Screenwriter Edmund North's script is literate and sometimes playful, with nearly subliminal "Christ themes" centered on Klaatu. North's script also, mercifully, resists the temptation to turn the friendship between Klaatu and Helen into a romance; it's virtually the only SF film of the 1950s without a rote subplot of this kind. Composer Bernard Hermann graced *TDTESS* with perhaps the finest score of any science fiction film ever, making superb use of the eerie electronic wailing of the theramin. Last but not least, designers Lyle Wheeler and Addison Hehr gave science fiction one of its all-time great icons in Gort, the eight-foot robot that accompanies Klaatu on his mission.

The posters for *TDTESS* are highly collectible, if somewhat more conventional than the film itself. 20th Century Fox seems to have hedged its bets on its "adult" sci-fi film by designing a promotional campaign centered on the robot Gort and scenes of mass panic and destruction. Nonetheless, the imagery on all *TDTESS* posters is vivid and memorable. The half-sheet shown here is, oddly, the only poster from the film to portray Klaatu. ☾

The Day the Earth Stood Still. © 1951 20th Century-Fox Film Corporation. Half-sheet, 22 x 28 inches.

Red Planet Mars

➤ 1952

This striking poster represents one of the most unusual films described in this book. It's not *good*, mind you, or entertaining, but it *is* unusual. *Red Planet Mars* has no futuristic settings, no monster suits, no spaceships—scarcely anything of visual interest, in fact, just some rather silly ideas. The film's sole science fiction element consists of radio messages from Mars, which turn out to be from God. Perhaps I should explain.

Red Planet Mars was adapted from a play, and looks it. Most of the film takes place on two sets, the radio laboratory of Chris Cronyn (Peter Graves), and that of an ex-Nazi scientist in hiding, Franz Calder (Herbert Berghof). Cronyn has used an advanced radio, built from a design of Calder's, to contact intelligent life on Mars. Calder, in turn, is secretly listening in on Cronyn's experiments. Calder is in the pay of Evil Russians; this rather optimistic idea that Nazis and Communists are natural allies pops up frequently in the McCarthy-dominated early 1950s. The commie overlords want the Martians' advanced scientific knowledge (which they are automatically assumed to have, being Martians).

When Cronyn's Martian messages are released, everyone seems to believe that any technology mentioned by the Martians will soon be transferred to Earth, which leads to a massive inferiority complex on civilization's part. For instance, a message claims that Martians can feed a thousand of their own people with the produce of a single acre, and farm prices collapse. A similar message about power from "cosmic energy" throws all the coal miners out of work. Soon, a worldwide depression has set in. As the West descends into economic chaos, the Kremlin gloats.

But wait! It's those commies' turn next. The radio messages shift to spiritual topics, and soon the Martians are beaming paraphrases of the Sermon on the Mount. These messages initially seem to be from Christian Martians, but soon everyone seems to think they're coming directly from God. This causes a worldwide religious revival. In Russia, the peasantry hear of the miracle on Voice of America, rise up and overthrow their communist leaders (*that'll* never happen, right?). About this time, though (first plot twist), Cronyn is visited by Calder, who reveals that *he* created the Martian messages to destroy Western economic confidence. However, (second plot twist) Calder *didn't* send the religious messages; he assumes Cronyn *did*.

As the two scientists confront one another, another message from Mars (God?) begins to come in, throwing Calder into a frenzy. Everyone is destroyed in an explosion inadvertently triggered by the gun-toting Nazi. At the end, Cronyn is praised by an Eisenhower-clone President, angelic choirs warble and a final title says "The Beginning."

Amen. Unfortunately, even if you can buy the premise and a half-dozen associated absurdities, *Red Planet Mars* is little more than a curiosa. The writing is generally poor, and the acting is bad in a little-theater sort of way, with a lot of unmotivated and over-emphatic declaiming. But it *is* different. (Although *not* unique. *Red Planet Mars* would seem to owe something to another "Radio God" story from 1950, *The Next Voice You Hear*, which starred James Whitmore and Nancy Davis, later Reagan.) ☾

Red Planet Mars.
© 1952 United Artists. Insert, 14 x 36 inches.

It Came From Outer Space

➤ 1953

This eye-popping Joe Smith poster provides fitting hype for one of best and most influential science fiction films of the 1950s.

It Came From Outer Space.
© 1953 Universal-International Pictures.
One-sheet, 27 x 41 inches.

It Came From Outer Space is an important landmark for a number of reasons. First, as the poster will not let you forget, it was one of the first 3-D releases, although it's nearly impossible to see it in its original form today. Also, the movie introduced or at least codified several signature themes of the '50s science fiction canon—the young, virile, regular-guy scientist (played incessantly, though not in this film, by John Agar); the Southwestern desert setting as a suitably eerie backdrop, later seen in *Them!*, *Tarantula* and many other films, and the Friends-and-Neighbors-Turning-Alien gambit, which reached its fullest development in 1956's *Invasion of the Body Snatchers*.

Perhaps most importantly, *Outer Space* marked the beginning of an extraordinary series of genre projects by director Jack Arnold. On the strength of this imaginative and financially successful movie, Arnold was able to position himself as Universal's "science fiction specialist," turning out a string of memorable projects including *The Creature From The Black Lagoon*, *Tarantula*, and his finest film, *The Incredible Shrinking Man*. Arnold was an energetic storyteller with a talent for unusual and haunting visual compositions; even his minor works are a distinct cut above run-of-the-mill '50s pictures.

Outer Space is a classic Invaders From Elsewhere story that, like *Day the Earth Stood Still*, subverts the era's paranoia by making its aliens more sympathetic than some of the human cast. Amateur astronomer George Putnam (Richard Carlson) and his fiancé Ellen (Barbara Rush) observe a "meteor" falling in the lonely Arizona desert. Rushing to the scene, they find a huge crater. Putnam climbs down and discovers an enormous, globular spaceship half-buried in the crater's wall. (A tremendously atmospheric shot of Putnam standing, dwarfed, before the giant sphere is one of the most famous images in '50s SF.) The spaceship is almost immediately buried by a landslide, and at first no one believes Putnam's story; even Ellen is skeptical.

Soon after, several local townspeople are replaced by aliens from the buried ship, who have the ability to take on human appearance. The aliens, we learn, were on a peaceful mission to another planet when they accidentally crashed on Earth. Now they're "borrowing" the forms of locals to obtain the equipment they need to repair their ship, meanwhile keeping the duplicated people as hostages. Even Ellen is duplicated; in a famous, dreamlike sequence, a false "Ellen" lures Putnam across the desert at night to a deserted mine where the aliens are hiding. Putnam discovers the aliens' secret, comes to trust their intentions and finally is forced to defend them from a hot-headed local sheriff (Charles Drake).

Outer Space benefits tremendously from its origin as a Ray Bradbury story treatment. The script was written by Harry Essex, but, as Bill Warren has shown, Essex produced substantial portions of Bradbury's dialogue practically verbatim. An eerie and oddly elegaic scene featuring a thoughtful telephone lineman—"sometimes you think that the wind gets into the wires and hums and listens and talks..."—comes closer to capturing the quality of Bradbury's verbal poetry than most of the films and TV shows based on his novels and short stories. ☪

Target Earth

➤ 1954

Here's Good Robot Art on one of the better genre inserts of the 1950s, with a near-perfect balance of graphic elements (even if Richard Denning *does* look a bit bug-eyed).

Target Earth is an ultra-low budget SF programmer from Allied Artists that rises above the bottom rung via an atmospheric opening and some interesting characters. Also, the robots are sort of cute.

As *Target Earth* opens, a young woman, Nora King (Kathleen Crowley), wakes up to find herself alone in her boarding house. She'd attempted suicide the night before, through an overdose of sleeping pills. She quickly discovers that the unnamed city she lives in is deserted. Nora meets Frank Brooks (Richard Denning), who'd been mugged the night before; he, too, was deeply unconscious while the city emptied. Nora and Frank in turn find another couple, Jim Wilson (Dick Reeves) and Vicki Harris (Virginia Grey). They're tacky but good-hearted slobs who are taking advantage of everyone's absence to drink the best bars and clubs in town dry. In all, these opening scenes are nicely mysterious, reminiscent of a decent *Twilight Zone*.

Unfortunately, a mystery explained is a mystery no more. The little band learns that the apparently empty town is infested with big boxy robots armed with death rays mounted in their heads. Frank finds a newspaper that fills in the rest of the story. The town was evacuated on the approach of an invincible robot army that materialized nearby and wiped out all opposition (many stock-footage planes are destroyed with cheap optical effects). The group, now led by Frank, the hero type, begins living furtively in a hotel. Intercut with these scenes is a subplot involving a scientific team that is studying a deactivated robot, which malfunctioned because something—what?—cracked its seemingly indestructible faceplate.

Meanwhile, back in the hotel, Nora and Frank find each other, as it were; she's a young widow who'd thought she'd never love again, etc. Jim and Vicki also realize they love each other, in second-banana, comedy-relief fashion. The lives of the four refugees are further complicated by the arrival of a homicidal maniac, also trapped in the deserted city. And those scientists are getting closer to the robot's secret...Wait! You don't suppose sonic vibrations would do the trick, do you?

We never learn why the robots are here or where they came from, although both the scientists and Frank guess that they're Venusian. Frank rather endearingly admits he learned about Venus by reading science fiction magazines. Science fiction fans are seldom portrayed as manly heroes; it's a pity this fine trend didn't catch on.

Target Earth was based on a 1953 novelette by Paul Fairman, who also wrote the short story that became *Invasion of the Saucer-Men*. Fairman was, I assure you, an obscure writer of little merit—yet his work inspired, if that is the word, two films, while several metric tons of quality SF remain utterly ignored by Hollywood. It gives one much to ponder. ☾⋆

Target Earth.
© 1954 Allied Artists.
Insert, 14 x 36 inches.

Earth Versus the Flying Saucers

➤ 1956

Earth Versus the Flying Saucers is one of Ray Harryhausen's few "pure" science fiction films. After this and 1957's *20 Million Miles to Earth*, he turned more or less permanently to storybook fantasies such as *The Seventh Voyage of Sinbad*, a genre apparently closer to his heart. (Harryhausen did occasionally return to science fiction in such films as *First Men in the Moon*, but the later pictures are historical or prehistorical pieces, and lack the lab-coat and raygun themes of his '50s work.)

Ray Harryhausen occupies a special niche in film history, as the only true special effects *auteur*; his name has become as synonymous with his films as Welles' or Godard's. With few exceptions, his films were written, directed, and produced by relative nonentities; Harryhausen always provided the guiding vision. No one who regards his films with fondness ever refers to *Jason and the Argonauts,* say, as anything but a "Harryhausen movie," in precisely the same sense that *Lawrence of Arabia* is called a "David Lean film."

Earth Versus, as its fans usually call it, is generally regarded as minor Harryhausen; it's his only film that doesn't feature at least one of his disturbingly "alive" animated monsters. *Earth Versus* was designed to capitalize on the postwar flying saucer craze, which began in the late 1940s and reached a culmination of sorts with the great Washington, D.C. flap of 1952, when for months, it seems, residents of the city could scarcely go out of doors without having their hats knocked off by silvery disks from Beyond. Harryhausen reportedly was intrigued by the challenge of putting his customary dynamism and "life" into an inanimate object, and his flying saucers are by far the best put on film during the era.

As with Harryhausen's other science fiction films, *Earth Versus*' plot is comic-book simple. Our scientist-protagonist, Russell Marvin (played by *The Day the Earth Stood Still* alumnus Hugh Marlowe), heads a government rocket project that has launched several satellites only to see them destroyed in space by a mysterious force. The rocket base soon comes under attack by flying saucers, which had also destroyed the satellites. Marlowe's scientist eventually establishes contact with the aliens, and learns that they are the survivors of a dying world who seek to colonize Earth, by force if necessary. By the film's end, naturally, Marvin devises an anti-flying saucer ray. In a thoroughly enjoyable climax, earth's forces use the ray to foil an alien raid on Washington, D.C., and saucers crash into every recognizable landmark larger than a mailbox.

Harryhausen's films have undeniable shortcomings, and some fans lament the fact that the animator didn't work within the framework of the studio system, which might have offered him better actors and directors. Harryhausen, however, who seems a fiercely private man, opted for the freedom of independent, low-budget production. It was a personal choice, deliberately made, and one I respect.

Unfortunately, the posters for most of Harryhausen's films are rather drab and dull. *Earth Versus* is a glorious exception. All pieces from the film are excellent, but the one-sheet pictured here, with its deep, saturated colors, is the finest. The claustrophobic composition, with totemlike aliens marching serenely beneath saucer spotlights, makes this poster an expressionist classic of the genre. ☾★

Earth vs. the Flying Saucers. ©1956 Columbia Pictures Corporation. One-sheet, 27 x 41 inches.

It Conquered the World

➤ 1956

Like Roger Corman's other early science fiction films, *It Conquered the World* has been lavishly praised and subjected to much deep-thought film criticism—pretty weighty baggage for a ten-day, $80,000 quickie featuring a giant cucumber menace. Nevertheless, *It Conquered* does have an interesting, if not original, premise and some surprisingly grim plot twists (a Corman specialty).

The Invader from Elsewhere in *It Conquered* is a super-intelligent Venusian that does indeed resemble a conical cucumber with muscular-looking crab claws. The alien is summoned to Earth by a demented scientist, Tom Anderson (Lee Van Cleef), who believes it will free us from the tyranny of our emotions, ushering in a new era of order and scientific reason, etc. The alien establishes itself in a nearby cave and sets its plans for conquest in motion, with Anderson as its collaborator. Anderson, who communicates with the creature by radio, identifies the key leaders in the immediate area; as in so many of these films, the stated goal is world conquest, but the actual battle revolves around one little town. The leaders are attacked by batlike creatures produced by the alien, that have, and I quote, "radiological electrode-type things in their beaks." One sting from a bat-critter makes the victim a willing slave.

Soon the alien is the town's hidden master, in control of the police and local military authorities. (This aspect owes a lot to *Invasion of the Body Snatchers*, released earlier that year.) Only Paul Nelson (Peter Graves), heroic scientist and Anderson's friend, resists the takeover, even shooting his own wife when she becomes possessed by the alien. This scene, by the way, delivers a fairly potent shock, since it flies in the face of all our expectations; heroes just don't *do* this sort of thing. Paul does, though, and ultimately rubs out several other possessed friends and coworkers. Meanwhile, Anderson's wife, Claire (Beverly Garland), has had just about enough of her husband's new friend, and sets out to blast it with a shotgun. She fails, and is crunched by a rubbery claw, but her death makes Anderson comes to his senses. He kills the alien with a blowtorch(!), dying in the process, and Nelson delivers a speech about Man's Destiny over their carcasses.

And now, a word of praise for Paul Blaisdell, a name that appears several times in this book. Blaisdell produced a number of the era's most memorable monsters, including the cone-shaped monster from *It Conquered*, whom he affectionately dubbed Beulah. In an era when special-effects technicians have titles like "third assistant latex foam specialist," it's instructive to recall that Blaisdell was virtually a solo act, producing makeup, models and a wide variety of special effects on dismally small budgets. Blaisdell and his ingenious creations seem to have been systematically abused by the skinflint producers for whom he worked, and he was nearly forgotten when he died in 1983. Recent years have seen new interest in Blaisdell's work. While his monsters aren't exactly convincing or frightening, they *are* charming, and very much a part of the history of the genre.

This Albert Kallis poster faithfully renders Beulah's pumpkin grin, and demonstrates once again how Kallis could lend a touch of class to virtually any concept, no matter how unlikely. ☾★

It Conquered the World.
©1956 American International
Pictures. Insert, 14 x 36 inches.

Invasion of the Saucer-Men

➤ 1957

This intensely strange little movie has become a fan favorite in recent years, largely on the strength of make-up wizard Paul Blaisdell's bug-eyed monsters—and not, I hasten to add, because of the film's merits as a work of entertainment.

According to a *Cinefantastique* retrospective on Blaisdell, *Invasion of the Saucer-Men* began as a serious (more or less) film, the first to focus specifically on the "little green men" of the '50s flying saucer craze. During the film's production, however, it "just sort of collapsed" into a comedy, as Blaisdell put it. The result is a weird mishmash that veers from low-grade slapstick to some fairly gruesome, if unconvincing, violence, all larded over with an exceptionally irritating "comic" soundtrack.

Saucer-Men, oddly enough, is one of the handful of 1950s SF movies based on an actual written work, albeit a pulp short story of no particular merit ("The Cosmic Frame" by Paul W. Fairman). The film concerns the invasion of a small-town's Lover's Lane by swollen-headed, bulging-eyed midgets from Beyond. The aliens kill an over-curious passerby (Frank Gorshin, the best Riddler on the *Batman* TV series) by injecting him with a lethal dose of alcohol delivered through their needlelike claws. Later, they inject another man in his *face*, in closeup. An alien tries this trick on a bull, and gets one of his huge eyes bloodily gouged out. Remember, this is a *comedy*, so yock it up.

The aliens *frame* a local teenager, Johnny (Steve Terrell) for the killing, by making it appear to be a case of hit-and-run(!). Johnny and his best girl, Joan (Gloria Castillo) have seen the aliens, but naturally no one believes these kooky teeners. As in most AIP films, adults here are cement-headed kid-haters, even though these teenagers are about as unruly as Mormon missionaries. Johnny and Joan round up "the gang" from Lover's Lane and track down the aliens themselves. Learning the aliens' weakness—light—they're able to destroy the whole bunch with their auto headlights.

Blaisdell's Saucer-Men are intriguing, and, as always, his special effects are as good as can be expected, considering the money available and the time allowed to produce them (one day, according to his partner, Bob Burns). Even so, *Saucer-Men* is fairly dismal by any objective standard. Unsurprisingly, most of the laughs to be found here are of the unintentional variety, and the "so-bad-it's-good" crowd seems to have adopted the film as a, uh, classic. Ironically, though, the attempts at "comedy" actually work *against* the unintended humor; the utter straight-facedness of a *Teenagers from Outer Space* is in large part what makes it so funny.

The poster art for *Saucer-Men* is one of Albert Kallis' finest science fiction posters, perhaps *the* finest. All posters for the film feature the spectacular and richly colored artwork shown here, which by the way portrays the Saucer-Men at about four times their "actual" size, and toting a Woman in Peril in the classic fashion. In the last five years, demand for *Saucer-Men* has risen to levels equalled only by titles such as *Forbidden Planet* and *The Creature From the Black Lagoon*—pretty heady company for this self-basting Butterball of a movie. ☪

Invasion of the Saucer-Men. © 1957 American International Pictures. Half-sheet, 22 x 28 inches.

The Brain Eaters

➤ 1958

This tightly-rendered poster may be too intense to decorate your breakfast nook, but it's still one of the most interesting images of the era. However, the title is misleading, as is the ad copy. They don't eat brains, and they're not slimy—they're more like fuzzy carpet slippers.

The Brain Eaters concerns parasitical carpet-slippers from deep beneath the Earth who drill up to the surface in search of human prey. They control humans by mounting a victim's back and boring holes in the neck with their pipe-cleaner antennae. This process turns the victim into a zombie-type slave. These slaves transport other parasites around a nearby town in glowing goldfish bowls, and soon the mayor's office, the police, and the phone company have all been infiltrated.

The parasites are opposed by a small group consisting of a he-man scientist (Edwin Nelson), an insecure guy (Alan Frost), their respective love interests (Joanna Lee and Jody Fair) and a blustery senator (Jack Hill, whose carpet-chewing performance is not as endearing as it seems intended to be). The insecure guy's father is the mayor, and the first person possessed by a parasite; later on, despite the fact that the aliens have targeted authority figures, someone expresses surprise at the idea that the parasites might be intelligent.

Still later, the group discovers a dying scientist who had been possessed by the parasites. He gasps the word "Carboniferous" before dying, and the hero-scientist understands that, since the man was apparently referring to the "Carboniferous Age" [sic], the parasites must come from underground. (Huh?) Ultimately, the scientist-protagonist makes a Heroic Sacrifice in destroying the parasites. Hint: they don't like electricity.

Science-fiction fans may recognize that *Brain Eaters* screenwriter Gordon Urquhart's basic setup—alien parasites that control their victims while riding on their necks—is taken from Robert A. Heinlein's classic paranoid novel, *The Puppet Masters*. Heinlein *also* thought he recognized a certain similarity and sued (later settling out of court, according to Bill Warren). *Brain Eaters* is a particularly flagrant example of this sort of plagiarism, but it's hardly unique—note, for instance, the close resemblance between Richard Matheson's novel *I Am Legend* and the film *Night of the Living Dead*. Writer Harlan Ellison, among others, has bitterly criticized this tendency of some filmmakers to treat literary SF as a sort of idea junkyard, to be mined freely without regard for creators' rights.

Of the cast, Edwin Nelsons delivers the only performance that can really be called professional; the film rises to a dim sort of life in his best scenes. Nelson, a regular player in Roger Corman's movies at this time, later shortened his name to "Ed" and became a star of TV's *Peyton Place*. Also worth mentioning, in a brief role as a human emissary of the slipper-monsters, is Leonard Nimoy. His character here is a solemn and unemotional scientist—not a real stretch for him, as we later came to learn. ☪

The Brain Eaters.
© 1958 American International Pictures.
Insert, 14 x 36 inches.

The Brain From Planet Arous

➤ 1958

Continuing with our Brains Out for Trouble survey, we turn now to the lurid but appealing poster to *The Brain From Planet Arous*. First of all, it's pronounced "eris," not "arouse," so wipe those silly smirks off your faces.

The Brain from Planet Arous is a weirdly energetic and imaginative movie, albeit absurd. It's the story of an alien criminal, Gor, who comes to Earth with *extremely* ambitious plans, not merely for worldwide but *universal* conquest. Gor is an engaging villain, in a dopey sort of way. After all the unemotional aliens in this book, it's refreshing to meet one who cackles with Snidely Whiplash glee over his own fiendishness. Gor comes from a race of floating brains, as portrayed on the poster inset. Arousians (Arousites?) have dangling spinal-cord tails and cat's eyes, and possess tremendous powers, being able to project bursts of lethal radiation powerful enough to destroy entire continents. In addition, they can possess humans, literally inhabiting their bodies and controlling their wills, a fate that befalls nuclear scientist Steve March (played by the ubiquitous John Agar).

March's fiancé, Sally (Joyce Meadows), quickly senses a change in Steve/Gor, not least because Gor is a randy little brain, who enjoys the "primitive" joys of heavy petting; it's implied that plain old Steve wasn't exactly a firecracker. Steve/Gor sets out to conquer the Earth, as a stepping-stone in his ultimate plan to conquer his homeworld of Arous and the universe at large. He stares at an airplane overhead and destroys it with a glance from eyes that become enormous and silvery, as per the poster. He repeats this trick for the military and a delegation of diplomats, zapping a recalcitrant general and destroying a sizeable chunk of nearby desert.

Meanwhile, an increasingly suspicious Sally is contacted by another brain, Vol, who's some sort of Arousian cop. Vol tells all, and reveals Gor's weakness; every twenty-four hours, he must leave March's body to absorb oxygen. During this time, a freed Steve might kill Gor by striking him at a special place, identified with a human brain-chart as the "Fissure of Rolando." Sally leaves a note to this effect where Steve will find it, and luckily he discovers it during the brief period when Gor's reoxygenating. In spite of the big deal made about that "Fissure of Rolando," Agar kills the brain by whomping it randomly with an axe. When Sally explains about Vol and his warning, Steve *refuses to believe her*, saying "You and your imagination"—one of the great *non sequiturs* in cinematic history, considering what Steve's just been through.

Planet Arous is directed competently by Nathan Juran; as with *Attack of the 50 Foot Woman*, he's credited as "Nathan Hertz," the name he reserved for basement-level work such as this. (Juran apparently was more proud of his collaborations with Ray Harryhausen, such as *The Seventh Voyage of Sinbad*—and rightly so.) The movie is a prime example of John Agar's mid-career slide, roughly halfway between 1948's *Fort Apache* and 1966's *Zontar, The Thing From Venus*. In his dual role as Steve March and space menace Gor, Agar is wooden but likeable, as always—too likeable to be an alien bent on galaxy-wide conquest, unfortunately. ☾⋆

The Brain From Planet Arous.
© 1958 Howco International.
One-sheet, 27 x 41 inches.

The Crawling Eye

➤ 1958

As is so often the case, this interesting poster has damned little to do with the film in question, although it does feature tentacled creatures who are mostly eyeballs.

The Crawling Eye is an English film, released in that country under the less sensational title *The Trollenberg Terror*. Several writers have commented on the film's obvious resemblance to screenwriter Nigel Kneale's *Quatermass* films, which concern a heroic scientist's battles against a series of alien menaces. Like the *Quatermass* movies, *The Crawling Eye* originated as an English television series. The film also echoes Kneale's work in its eerie atmosphere and its generally adult and imaginative approach. But while *The Crawling Eye* strives to be more than a simple monster movie, its good moments never add up to a coherent whole.

The Crawling Eye is set in Switzerland, near a high peak called the Trollenberg. Alan Brooks (Forrest Tucker), an American scientist, has come to the area to meet with a colleague who runs an observatory on the mountain. They come to suspect a link between a series of local disappearances and murders and a mysterious, unmoving, radioactive(!) cloud high on the Trollenberg. An Englishwoman, Anne Pilgrim (Janet Munro), enters the story; Anne is a psychic who is peculiarly drawn to the mountain.

We soon learn that sinister extraterrestrials have settled on the Trollenberg. The cloud that hides them also supplies them with the radioactivity, intense cold, and low atmospheric pressure they apparently need to survive. The aliens are aware of Anne's psychic link with them; they capture and brainwash various locals and send them to kill her. There's also a suggestion that these men are already dead, and thus are zombies of some sort, but this is never really explained. Eventually, the aliens move in person against the local populace. Brooks evacuates everyone to the fortress-like observatory, which soon is under siege by the giant, squishy-looking eye-beasts. However, Brooks now knows that heat is the aliens' weakness, and by radio summons a single jet bomber that blasts them with napalm, rather too easily disposing of the menace.

The Crawling Eye was scripted by Jimmy Sangster, a prolific screenwriter of Hammer horror movies in the 1950s and '60s. His dialogue is often crisp, but the plot fails to fall together. The link between Anne and the aliens seems important, but we never learn why; her abilities never add to the story. The aliens' habit of decapitating their victims is ghoulish fun, but there's no reason for it. And why are they here? What do they want? Without having seen the original teleplay, it's impossible to say whether *The Crawling Eye*'s many unanswered questions reflect its origin as a much longer TV series. But the story feels overstuffed; it's crammed with portentous incidents and happenings that aren't adequately explained, and characters with so little to do that there seems to be no reason for their presence.

Still, the movie does have a certain claustrophobic intensity, and while the effects are wildly variable, effects man Les Bowie's eye creatures are queasily effective. In all, *The Crawling Eye* is considerably better than many genre films of its time, even if its execution mostly fails to match up to its ambitions. ☾

The Crawling Eye.
© 1958 Distributors Corporation of America. Insert, 14 x 36 inches.

I Married a Monster From Outer Space

➤ 1958

This is a one-joke poster, although I happen to like the joke. But there's a lot more to *I Married a Monster From Outer Space* than its silly name.

As film historian Tom Weaver has said, everyone who writes about this movie ends up apologizing for the title. But the outrageous monicker was purposely chosen by director Gene Fowler, Jr., in deliberate imitation of his surprise mega-hit *I Was a Teenage Werewolf*. Fowler intended the film purely as exploitation, but unlike many directors, he seemed incapable of intentional mediocrity. *I Married* is a surprisingly effective thriller, with some touches worthy of Fowler's friend and mentor, the German master of suspense Fritz Lang.

Bill Farrell (Tom Tryon) is waylaid on his way to his wedding to Marge (Gloria Talbott), and replaced by an extraterrestrial duplicate. A year passes before Marge discovers alien-Bill's secret, although she receives enough hints to know something's wrong—he's become cold and unemotional, dogs suddenly hate him, he no longer drinks alcohol (which is poison to the aliens). Marge learns Bill's secret when she follows him to the aliens' hidden ship. After this discovery, she learns that others in town are also alien imposters, including members of the local police.

When confronted, Bill tells Marge that the aliens are the survivors of a race from the Andromeda "constellation" (I assume he means "galaxy") whose women perished in a solar disturbance, and that they're here to interbreed with human women. In the film's only major gap in logic, Marge convinces her doctor of her story (which is, after all, pretty unlikely). The doctor organizes a posse that locates the spaceship and destroys the alien, with the help of two brave German shepherds. The real Bill and the others are freed unharmed.

This is all pretty standard fare—aloof aliens (why aren't they ever boisterous and excitable?), dogs that sense evil we can't, and so forth. The alien's infiltration of the town seems inspired by 1956's *Invasion of the Body Snatchers*. However, it's the execution of *I Married* that places it a cut above most science fiction films of its day.

Fowler fills the movie with interesting shadings. He takes pains, for instance, to suggest that the invaders have different personalities; some of false-Bill's alien cronies dislike living as humans, while others enjoy it, and "Bill" himself feels troubling stirrings of emotion for Marge. When Marge trails Bill to the alien vessel, there's a great scene in which the possessing alien drifts out of Bill's body like a vapor, leaving it an empty shell. Marge approaches the body and touches it, only to topple it. The body lies wide-eyed and motionless, its face illuminated by a shaft of light, as a beetle crawls across its eyes.

Gloria Talbott, is excellent as Marge, conveying her disappointment and growing fear quite convincingly. Tom Tryon as Bill is only mediocre, but his woodenness doesn't damage the story—he *is* an unemotional alien, after all. In later years, Tryon became a popular author, with bestsellers including *The Other* and *Harvest Home*. By some accounts, he was ashamed of *I Married a Monster From Outer Space*. He needn't have been. ☾

I Married a Monster From Outer Space.
© 1958 Paramount Pictures.
Insert, 14 × 36

Satan's Satellites

➤ 1958

Train wrecks! Rocket attacks! Boat chases! Axe-wielding robots! Aerial bombs! Underwater bombs! Shooting galore! It's hard to avoid exclamation points when discussing the science fiction work of Republic Pictures.

Satan's Satellites is actually a cut-down feature version of the 1952 serial, *Zombies of the Stratosphere*—which explains the heroes' otherwise mystifying habit of referring to their Martian adversaries as "zombies." Even '52 seems far too late, however; Republic serials didn't change much from the late 1930s on, giving this movie a curiously antique feel even for its time.

Satan's Satellites features Republic's greatest science fiction hero, the Rocketman, a leather-jacketed, bullet-helmeted, flying protector of Earth who zoomed through four serials, two feature-film condensations and a television series. (An excellent recent comic book series and movie called *The Rocketeer* were lovingly modeled on Republic's character.) The Rocketman suit was the star, rather than the man who wore it, possibly because Republic had no interest in producing a human star who could demand more money. At any rate, the Rocketman was played by three actors at various times, and confusingly given different character names, including "Jeff King" and the more grandiloquent "Commando Cody, Sky Marshal of the Universe."

Here, though, the Rocketman is rather blandly called Larry Martin (Judd Holdren) of the Interplanetary Patrol, an understaffed organization that seems to consist mainly of Martin and his sidekick/stooge Bob (Wilson Wood). The patrol is pitted against a similarly skimpy Martian invasion party of three, Marex (Lane Bradford), Elah (Robert Garabedian), and Narab (Leonard Nimoy!). The Martians are human, but wear tights featuring cowls and wide, metal-studded leather belts, which make them all look vaguely like medieval executioners.

Marex's orders are to plant a hydrogen bomb that will throw the Earth out of its orbit, so that Mars can assume our place around the sun and enjoy better weather. However, Marex didn't bring a bomb with him, and so, with the aid of human henchmen, he has to steal the necessary parts and build the bomb right here on Earth, which effort provides much of the ensuing plot. Larry and Bob are the only agents on this case, despite its importance, and they pursue the Martians and their henchmen through car chases, fist-fights atop speeding trains, boat chases, encounters with a homicidal robot, aerial dogfights, and endless gun battles. The last-week's-cliffhanger-and-this-week's-escape format of the serial is truncated to bring the thing into feature length, but the film still consists almost entirely of one narrow escape from elaborate death followed by another.

One does not (or should not) apply ordinary cinematic standards to Republic serials, an artform as formal and ritualized as kabuki theater. Suffice it to say that, while serial buffs consider *Zombies/Satan's Satellites* to be one of Republic's lesser efforts, all the key elements are here, including gunfights that occur every five minutes and yet fail to produce a single injury. Note also that, despite repeated pummelings, leaps from trucks and whatnot, none of the human participants ever loses his hat.

Republic's science fiction posters match the charmingly antiquated look of the films themselves. *Satan's Satellites* is one of the best, a colorful scene of destruction that would not have looked at all out of place in a 1936 pulp magazine. ☾

Satan's Satellites. © 1958 Republic Pictures Corporation. One-sheet, 27 x 41 inches.

The Cosmic Man

➤ 1959

This poster is another personal favorite; it's beautifully colored, and something about the jagged bolts around the Cosmic Man's head has a nice Art-Deco feel.

The Cosmic Man seems sincere enough in its intentions, and has a few good moments, but its general incompetence makes it a drab and dull affair. The most interesting thing about the film is its obvious debt to *The Day the Earth Stood Still*.

An object streaks past the nation's radar defenses, coming to rest in bucolic Rock Canyon. The first investigators on the scene are Colonel Mathews (Paul Langdon), a hardened Cold Warrior, and Dr. Karl Sorenson (Bruce Bennett), "the famous scientist who discovered omicron radiation." They find a hovering, ball-shaped UFO. Mathews immediately wonders about the object's military potential; as in *Day the Earth Stood Still*, a line is immediately drawn between military paranoia and the scientific desire for understanding, and our sympathies are clearly with Dr. Sorenson. Mathews instantly dislikes peace-creep Sorenson. However, the authorities want Sorenson's help, so the two men are forced to work together. Their rivalry is sharpened by widow Kathy Grant (Angela Greene), owner of the local inn they use as a base. Her crippled son, Ken (Scotty Morrow), idolizes scientists, which doesn't hurt Sorenson's chances with the mom.

The investigators quickly learn that, as with Klaatu's ship, the UFO can't be moved, opened or penetrated. Meanwhile, Kathy receives an odd guest who speaks stilted English and dresses in such a way as to disguise his features (who might this be, kids?). At nearby scientific installations, a rash of odd incidents begins, including the apparent sabotage of equipment and records. At Sorenson's own lab, a mysterious black shape corrects an error in a vital blueprint, a direct steal from a similar scene in *Day the Earth Stood Still*. Sorenson suspects that something from the UFO—heck, let's call it a Cosmic Man—is responsible for these events.

The Cosmic Man (John Carradine), a caped humanoid seen in negative, confronts Sorenson and Mathews in Kathy's inn. In a windy speech, he explains that Peace and Understanding are good, while Violence and Ignorance are not; mankind must clean up its act before it explores space. Kathy doesn't recognize the alien's distinctive voice as that of her mysterious guest, who she later finds playing chess with Ken. The Cosmic Man appears to kidnap the child, but releases him in a final confrontation at the UFO. Despite Sorenson's efforts to stop them, the army manages to zap the alien with a magnetic device. He falls, unconscious or dead, but a ray from the UFO sucks him up, and both sphere and alien disappear. In a sickly sweet coda, redolent of Klaatu's Christlike nature, we learn that the Cosmic Man has cured Ken's paralysis.

Cosmic Man was directed in lackluster fashion by Herbert Greene and written by Arthur C. Pierce, who also scripted the even duller *Beyond the Time Barrier* and stayed active in barrel-bottom SF through the lean years of the later 1960s. Most performances are fair at best, although John Carradine's mellow hamminess always adds enjoyment to any film, no matter how wretched. Also comparatively good is Bruce Bennett, a former Olympic shot-putter whose most famous role came in *The Treasure of Sierra Madre*. ☾

The Cosmic Man. © 1959 Allied Artists. One-sheet, 27 x 41 inches.

Teenagers From Outer Space

➤ 1959

Okay, so this *isn't* a particularly beautiful poster. Still, comedy has its place. Besides, the ad copy used here *has* to be a high-water mark in this peculiar school of prose.

Teenagers From Outer Space is a charmingly inept movie that hasn't achieved the same badfilm notoriety of *The Giant Claw*, say, or all-time classic *Plan Nine From Outer Space*. It's certainly a contender, though; it's briskly paced, with a number of laugh-out-loud moments and an unforgettable giant-lobster menace.

In *Teenagers*, a saucer with a drill-bit bottom(!) arrives on Earth and screws itself into the ground(!!) upon landing. The aliens wear jumpsuits decorated with duct tape and look like bellhops. Their evil natures are denoted by the fact that they all speak in deep, booming voices and don't use contractions. The aliens are here to use the Earth as pasturage for their primary food source, giant Gargons. The one Gargon we see is played by a lobster. As they exit their spaceship (which seems *far* too small to hold all of them; the effect is of those little circus cars that hold dozens of clowns), one of the aliens blasts a little dog with a disintegrator ray, which turns the pup into a perfectly articulated dog skeleton.

This Evil act offends a sensitive, troubled alien, Derek (who, despite the title, looks to be the only alien present on the sweet side of thirty). Derek finds the dog's tags among the bones, concludes the Earth is home to intelligent life, and stages an abortive mutiny against his fellows, since innocent humanity doesn't deserve to be used as fodder for grazing lobster herds.

Derek's overpowered, but escapes into a nearby town, where—despite his bellhop's uniform and his lack of money or contractions—he's *immediately* offered free lodging and clothes by a garrulous duffer and his pretty, teenaged daughter, who's soon falling for sensitive (not to say callow) Derek. One of the evil aliens tracks Derek to town, disintegrator blazing, and soon high-school bio lab skeletons are being found all over the place. Meanwhile, in the hills, the citizenry begins to fall prey to an enormous, screaming lobster, which is seen only in silhouette, even in bright sunlight.

Teenagers From Outer Space suffers from uniformly amateurish acting, and all the usual absurdities engendered by a miniscule production budget. At one point, the alien's leader says they'll "wait until the sky is light enough," when the scene appears to be shot at high noon in blazing desert sun. Later, it's night-time inside a car, but not in the scenery the car's passing through. Interestingly for collectors, the disintegrator used by the aliens is actually a Buck Rogers cap pistol, which today fetches a pretty penny as one of the most highly prized toy ray guns ever made.

Still, the movie's not dull. Unlike a lot of these films, *Teenagers* has a giddy energy that keeps it moving right along. Writer Bill Warren took some pains in researching this movie, and according to him, the Tom Graeff who wrote, directed and produced this movie is also the "David Love" who starred as Derek. Apparently, Graeff never made another film; but at least we have *Teenagers From Outer Space* as a document of his peculiar talents. ☾

Teenagers From Outer Space. © 1959 Warner Brothers. One-sheet, 27 x 41 inches.

The Atomic Submarine

➤ 1960

This explosive poster is one of Reynold Brown's most successful of the era. Brown was an aeronautical illustrator in the 1940s, and his work for *The Atomic Submarine* seems to reflect an enthusiasm for military hardware. The movie itself has some ingenious ideas and a competent cast, but it's ultimately torpedoed by a terrible script. (Thanks for letting me get that out of my system.)

The Atomic Submarine opens in a near future featuring regular cargo and passenger submarine shipping that passes beneath the polar ice. (The movie is obviously inspired by the 1958 polar voyage of the U.S.S. *Nautilus*, the first nuclear submarine.) These polar routes are disrupted by a mysterious force that destroys subs and surface vessels. The submarine *Tiger Shark* is dispatched to stop whatever's responsible for the sinkings. The sub's complement includes Captain Dan Wendover (Dick Foran); Commander "Reef" Holloway (Arthur Franz), a brass-*cojoned* tough guy; sensitive, Montgomery Clift-ish scientist and diving-bell operator Dr. Carl Nielson (Brett Halsey), and distinguished British scientist Sir Ian Hunt (Tom Conway).

These worthies learn that the ship disasters are the work of an undersea flying saucer(!) they dub the "Cyclops," due to its rotating beacon "eye." The *Tiger Shark* fires atomic torpedoes at point-blank range, which seems risky, but the Cyclops is unaffected. Captain Wendover, deciding to sacrifice his ship to end the menace, rams the Cyclops. The submarine survives but is trapped, wedged in the flying saucer's side. Via Nielson's diving bell, Reef leads a team into the Cyclops, which is "manned" by a tentacled, one-eyed creature.

The alien, as usual, is telepathic, and tells Reef that he's scouting worlds for his race to colonize; the Earth will do nicely, thanks, and he's just about to leave to report back. (As Fate would have it.) The creature kills several crew members, but Reef blasts it with a flare pistol and escapes. The *Tiger Shark* frees itself from the flying saucer, and its scientists reprogram an atomic missile with a torpedo guidance system. The alien ship takes off, but the heroes blast it with the modified missile, saving the Earth.

All this may lead you to expect action, but mostly the cast sits around improbably roomy submarine sets and *talks*. Narration meant to lend a documentary air to the proceedings is ludicrously overwrought, describing the effort to reprogram the missile as "foolish...insane...fantastic!" There are gaps in logic large enough to accommodate the *Tiger Shark*. For instance, if the Cyclops is a scout, why the heck is it destroying these ships and drawing attention to itself? And why would an atomic missile destroy the saucer when an atomic torpedo won't? Worst of all, Reef, our hero, is a real *jerk*, dismissing his friends' deaths with a clipped "fortunes of war," and later complaining that he lost his little black book on the flying saucer.

Even so, *Atomic Submarine* has an oddball surrealism that makes it modestly amusing. Arthur Franz's testosterone-glutted Reef carries on an outrageously overdone rivalry with peacenik Dr. Nielson that provides some laughs for the post-'Nam generation. Tom Conway, George Sanders' brother and a fine actor in the same ultra-urbane mode, looks utterly lost and, frankly, a little drunk. ☾★

The Atomic Submarine. © 1960 Allied Artists. One-sheet, 27 x 41 inches.

Village of the Damned

➤ 1960

Without a single flying saucer or foam-rubber beastie, this literate, understated chiller created some of the very best Invaders From Elsewhere.

Village of the Damned, based on a John Wyndham novel called *The Midwich Cuckoos*, concerns a most unusual invasion of Earth that begins in a small English village called Midwich. On a quiet morning, the town's entire population falls unconscious, including Gordon Zellaby (a fine, late performance by George Sanders) and his wife Anthea (Barbara Shelley). After several hours, everyone wakes up again, seemingly no worse for wear. A few months later, every woman in town capable of childbirth—twelve in all—is pregnant.

Naturally, this is disconcerting news; an unwed teenager is mortified, while a returning sailor's convinced his wife has been unfaithful. Anthea Zellaby is one of the pregnant women, and her husband is initially overjoyed. When the children arrive, however, they grow unnaturally fast. All have pale blonde hair and compelling, hypnotic eyes. One of the first hints of the children's powers comes when Anthea accidentally scalds her child with too-hot milk. As the tyke holds its enormous, unblinking eyes on her, she finds herself compelled to plunge her hand into a kettle of boiling water.

By the age of three, the children appear to be about ten, with superhuman intelligence and adult mannerisms. They share a group mind; what one learns all the others know. Dr. Zellaby studies the children while tutoring them. He's a devotee of pure intelligence who hopes the children may usher in a new era of progress. Meanwhile, the children have begun a reign of terror in Midwich, using their mental powers to force several villagers to commit suicide. Finally, Zellaby understands that the children must be destroyed. Knowing their ability to read minds is growing but limited, he shields his thoughts long enough to destroy them and himself with a bomb.

In *The Midwich Cuckoos*, the strange children are clearly extraterrestrial in origin; aerial observers see an alien craft in the village during the blackout period. *Village of the Damned* is equivocal on this point. Zellerby speculates that the women were impregnated with some sort of ray by an alien intelligence, but it's just his guess. The children, frank enough in most matters, refuse to discuss their origins. As for what happened during the blackout, and exactly why the children are here, we're left to guess. Some find this ambiguity annoying, but it adds more to the film's atmosphere than any "explanation" could.

The best thing about *Village* is the children. They're quiet, still and cold, and move with an eerie, serpentine deliberateness. Particularly chilling is Martin Stephens as the Zellaby's son, David, the children's spokesman. A year later, Stephens turned in similarly good work in the classic ghost story *The Innocents*.

It's nearly impossible to imagine an American SF film of the era being made with this restraint. Someone would've demanded at least one tentacled monster. MGM's British division, which made the film, instead insisted on a simpler gimmick. This poster, one of the few effective photo-montage images, highlights the movie's only significant special effect—the silvery glow that appears in the children's eyes when they're working their mojo on someone. It's a slightly silly effect, and completely unnecessary, but it gave the poster artists something with which to work. ☪

Village of the Damned. © 1960 Loew's Inc. One-sheet, 27 x 41 inches.

Bogey Persons

"Strange...a slice on each side of the throat. Fangs!"

—a police investigator
in *I Was a Teenage Werewolf*

Michael Landon as a monster created by science,
in one of the most successful exploitation films of
all time, *I Was a Teenage Werewolf*.

Phantom From Space

➤ 1953

Well, his secret power doesn't *really* menace the world, and no cities go up in flames as per the line art here. Mostly the Phantom indulges in more prosaic Bogey Person activities, such as scaring and manhandling a few bystanders. But then, understatement isn't really common in this artform.

Phantom From Space opens in a welter of military stock footage. A UFO streaks through U.S. air defenses, disappearing from radar screens near Santa Monica. On the ground, local radio and TV transmissions go haywire. Led by Hazen (Ted Cooper), members of the Federal Communications Commission attempt to track down the source of the disturbance, in "woodie" panel trucks with large, rotating aerials on top. Meanwhile, L.A. cop Lieutenant Bowers (Harry Landers) wrestles with a series of murders by a strange figure in a "diving suit." Eyewitnesses report the mysterious character killed in self-defense and—this is important—say there's *no head visible* in his helmet.

Soon Hazen and Bowers are comparing notes, figuring there may be a connection between their cases. (It's a given in these movies that all authority figures know and cooperate with each other.) The "diving-suited" figure, now dubbed the Phantom, is tracked to an oil refinery and nearly captured; he escapes by shucking his suit, tanks and helmet, revealing that he really *is* a phantom—he's invisible. The Phantom's gear is taken to a lab (actually L.A.'s Griffith Park planetarium) for study. A scientist, Dr. Wyatt (Rudolph Anders), discovers that the suit is intensely radioactive, which caused the broadcast disruptions. He handles the suit with rubber gloves, as if these would protect him from hard radiation. Wyatt's beautiful female assistant (natch), Barbara Randall (Noreen Nash), finds that the Phantom's breathing tanks contain methane and an unidentifiable gas.

Dr. Wyatt hypothesizes that the alien is invisible because it's a silicon-based lifeform, rather than carbon-based, as with terrestrial life. "Silicon! That's glass!" exclaims Bowers. At this point—after we've established that the Phantom is invisible, impervious to radioactivity and doesn't breathe oxygen—the detective reacts with surprise to the idea that he might be an alien.

Meanwhile, the Phantom is lurking nearby. He can live in our atmosphere for brief periods, but must return periodically for a refresher from his tanks. He does so more than once, despite our protagonists' rather feeble attempts to catch him. At one point Barbara is alone in the lab when the Phantom returns; he attempts to communicate with her by rapping on a table, while she discovers that he's visible under ultraviolet light. Shortly afterward, without explanation, the space suit dissolves. The Phantom, dying from exposure to earth's atmosphere, climbs high in an observatory dome (it's a well-equipped lab) and falls, Kong-style, more sinned against than sinner. In death, he's visible, a pale, bald, egg-headed man who looks a bit like James Arness as the Thing.

Phantom From Space is a creditable though cheap and sometimes-dull effort produced and directed by W. Lee Wilder, older brother of the famous comedic director Billy Wilder. W. Lee, as you may have guessed, failed to enjoy the same success in films as his kid brother. *Phantom* is probably his best genre effort, far better than his funny-awful *Killers From Space* and awful-awful *The Man Without a Body*. ☾

Phantom From Space. © 1953 United Artists. Half-sheet, 22 × 28 inches.

The Creature From the Black Lagoon

> ➤ 1954

While it's certainly no better than Jack Arnold's third-best film, *The Creature From the Black Lagoon* has entered the public consciousness more than any of his other works, generating a trainload of academese blather from film writers in its wake. But there's no denying that Jack Arnold's Creature is the most successful of the '50s Bogey Persons, and the last classic Universal monster, nearly as popular today as Frankenstein's Monster, Dracula, and the Wolfman.

Creature begins with the discovery of an ancient fossil in the Amazon River basin that appears to be an arm from some impossible half-man, half-fish. The fossil attracts the attention of a marine biologist, David Reed, (Richard Carlson) and his ambitious boss, Mark Williams (Richard Denning), who mount an expedition to seek more evidence of this bizarre creature. They're accompanied by David's fiancé, Kay Lawrence (the astonishingly beautiful Julie Adams), who Mark also loves. On reaching the site of the excavation, they find native workers brutally murdered. We know, though they don't yet, that there's a living Gill-Man nearby.

Their researches take them to the Black Lagoon, an area haunted by rumors of a deadly monster. Upon discovering the Creature, Mark becomes obsessed with the notion of capturing or killing it and hauling it back to civilization. David, our hero, opposes harming the monster and wants to study it in its native habitat. Meanwhile, the Creature has discovered Kay; he's obviously entranced by her. The party briefly captures the Gill-Man, but he escapes, nearly killing a scientist in the process. A surprisingly grim and bloody war then develops between the expedition and the Creature, culminating in Mark's death. The monster is wounded at the film's end, but not so much that he can't be made available for a sequel.

Part of *Creature*'s popularity doubtlessly is due to the monster suit itself, which was designed and produced by a Universal makeup team including artists Millicent Patrick and Chris Mueller and technician Jack Kevan. The monster's appearance is beautifully logical and plausible, and further benefits from Olympic swimmer Ricou Browning's fine underwater performance as the Creature (played on land by Ben Chapman).

As a film, however, *Creature* certainly is not without flaws. The script is strictly average, with characters that are little more than cardboard cutouts. Only Nestor Paiva as the crusty captain of the expedition's riverboat is memorable. The romantic triangle between Mark, David, and Kay feels perfunctory and leads nowhere. The science doesn't bear examination; the fossil Gill-Man is from the Devonian Period, "150 million years ago." That's 200 million years too soon for the Devonian, and improbably early in any case for an intelligent manlike creature.

What lifts *Creature* into minor-classic status is exceptional underwater photography and Jack Arnold's wonderfully atmospheric direction. Arnold's visual flair is nowhere shown to better advantage than in the film's most famous sequence, the eerie and erotic "water ballet" in which Kay swims unconcernedly in the lagoon, while beneath her, the fascinated Gill-Man follows, imitating her movements. (Interestingly, the Creature's crush on Kay clearly echoes *King Kong*'s vaguely racist White Goddess theme; one assumes the Creature could kidnap any number of native women, should his tastes lie in that direction, but this pale beauty in her snow-white bathing suit is clearly something special.) ☪

The Creature From the Black Lagoon.
© 1954 Universal-International Pictures.
Insert, 14 x 36 inches.

Tobor the Great

➤ 1954

This attractive and hard-to-find poster depicts the remaining member of the Big Three Club of 1950s robots. Tobor never achieved the fame of his cinematic brothers Gort and Robbie, but judging from the prices this one-sheet fetches today, he certainly has a solid lock on third place.

This is a children's movie. More specifically, given the subject matter and the era in which it was made, it's a boys' movie, a wish-fulfillment fantasy about a boy and his best friend, a large and powerful robot. It's probably the first science fiction film made specifically for kids, and accepted on these terms it's quite good.

Professor Nordstrom (Taylor Holmes), omni-inventor and genius, has invented Tobor (robot spelled backwards; did you get it right away?) to pilot interplanetary space probes. He's assisted by Dr. Ralph Harrison (Charles Drake), the titular hero, his beautiful daughter Janice Robertson (Karin Booth), Harrison's love interest, and a widowed mother. Janice's son is "Gadge" (Billy Chapin), an eleven-year-old electronics whiz who lives in the professor's *great* laboratory-house, and plays with a *lot* of *neat* stuff and probably gets to stay up as late as he wants, all the time—in short, he's everything a robot-struck boy of 1954 wished *he* could be. It's love at first sight for Gadge and Tobor, of course.

During Tobor's development, however, the professor is watched by a pipe-smoking, foreign-sounding spy who wants the robot's secrets for an unfriendly power. He says things like "Our employers do not forgiff miztakes" to his henchmen. The film never specifies just for whom he works; possibly it's the same outfit that employs Boris Badenov. At any rate, he lacks only a placard saying "spy" hanging around his neck.

Tobor is equipped with a form of ESP, and when Nordstrom and Gadge are kidnapped by the spy ring and threatened with torture, the boy mentally summons his robot pal. Tobor smashes his way into the spies' farmhouse lair and saves the day, personally capturing their chief and carrying Gadge to safety in his arms. Then, in a disconcertingly abrupt ending, Tobor is sent on his space mission, with no specific mention of when or if he will return. At least one writer has complained rather bitterly about this ending—Tobor's this big, lovable hero, and they're just going to shoot him into space? However, in the film's earlier scenes, the mission for which he's been constructed is specifically described as exploring space and returning to report. I choose to believe that Gadge and Tobor will see each other again someday.

Tobor's design has also been criticized, and it's true that he lacks both Gort's elegant simplicity and Robbie's pleasing lines. They're like sports cars, while Tobor's an ungainly pickup truck of a robot, with knobs and handles and geegaws on every surface. But again, Tobor looks just like a kid's idea of a robot. His appearance fits the spirit of the film perfectly.

The woman Tobor carries in this image bears no resemblance to anyone in the cast. She *does*, however, look remarkably like the blonde toted by both Gort and Robbie in *their* posters. Who was she, this mysterious Woman in Peril? Why did she spend so much time around robots? ☾⋆

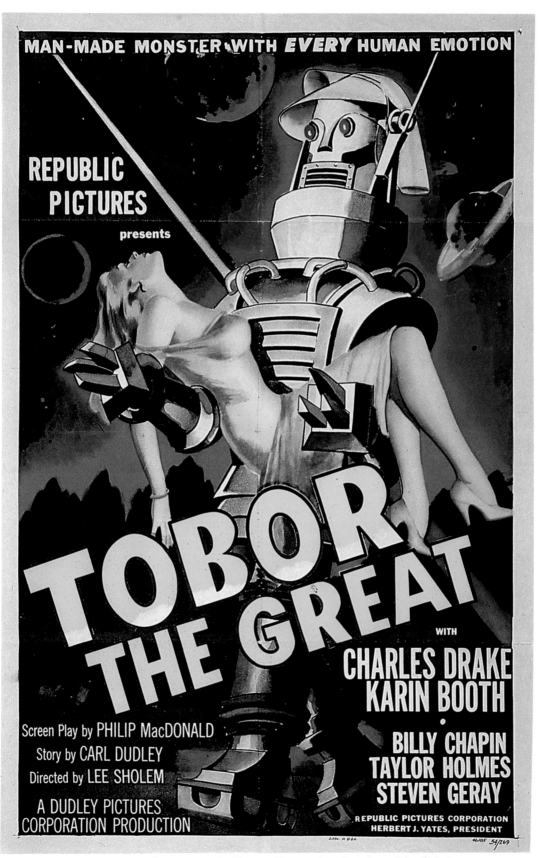

Tobor the Great. © 1954 Republic Pictures Corporation. One-sheet, 27 x 41 inches.

Devil Girl From Mars

➤ 1955

The *Devil Girl From Mars* poster is probably the most attractive and most valuable of science fiction's *femmes fatales*. The film itself is easily one of the strangest discussed in this book.

Devil Girl was made in the mid-1950s, but its story would have seemed dated and childish in a 1930 issue of *Wonder Stories*. It's hard to imagine audiences then, now, or *ever* taking the movie's absurd premises seriously, but the mostly competent British cast plays it absolutely straight, without a hint of tongue in cheek, which accentuates *Devil Girl*'s weird, other-worldly quality.

The film opens with a scientist and a reporter travelling together in the Scottish Highlands, searching for a reported fallen meteor (which turns out to be...but you've guessed that already). They stop at a remote inn where an escaped murderer is being sheltered by his barmaid girlfriend. Also staying at the inn is a beautiful model (played by Hazel Court, who starred in several of Roger Corman's Poe movies); the model and the brash reporter/hero are instantly attracted to one another.

Before we've had much character development, though, the Devil Girl arrives noisily, in a spaceship that looks like a child's top mated with a hubcap. The D.G., who calls herself Nyah, is clad in an unsavory-looking black leather ensemble complete with mini-skirt, skullcap, and floor-length cape. Nyah explains that Mars has suffered a destructive war between the sexes that left women in control. Now their men are dying out, and Mars needs virile new blood to keep its civilization alive.

Nyah sounds a lot like *Bewitched*-period Agnes Moorhead and has a bad attitude toward Earth-types, whom she calls "fools," "primitives," and "savages." (She's a bit of a bore.) She disintegrates a minor character and throws an electronic force-field around the inn, holding its occupants prisoner. Bullets, predictably, don't stop her. When angered, Nyah demonstrates Mars' "superior knowledge" by summoning Chani, one of the most laughable robots in science-fiction history, who resembles a mailbox with a gumball-machine head. Chani stomps around and disintegrates a tree, an old truck, and a barn while the cast tries to look terrified.

Later, Nyah boasts of Martian technology to the scientist, telling him that her ship is powered by "a form of nuclear fission, on a static negative condensity"(?). She gets hers when the escaped killer volunteers to board her ship and serve as breeding stock back on Mars; somehow—we never learn how—he redeems himself and saves mankind by sabotaging the saucer in flight. It explodes and the remaining cast members have a drink on the house.

Devil Girl was shot in three weeks and, to put it charitably, one doubts that its makers gave much thought to posterity. In the last few years, though, the film has become quite an item among connoisseurs of off-beat cinema, and its posters are extremely popular among collectors. This one-sheet is the best of the American posters. Also valuable is the British poster, which is similar to the American version but more richly colored; oddly, though, it portrays the Devil Girl in dark greys, as if she were carved of stone. ☾⋆

Devil Girl From Mars. A Spartan release, © 1955. One-sheet, 27 x 41 inches.

Revenge of the Creature

➤ 1955

This quickie sequel to the hugely successful *The Creature From the Black Lagoon* is a considerable letdown from the first film, but Jack Arnold's competent direction gives it a few effective moments.

Revenge opens with an expedition sent by an "Ocean Harbor Park" in Florida—similar to, and played by, California's Marineland—to capture the Gill-Man (Ricou Browning, reprising his role from *Creature*), who apparently didn't perish in the first film after all. After a brief but atmospheric return to the Black Lagoon, the expedition succeeds in capturing the monster, far too quickly and easily in view of his formidable resistance in the first movie. The Creature is transported back to Ocean Harbor, where he becomes a new exhibit. Biologists Helen Dobson and Clete Ferguson (Lori Nelson and genre stalwart John Agar) study the Gill-Man, and fall in love in a predictable and uninteresting fashion. The monster, in turn, becomes attracted to Helen, repeating his proclivity for interspecies lust noted in the first film. After escaping from its tank, killing an Ocean Park employee, and overturning a car, the Gill-Man runs into the ocean.

Presumably a search ensues, and newspaper headlines report Creature sightings up and down the eastern seaboard; actually, though, the Creature's lurking nearby, eyeing Helen from the shrubbery. Clete and Helen decide to take a river cruise (ducking their responsibilities in connection with the search, one assumes), and after shadowing them for awhile, the Gill-Man grabs Helen out of a crowded restaurant and makes for the beach. Clete and the cops follow, and the monster falls into the surf in a hail of bullets. And that's the end of the Gill-Man, unless—you don't suppose... (See *The Creature Walks Among Us*.)

Revenge is a slight affair, with a tired air, a desultory script, and mostly limp dialogue. The film's best moments are in the brief, opening Black Lagoon sequences; the monster seems diminished, somehow, in the Marineland setting. Even so, Arnold manages to create some surprisingly good scenes. The Creature's escape from the water park begins with a dynamic shot designed for 3-D, in which the Gill-Man *erupts* from the water directly at the camera. (*Revenge* was the last 1950s film made in 3-D, but was rarely shown as such, as the craze was dying.)

The first film's "water ballet" scene is re-staged in *Revenge*, but with an added twist; just as the Gill-Man reaches for Helen, Clete embraces her and kisses her, while the monster looks on (in envy?). Later, Helen sits before a vanity in her nightclothes while the Gill-Man watches her, gasping for air, fishlike, in a way that also suggests his loneliness and sexual frustration. A final trivia note: keep your eyes open for Clint Eastwood's first film role, as an Ocean Park lab assistant with a mouse in his pocket.

As can be seen here, posters for *Revenge* are quite nice, with a fine Reynold Brown portrait of the Gill Man. *Revenge* posters are much sought after, not so much because of the film's merits, but because they represent the last great Universal monster, and can be purchased for considerably less than *The Creature From the Black Lagoon* paper. ☾

Revenge of the Creature.
© 1955 Universal-International Pictures.
Half-sheet, 22 x 28 inches.

The She-Creature

➤ 1956

This poster, designed by Albert Kallis, features what may be monster-maker Paul Blaisdell's finest creation.

The She-Creature was inspired by a 1956 bestseller, *The Search for Bridey Murphy*, a nonfiction account of a series of hypnotic experiments involving a Colorado woman named Virginia Tighe. The hypnotized Tighe, speaking in an Irish brogue, recounted memories of a previous life as a nineteenth-century Dublin woman named Bridey Murphy, complete with a wealth of obscure historical detail. The "Bridey Murphy" phenomenon was a ten-day wonder that collapsed after the *Chicago American* newspaper published a story debunking Tighe's claims. (Interestingly, the *Denver Post* subsequently proved that the *Chicago American*'s "debunking" itself was largely fiction! "Bridey Murphy" remains an unsolved mystery.)

The She-Creature concerns a villainous hypnotist, Lombardi (inadequately played by Chester Morris) who can send his gorgeous assistant Andrea (Marla English) back through the ages, revisiting each of her past lives, including a life at the dawn of time, as a savage, aquatic monster—as the script puts it, "A creature out of time...the first life form of someone living today, over a million years old." The syntax is as muddled as the movie's metaphysics, but the upshot is that Lombardi can make these previous incarnations manifest themselves physically. In this way, he resurrects the murderous She-Creature and sends her on a killing rampage along a nearby beach.

Lombardi's "predictions" of the ensuing murders vault him into prominence as a society psychic, with a following of wealthy matrons. Lombardi arouses the suspicions both of a police lieutenant and a psychic researcher, Dr. Erickson (Lance Fuller), who falls in love with Andrea. The She-Creature kills the policeman, but Andrea's love for Erickson protects the scientist; instead, the monster slays Lombardi and returns to the sea.

The She-Creature herself is an engaging if improbable monster, with horns, antennae, claws, a tiny pair of wings(!), and prominent breasts. Paul Blaisdell's ingeniously constructed sculpted-foam and latex suit included built-in leverage for the arms, so that the She-Creature's victims could be lifted more easily. As usual for Blaisdell's monsters, it also included a number of features, such as blinking eyes and a swishing tail, that the hamfisted director didn't bother to use.

For years, movies like this were completely dismissed by fans of "serious" science fiction and horror. More recently, though, there's been a great deal of new interest in AIP's genre films and Paul Blaisdell's monsters in particular, so much so that the unwary might be led to believe that *The She-Creature* is a minor classic like *I Married a Monster From Outer Space*, or at least an entertaining romp like *Attack of the Crab Monsters*. Sadly, it's neither. Despite an interesting premise and a great monster, the script is achingly bad and the acting barely adequate. The monster is the most entertaining part of *The She-Creature*, and she's just not enough to carry the movie. ☾★

The She-Creature.
© 1956 American Releasing Corporation.
Insert, 14 x 36 inches.

The Phantom From 10,000 Leagues

➤ 1956

This whimsical poster, featuring a petulant bull terrier of a sea-monster, was one of Albert Kallis' first science fiction designs. The sexual imagery is unusually explicit. Note the lust in those puppy eyes, and the provocative "make-a-wish" thigh-grabbing.

The Phantom From 10,000 Leagues is as pure an example of exploitation as you're likely to see. It seems pointless to criticize its failings, since it amply accomplished its makers' single goal—it made money. Actually, the film is competently acted and no worse-looking than many other 1950s movies; its biggest failing is an extraordinarily convoluted and incoherent plot. As far as I can tell after two recent viewings, *10,000 Leagues* goes something like this:

Near a small California beach community, horribly burned corpses of boaters and swimmers are washing ashore with depressing regularity. It's no mystery to us, though; we immediately get to see the Phantom, a mutated, radioactive sea-beast played by a *really* dumb man-in-suit, with a pop-eyed, vaguely lionish head—in all, it looks a bit like Cecil the Seasick Sea Serpent of the old cartoons. The monster's guarding a brightly glowing deposit of uranium ore. Exposure to the radioactive light is also deadly, and it's not entirely clear whether the deaths are due to the monster or the burning light.

Two men are looking into the deaths—Bill Grant (Rodney Bell), a federal investigator, and oceanographer Ted Stevens (Kent Taylor). Their prime suspect becomes Professor King (Michael Whalen) of the nearby Pacific College of Oceanography. He's very nervous and defensive and given to sneaking around the beach at night. King is conducting a secret experiment behind locked doors, which, we soon learn, involves exposing a turtle to the same sort of glowing radioactivity we saw near the Phantom. Stevens begins snooping around as a tourist named "Baxter." King is wise to Stevens, though, because he has a book of Stevens' that features a huge picture of him on its front cover (odd marketing strategy, that).

Things are further complicated by the fact that King's secretary (Vivi Janiss) secretly hates him, because she blames him for the (largely unexplained) death of her son. She thinks King is behind the beach deaths, and spills her suspicions to government gumshoe Grant. But wait! There's more! King's assistant, Thomas (Philip Pine) is *also* sneaking around; he's in the pay of an Unfriendly Foreign Power that wants King's secrets. He spends a lot of time laying in wait on a local hillside with a speargun, attempting to murder Stevens, and eventually spears the secretary instead for reasons that are none too clear. As you can see, quite a lot of plot is riding on the Phantom's rubbery shoulders.

10,000 Leagues was produced by Jack and Dan Milner, brother film editors turned independent producers of no distinction (their other claim to fame is the arguably worse *From Hell It Came*, featuring a demonic tree stump). The movie was released on a double bill with Roger Corman's first science fiction film, *Day the World Ended*. This combination's success prompted AIP to release a long string of thematically related double features—two SF pictures, two juvenile-delinquent movies, etc. History, of a sort, was made. ☪

The Phantom From 10,000 Leagues. © 1956 American Releasing Corporation. One-sheet sheet, 27 x 41 inches.

The Creature Walks Among Us

➤ 1956

This last and, to many, least of the *Creature* series actually is somewhat more effective than *Revenge of the Creature*, in that the third installment contains some fairly powerful scenes that aren't merely rehashes of the original film. For *Walks Among Us*, Jack Arnold passed directorial duties to his assistant, John Sherwood. Sherwood's strange little film tosses aside the established Creature formula with mixed results.

Walks Among Us opens with our third expedition to capture the Creature. The current effort is headed by an unpleasant scientist, Dr. Barton (Jeff Morrow). His geneticist colleague, Dr. Morgan (Rex Reason), serves as moral opposite. Dr. Barton wants to perform a rather peculiar experiment on the Gill-Man; he wants to alter the monster's genetic structure by tinkering with his blood chemistry. (Bio students may recognize this as Lysenko's heresy—the idea that, for instance, a giraffe feeding on successively higher leaves will eventually develop "longer-necked" genes.) Barton wants to do all this so that one day humanity can withstand the pressures of space travel (huh?). The Gill-Man confronts the expedition members, and in the ensuing struggle he's severely burned and then captured.

Much to the scientists' surprise, when they examine the monster they find functional lungs and human skin under his burned gills and scales. Barton is elated by this discovery, which he believes confirms his theory (why?), and transfers the monster to his California laboratory. Soon, the Gill-Man is a more conventional, air-breathing hulk. He isn't much uglier than a wrestler, and he's grown a barrel chest he didn't have before; in his roughly made clothes, he looks and acts faintly like Frankenstein's monster in pajamas. He's a sad sight, and his longing looks toward the sea come close to real pathos.

Meanwhile, among the human cast, torrid doings heat up. Barton is insanely jealous of his beautiful but aloof wife Marcia (Leigh Snowden). A seedy hired hand makes an unsuccessful pass at the wife, and Barton kills him in a fit of rage. Barton tries to hide his crime by dumping the body in the Creature's cage, but it doesn't get him much of anywhere; the monster immediately breaks free, pursues Barton and kills him, after first sparing Morgan and the wife. In the movie's final scene, the Creature is seen walking morosely to the sea, and presumably suicide, since he's lost his gills—although there's plenty of room for a sequel that never came to be.

Walks Among Us reunites *This Island Earth* stars Morrow and Reason, but here, without that film's better-than-average script, both men revert to their normal, wooden screen personas. The film's best feature is its recurrent and well-handled suggestion that the sad-looking former Creature longs to return to his aquatic world. Would that it had been.

The one-sheet and most other posters from *The Creature Walks Among Us* feature the poor, pants-wearing schnook the Gill-Man becomes in the film. The insert pictured here is the most desirable piece with collectors, simply because it's the only poster depicting the real, *bona fide* Gill-Man. It's how he would have wanted to be remembered. (On the other hand, I can't shake the idea that the monster, as pictured here, looks a great deal like Marlon Brando.) ☾

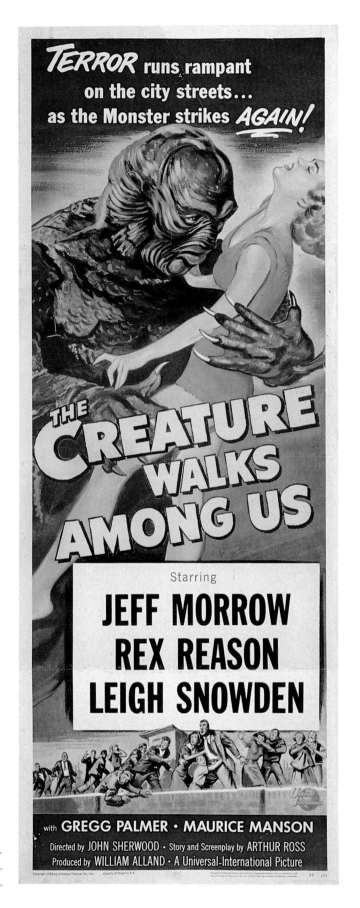

The Creature Walks Among Us.
© 1956 Universal-International Pictures.
Insert, 14 x 36 inches.

Not of This Earth

➤ 1956

Here's an especially fine Bogey Person poster, a starkly beautiful image that just *oozes* paranoia. As is so often the case with AIP films, the image shown here has nothing to do with the actual story; the intriguing eye-monster doesn't even appear in the movie. Even so, it's one of the era's more entertaining SF films.

Not of This Earth perfectly demonstrates the strengths and limitations of Roger Corman's output of this period. The movie is technically unimpressive—in prints I've seen, at least, it has a flat, washed-out look, suggestive of inferior film stock—but the storyline is consistently inventive. Compared with most of the science fiction films of the day (and indeed to many of Corman's other films) the movie uses some relatively sophisticated concepts, and contains some of the earliest cinematic references to telepathy and matter transmission, longtime staples of literary SF.

Not of This Earth combines an invasion story with an interesting science fiction-inflected vampire theme. "Paul Johnson" is the name adopted by an alien from Davanna (Paul Birch), a world whose people are slowly dying due to mutations produced by centuries of atomic warfare. The Davannans suffer from a bizarre form of anemia that literally evaporates the blood in their veins, and only constant transfusions can keep them alive. Johnson is scouting the Earth as a potential new source of blood. He can control people with a form of hypnotic telepathy, and kills his victims with radioactive blasts from his milky-white eyes, normally hidden beneath dark sunglasses. He then drains their blood with an odd pump he keeps in a metal briefcase.

Periodically, Johnson sends blood shipments back to Davanna via a teleportation device tucked away in a closet(!). The Davannans plan to take our blood if it's suitable for their purposes, and destroy the Earth if it's not, which seems petulant, to say the least. The alien gets his comeuppance via a tough-cookie nurse he hires to administer his own transfusions (Corman regular Beverly Garland) and the nurse's boyfriend, a tough cop (Morgan Jones). A typically downbeat Corman ending suggests that more Davannans are on their way, ready to finish their mission here.

Paul Birch is excellent as Johnson, whose intelligence, fatalism and stiff, unemotional dignity are rather appealing. We actually come to sympathize with the Davannan's plight, and perhaps even root for him a bit. In comparison, Morgan Jones is a cypher, and Beverly Garland is...well, Beverly Garland, spunky as always, but little more. The remaining cast standouts are also Corman regulars—Jonathan Haze is a good-natured weasel who becomes Johnson's valet, while Dick Miller steals the film's best moment as a sleazy vacuum-cleaner salesman who fast-talks his way into Johnson's house only to end up hooked to his blood pump. This edgy scene represents one of Corman's earliest experiments in blending humor and suspense, a formula he would use extensively in films like *Little Shop of Horrors*.

Not of This Earth was released on a double bill, as were most AIP films in this period; its co-feature was *Attack of the Crab Monsters*. According to their screenwriter, Charles B. Griffith, the films made a tidy 400-percent profit for American International in their first week of release. ☪

Not of This Earth. © 1957 Allied Artists. One-sheet, 27 x 41 inches.

I Was a Teenage Werewolf

➤ 1957

This eye-catching image effectively promoted one of the most famous films ever made. *I Was a Teenage Werewolf* made *big* cash at the box office—according to its director, the $82,000 feature made up to $8 million, putting AIP into the black for the first time—and generated a flurry of "teen"-oriented SF and horror films in its wake. Much of its fame rests on its unforgettable title, coined by AIP co-founder James Nicholson; however, it's also an entertaining, well-directed movie featuring an energetic starring performance by Michael Landon.

Teenage Werewolf, like *Not of This Earth*, is a science fiction twist on a traditional horror theme. It's also the perfect apotheosis of American International's style. AIP essentially discovered teenagers as a separate market, and the movie certainly reflects their point of view; teens are the only fully realized characters, while adults are either oppressors or ciphers who Just Don't Understand. (On the other hand, they're also AIP teenagers—incredibly clean-cut twenty-eight-year-old teens who wear ties and drink sodas in jive joints till all hours.)

Landon plays Tony Rivers, a troubled and angry kid who can't adjust to life in his sterile hometown. Tony fights constantly and is skirting dangerously close to trouble with the law. His girlfriend Arlene (Yvonne Lime) persuades him to see a local psychiatrist, Dr. Brandon (Whit Bissell). This is a mistake, however, as Brandon happens to be a mad scientist who's shopping for an experimental subject. Brandon uses a combination of hypnotism and drugs to cause Tony to regress to an earlier stage in human evolution—a stage in which we were werewolves, apparently. (As with *She Creature*, this seems inspired by the "Bridey Murphy" craze.)

Tony the werewolf kills a friend in an atmospheric chase through woods at night; later, he changes again at school, stalking and slaying a girl in his high-school gym. A remorse-stricken Tony unwisely goes to Dr. Brandon for help, and Brandon even more unwisely changes Tony back into a werewolf. Tony kills his tormentor before perishing in a hail of police bullets.

Teenage Werewolf's mediocre script was written by Aben Kandel, here billed as "Ralph Thornton." Kandel worked with producer Herman Cohen on several other SF and horror films, none of them as good as this. Within the limitations of Kandel's often-poor writing, however, Landon does an excellent job, convincingly portraying Tony's internal turmoil. Landon, who did his own stunts, is also a good monster, probably the most agile and athletic werewolf in films. (Landon was allegedly signed for *Bonanza* on the strength of this performance.) *Teenage Werewolf* also benefits tremendously from Gene Fowler, Jr.'s intelligent direction, as well as Joseph LaShelle's fluid and elegant camera work. Tony's personality is sketched in boldly, in explosively powerful scenes, and the werewolf's "stalking" sequences are well-paced and frightening.

The poster is an Albert Kallis design executed by Reynold Brown. AIP's accelerating production schedule had by this point forced Kallis to rely on freelancers such as Brown to meet the studio's ever-growing demand for colorful and exciting graphics. While the poster looks more like a Kallis than a typical Brown, it's quite successful; the poster for the 1981 werewolf tale, *The Howling*, relied on a variation of this design. ☾

I Was A Teenage Werewolf. © 1957 American International Pictures. One-sheet, 27 x 41 inches.

The Invisible Boy

➤ 1957

This beautiful poster is becoming increasingly popular as a sort of "poor man's *Forbidden Planet.*" It has a very nice image of Robbie the Robot, most genial Bogey Person of all, obtainable for a tenth or less of the skyrocketing prices commanded by *FP* posters.

The Invisible Boy was the second film made by Robbie, one of the few special effects to have its own career ("he" also appeared in a *Twilight Zone*, a *Lost in Space*, several commercials, etc.) *Forbidden Planet* screenwriter Cyril Hume and producer Nicholas Nayfack also wrote and produced this movie, which is sometimes called an "unofficial sequel" to *FP*. It's an unfortunate connection in a way, because *Invisible Boy* is a charming if modest film that deserves attention in its own right.

The boy in question is Timmie (Richard Eyer), an all-American boy whose father is computer genius Dr. Merrinoe (Philip Abbot). Dr. Merrinoe is in charge of the top-secret "Super Computer," one of those enormous, Eniac-inspired '50s-style computers (funny how so few SF books or films of the era anticipated computers getting *smaller*). Merrinoe's a scientific whiz, but he's an overachiever as a father; he's worried that ten-year-old Timmie "can't even play a decent game of chess!" Merrinoe decides to let the Super Computer, which is capable of synthetic speech, tutor Timmie. The computer, however, has its own agenda; unbeknownst to the scientists, it has achieved self-awareness, and is (of course) bent on world conquest.

At this time, we also learn that one of Merrinoe's colleagues, the now-deceased Professor Greenhill, was an eccentric who claimed to have invented a time machine and visited the year 2309. Merrinoe and his fellow scientists (an amazingly incurious bunch, by the way) disbelieved the professor's claims, but have kept various futuristic components of his in storage. The Super Computer hypnotically enhances Billy's technical knowledge so that he can build Robbie from these components, and then secretly reprograms the robot to be its slave.

But why an *invisible* boy? After Timmie is punished for dangerous play—specifically, *flying* in an enormous kite built by Robbie; parents never let you have *any* fun—Robbie helpfully concocts an invisibility formula for the boy. Timmie has an entertaining series of adventures while invisible, including evening the score with a schoolyard bully. Meanwhile, the Super Computer uses Robbie to seize control of the project's scientists, one by one, by implanting radio control devices in their *skulls!* (Ow!) And then Robbie faces down an entire army! And then he and Timmie are *launched into* space in a satellite! And then they single-handedly save *the entire world!*

Invisible Boy is *stuffed* with incidents, enough for a whole series of movies, and they flow beautifully, with the ease of a ten-year-old's tall tales. The point of view is consistently that of its boy-protagonist, meaning that, from an adult's perspective, the film's logic is distinctly askew, lending a pleasantly surreal feeling to the proceedings. *Invisible Boy* is a kid's movie, in the very best sense, ranking with *Tobor the Great*, *Invaders From Mars,* and *The 5,000 Fingers of Dr. T*. Like these small-scale classics, *Invisible Boy* captures the imaginative freedom of childhood without condescending to the kids or boring its adult audience. ☪

The Invisible Boy. © 1957 Loew's Inc. Title card, 11 x 14 inches.

The Astounding She Monster

➤ 1958

Great poster; one of Albert Kallis' most memorable images. As for the flick: I tell you, they just *do not* make movies like this anymore. *The Astounding She Monster* has *got* to be the longest fifty-nine-minute feature in history.

She Monster concerns a mysterious visitor from a downed meteor whose touch can kill, a talent partly explained by her "radium coating"—actually a glittering Spandex jumpsuit. (She has really odd eyebrows, too.) As the film opens, we see beautiful heiress Margaret Chaffee (Marilyn Harvey) kidnapped by a gang led by Nat (Kenne Duncan) and his frowsy moll, an ex-society dame named Esther (Jeanne Tatum).

On the lam, the gang decides to hole up at the mountain cabin of geologist Dick Cutler (Robert Clarke)—"the ever-present innocent bystander," as the narrator helpfully informs us. Dick and Margaret are, of course, attracted to one another. Esther has a drinking problem, a character trait subtly conveyed by the fact that virtually every line she has in the picture—and she has way too many—is a demand for booze. Nate affectionately refers to her a "lousy drunk"; "I prefer to be referred to as an alcoholic," Esther replies, with a fine *hauteur*.

Just as you begin to think you've wandered into some hellish amateur production of *The Petrified Forest*, the She Monster drops in. Bullets have no effect on her. She rubs out some of these people; can you guess which ones? I *thought* you could. Geologist Dick examines the body of a She-Monster-slain gunsel and immediately diagnoses the cause of death as radium poisoning. This knowledge is all he needs to devise a weapon, an acid that eats through the She Monster's Spandex togs.

The movie's crowning, if leaden, irony comes with a final revelation that the fallen She Monster was an emissary from a superior civilization, sent to establish peaceful contact with the Earth. Which makes very little sense, considering that the film's taunting narration heralds her arrival with a stern "Evil unto evil," and refers to her "universal cunning." And then there's the little matter of her murder of most of the human cast, an adorable collie dog, and even a bear.

I'm constantly forced to find different ways of describing lowest-budget filmmaking; one thinks of the Eskimos and their dozens of words for "snow." To call this movie cheap-looking, though, is to flatter it. It's *impoverished*. There's one, count it, *one* set, of Dick Cutler's mountain cabin, and all the characters run from it, fleeing the She Monster, and then come *right back*, again and again and *again*. The She Monster's odd habit of exiting scenes by walking backwards is due to the fact that the rear of her costume kept coming apart.

This sinister and evocative image is generally regarded as one of Albert Kallis' finest works, and *The Astounding She Monster* currently is one of the hotter titles in the science fiction poster market. Collectors seem to have a fondness for deadly (or at least alien) ladies, and since the late 1980s, the market has seen intense demand for *The Astounding She Monster* and several of her sisters, notably the *Devil Girl From Mars*.

☾⋆

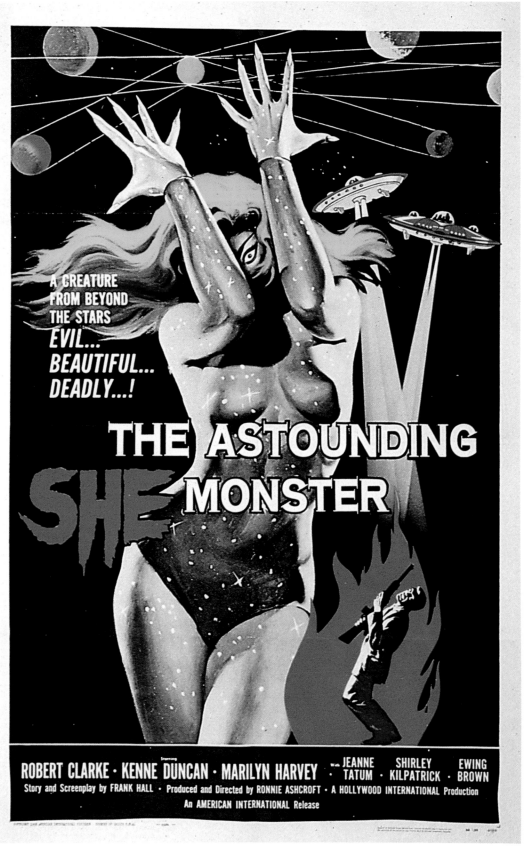

The Astounding She Monster. © 1958 American International Pictures. One-sheet, 27 × 41 inches.

Fiend Without a Face

➤ 1958

Fiend Without a Face has haunted a lot of subconscious minds over the years since its release. One scholarly work I've seen devotes a dozen pages of feverish Jungian analysis to the movie, calling it a "Promethean myth of individuation." (Really.) Even people who haven't seen the film in decades remember it vividly, although you may have to remind them it's the one with the "jumping brain monsters."

Fiend is a British-made film, loosely based on an early 1930s pulp horror story, "The Thought Monster," by Amelia Reynolds Long. The movie has become a classic largely on the strength of some top-notch special effects work in its final reel. The rest of the film doesn't measure up to its climax, but at least for once a monster-attack payoff really delivers.

As *Fiend* opens, a sentry patrolling a U.S. Air Force base in Canada's northern wilderness is killed by an invisible creature. The base is conducting secret experiments with an atom-powered radar device. No points for guessing there's a connection. Mysterious killings continue, and the local rubes decide (with some justification, as it turns out) that the air base is responsible. Major Jeff Cummings (Marshall Thompson), our hero, investigates the killings, in the process falling in love with the sister of the first victim. A great deal of semi-coherent plot ensues—including a longish digression in a cemetery that's never effectively explained—before Cummings discovers that the Fiends responsible for the killings are the product of a local scientist's ESP experiment gone awry, and that they somehow need the energy produced by the air base's atomic pile to live.

This brings us to the film's monster sequences; as indicated above, these bogeys do *not* disappoint. The Fiends were created through stop-motion animation by a German effects team, Florenz von Nordhoff and K.L. Ruppel, whose efforts approach those of Ray Harryhausen and easily top any other stop-motion work produced during the 1950s. As seen in the poster (which for once is accurate) the Fiends are *literally* brains with eyestalks, tendril legs and whiplike, spinal-cord tails. They *jump* on people, and suck their brains and spinal cords out, with a horrible *crunching, slurping, slobbering* sound! And when they're shot or bludgeoned, they burst open, gushing nasty puddles of *black goo*! Neat, huh? It's pretty easy to imagine the impact these critters had on twelve-year-old boys. According to producer Richard Gordon, English censors refused to pass the film without extensive cuts, and even the American print had to be trimmed slightly.

Two final odd notes, from the perspective of 1993. First, when we initially meet Major Cummings, he's taking a tablet, and a friend tells him he should try sleep instead of benzedrine. For me, at least, knowing the hero's a speedfreak certainly puts a different spin on his subsequent actions. Second, the film displays an amazingly cavalier attitude towards atomic power. During a routine test, the major orders the atomic pile pushed beyond its limits. A technician tells him the reactor may go out of control, then shrugs, smiles and says "It's your funeral...mine too, probably." *And everybody else's downwind for a thousand miles,* we think. ☾⋆

Fiend Without a Face. © 1958 Loew's Inc. One-sheet, 27 x 41 inches.

4D Man

> 1959

Here's an interestingly expressionist image of a unusual SF Bogey Person—the vampire as wraith, who can literally walk through walls.

Like *Not of This Earth*, *4D Man* is a modest but intriguing science fiction twist on vampirism. The film was produced by Jack Harris and Irvin Yeaworth, Jr., and directed by Yeaworth, the team that also made *The Blob*. *4D Man* has a low-budget look, some mediocre acting and a god-awful brassy jazz score. But intelligent ideas, a good script and a thoughtful performance by Robert Lansing as the 4D Man make it surprisingly adult, one of the better offbeat SF stories of the period.

Maverick physicist Tony Nelson (James Congdon) is searching for a way of penetrating solid matter through the fourth dimension. (In most genre films, the "fourth dimension" is assumed to be time, often with references to "Einstein's theory"; here they mean another spatial dimension.) Several years before, while experimenting with a device that amplifies atomic fields, Tony succeeded in pushing an ordinary pencil through a solid plate of steel—not punching a hole in it, but somehow *intermingling* the pencil's atoms with the steel. Importantly, he believes the atomic-field amplifier worked on his brain, not the steel; that he *willed* the pencil through the steel. Now, Tony is obsessed with duplicating his results.

His brother, Scott (Lansing), also a scientist, has been exposed to radiation in the course of his research. This has altered his brain waves, making them much stronger than normal. While imitating Tony's experiment, he suddenly succeeds in thrusting not just a pencil but his *hand* through a steel plate. The next day, Tony and Scott discover that the atomic-field amplifier wasn't working properly; Scott performed the trick by *mental power alone*. Soon, Scott can go "4D" at will, and in this state penetrate or pass through any physical barrier.

At first he enjoys the power. He can reach into jewelry-store windows, pluck letters from inside mailboxes—he even robs a bank for sport. But Scott soon finds that 4D comes at a terrible price, aging him by decades within a few days. Then he discovers that contact with another human while he's in 4D drains that person of his or her life force and transfers it to Scott. His first kill is accidental, but soon he's driven to steal life from his boss, a rival, even a little girl....

This sounds, if not typical, then at least predictable. What makes *4D Man* interesting is the emotional framework *behind* the monster story. Tony is younger than Scott, irresponsible and impetuous. Scott is responsible, intelligent and warm, but staid, insecure, a little too tightly wrapped. Scott loves his research assistant, Linda (Lee Meriwether), who's dating him but does not love him in return. When the more dynamic Tony comes on the scene, he and Linda are quickly drawn to one another; guilt and anger between the brothers drives much of the plot.

Lansing's performance is remarkable, particularly as Scott's rigid control begins to crack under the strain of the 4D power and its terrible cost. James Congdon's Tony is only fair; he doesn't seem like someone who could take a woman away from Lansing. Even so, *4D Man* contains some intriguing emotional shadings, among characters much more subtly drawn than most of their counterparts in '50s SF. ☾⋆

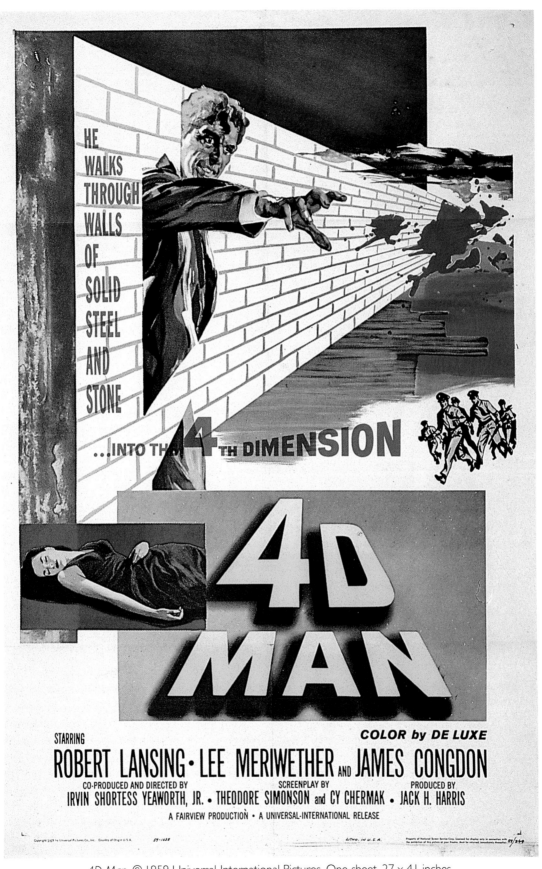

4D Man. © 1959 Universal-International Pictures. One-sheet, 27 x 41 inches.

The Wasp Woman

➤ 1960

The Wasp Woman is one of the most visually appealing of all the enormous-bug posters of the 1950s era. Alas, it's also one of the most misleading. One trusts it will come as no surprise to learn that this Roger Corman film has absolutely nothing to do with the arresting image shown here. This is unfortunate, as a human-headed wasp the size of a boxcar arguably would have made for a far more interesting movie.

The Wasp Woman concerns a rejuvenative drug extracted from the "royal jelly" of wasps (a substance I don't believe exists, by the way). The drug is refined by a vaguely European scientist named Eric Zinthrop (Michael Mark), for a cosmetics company run by aging beauty Janice Starlin (Susan Cabot). Starlin serves as her company's sole model and cover girl, and the firm is experiencing declining sales because the fortyish Starlin's looks are beginning to fade. (This is suggested by a frumpy hairdo and some dark circles under her eyes, and yes, ladies, there are some pretty unsavory sexual politics going on here.) Starlin and Zinthrop strike a deal; she wants to be young again and he wants her to sponsor his research. It's hard to see any sin in this, but the film's teeth-gritting trumpet-and-xylophone-based score portentously signals its disapproval of the deal.

Starlin insists on becoming Zinthrop's guinea pig for his wasp jelly experiments, and indeed begins to grow younger (the dark circles go away.) Then Zinthrop is removed from the scene by a clunky plot device; he's struck by a truck and rendered amnesiac. Soon, youth-hungry Starlin is mainlining wasp extract and periodically becoming a deadly Wasp Woman, slaying her victims by night and attending marketing meetings by day. At one point, a recovering Zinthrop indicates that she may be *devouring* her victims, which seems like a pretty tall order for five-foot-two Susan Cabot.

The Wasp Woman was shot in less than a week, for about $50,000. The film was shot during Corman's most prolific period; the legendary director was entirely capable of shooting a film a week in those days. The movie looks like a quickie knockoff of *The Fly*, but the plot situation plays out more like *Doctor Jekyll and Mr. Hyde*. Once the Fly had become the Fly, there was no turning back, but the Wasp Woman changes back and forth, and seems to have little memory about her transformations (although the film is none too clear on this point). Unfortunately, the Wasp Woman makeup is poor even by Corman's standards, resembling nothing so much as a goggle-eyed Mardi Gras mask.

Still, even the least of Corman's pictures contain a grace note or two; here it's mostly Susan Cabot's performance in the lead role. Cabot was a darkly beautiful actress with a rare gift for projecting both intelligence and menace, qualities used to good effect in *The Wasp Woman*. She left films shortly afterward, dissatisfied with the type of work she was getting, and had a brief fling with Jordan's King Hussein(!) before becoming active on stage and in television. Sadly, Susan Cabot was murdered in 1986.

Despite its positive points, *The Wasp Woman* is a distinctly minor Corman film. Once again, a beautiful poster makes a large promise it has no intention of keeping. ☾⋆

The Wasp Woman. © 1960 Allied Artists. Half-sheet, 22 × 28 inches.

X—The Man With the X-Ray Eyes

➤ 1963

X—The Man With the X-Ray Eyes may well be Roger Corman's best SF project to date. Corman's direction here has a depth and assurance far beyond his earlier work, and for once some of the subtleties his worshippers invariably find actually seem to be present. *X* has considerably more on its mind than simple shocks; it's a bleak, chilly fable with a sting in its tail.

X is a tragedy of Icarus, the fall of a man with a fatal desire to exceed human limits—in this case, to see more than anyone has before. Dr. James Xavier (Ray Milland) is obsessed with human vision. As he points out, people see only a small portion of the electromagnetic spectrum. Xavier believes that broadening that range could yield any number of wonders, including the ability to see directly into the human body, diagnosing illness with far greater accuracy than any X-ray. Using himself as a guinea pig, he succeeds in developing a drug that expands his powers of vision.

At first the power seems harmless enough; there's a humorous scene in which he realizes he can see through pretty girls' clothes. But soon, Xavier finds the people around him are blind in more ways than one. The foundation supporting his experiments cut off his funding. He uses his gift to save a girl during a delicate operation, but finds himself threatened with malpractice. Finally, an agitated and increasingly desperate Xavier accidentally kills a friend who attempts to restrain him, initiating a relentless downward spiral. The remainder of the film plays out in a series of increasingly expressionist scenes. The fugitive Xavier becomes a carnival mind-reader, "Mentalo," and later "the Healer," who, for a fee, diagnoses the diseases of the slum dwellers around him.

Xavier is found by his colleague and love interest, Dr. Diane Fairfax (Diana Van Der Vlis). Xavier by now is partly deranged, unable to rest, always bathed in light, for eyelids can't stop vision that can penetrate steel and brick; he'd "give anything—anything! to have dark." People look like "dissections" to him now, all bones and organs; he fails to recognize Diane when she finds him playing the Healer. The two go to Las Vegas, where Xavier attempts to use his X-ray vision in the casinos to raise money to complete his research. The plan backfires when his powers cause the casino crew to assume he's cheating.

Xavier flees into the desert, ultimately stumbling into a tent revival. By this time his eyes are eerie black voids. With them he can see to the "center of the universe, the eye that sees us all!" A sinister preacher denounces Xavier as a sinner, and the parishioners echo the words: "If thine eye offend thee, pluck it out." With a look of mingled anguish and relief, *he does so.* Roll the credits. Brrr.

The *X* poster is a particular favorite of mine, and a relative sleeper on the poster market. Collectors don't seem to prize it much, probably because it lacks overt science-fiction imagery. But, to me at least, the one-sheet's rich colors and powerful, Deco-inflected design harken back to the classic posters of the 1930s. ☾

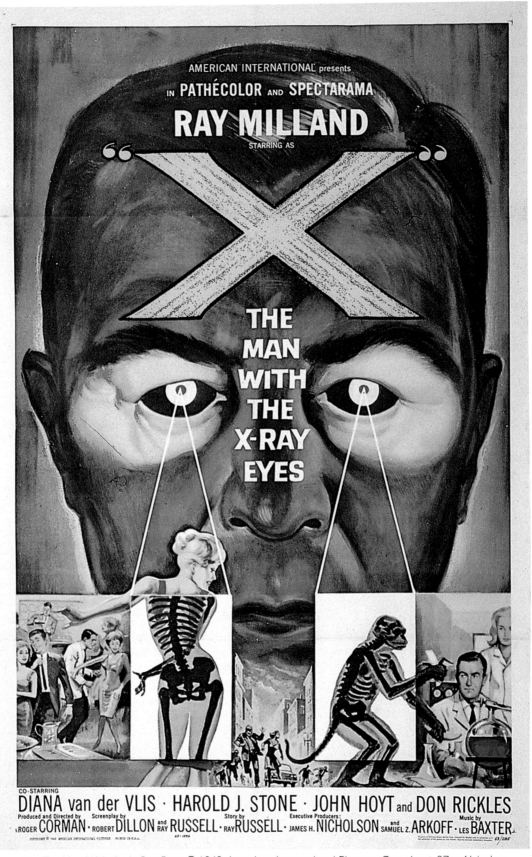

X—The Man With the X-Ray Eyes. © 1963 American International Pictures. One-sheet, 27 x 41 inches.

COLLECTING SCIENCE
FICTION MOVIE POSTERS

Movie posters are among the most sought-after of all collectors' items, and science fiction films from the period 1950-64 constitute one of the hottest categories in movie poster collecting. Many people feel that science fiction posters of this era are the last truly interesting vintage movie posters.

The 1920s and '30s were golden years for movie posters, as they were for American illustration in general. Most of the major studios printed their own posters, usually in richly colored stone- or zinc-plate lithography, and the best work of studio art departments was fully equal to that of contemporary giants of illustration such as Maxfield Parrish and Franklin Booth. By the 1940s, however, American movie posters had entered what historians Stephen Rebello and Richard Allen have termed "a decade of marked aesthetic decline." Lush and imaginative painting was gradually supplanted by photo montage and dully executed art. During the same period, the expensive and painstaking stone-lithography technique was replaced by faster and cheaper offset printing, which generally failed to reproduce the rich tones of the earlier process.

James Arness as *The Thing From Another World*. Fortunately, the disappointing makeup is seen only fleetingly in this otherwise effective thriller.

The 1950s science fiction boom, however, produced posters in marked contrast to the generally drab look of those for "serious film." Most '50s SF movies were exploitation vehicles targeted at teenagers; they were not, to say the least, regarded as important by film studios. Moreover, it was a common practice among bargain-basement studios (particularly American International Pictures) to use poster art to help sell movies to distributors. This required poster artists to produce paintings well in advance—often before the film was actually made. Such conditions made for posters that usually have little to do with the film they're selling, but also gave the artists freedom to devise eye-catching and imaginative works. Its artistic merits may vary, but at least 1950s SF poster art gives you the distinct impression that the artists had fun producing it.

Poster sizes

In the 1940s, movie studios began farming out movie poster printing and distribution chores to the National Screen Service Corporation (NSS), a company that specialized in posters and other promotional materials and theatrical "trailers" (the coming-attractions ads that run before the main feature). By the 1950s, nearly all American movie posters were produced by NSS.

NSS produced movie posters in a series of standard sizes derived from the size of the lithographic beds and plates used to print them. Sometimes, as with *The Day the Earth Stood Still*, a studio would prepare different art for each of the major poster sizes. Just as often, however, the various posters connected with a film use different arrangements of the same art.

The most common poster sizes are:

- **One-sheets** The "standard" 27 x 41 inch theatrical poster; today, virtually the *only* poster used in theaters. One-sheets are probably the most popular posters with collectors, although they are less rare than other sizes. 1950s SF one-sheets were often printed on relatively flimsy paper stock, and sometimes the colors are less vivid than those on other sizes. One-sheets typically were delivered to movie theaters folded, with one vertical fold and three horizontal folds. NSS sometimes shipped posters with three horizontal folds only; unfolded ("rolled") one-sheets from the '50s are almost unheard of.

- **Half-sheets** Posters roughly half the size of a one-sheet (22 x 28 inches), hence the name. Half-sheets are printed on heavier stock than one-sheets and usually feature brighter and more vibrant colors. During the 1950s, NSS often printed two different half-sheets for each film, denoted as A- and B-styles. Half-sheets commonly have a four-way, cruciform fold. Rolled half-sheets are uncommon but considerably less rare than rolled one-sheets.

- **Inserts** A tall, narrow poster (14 x 36 inches) printed on the same heavy stock and featuring the same generally superior printing as half-sheets. Occasionally, an insert's odd size makes for a clumsy balance of graphic elements—particularly on inserts featuring a "squeezed" version of a one-sheet painting—but when art is designed spe-cifically for the insert format, as with *Target Earth*, it can be striking. Inserts typically were folded horizontally at least three times, but rolled specimens pop up fairly often.

- **Window cards** A 14 x 22 inch poster on card stock. While other posters were displayed in theater lobbies, window cards were designed for display in area grocery-store windows and the like. For this reason, window cards have a wide blank space at the top to display the theater's name. This bugs many collectors, and it's fairly common to find window cards with the blank space trimmed off. For some reason, the printing on window cards often looks drab, but occasionally the size will shine; for instance, in my opinion the window card to *Them!* is the best poster available on the film.

- **Lobby cards** An 11 x 14 inch poster on card stock. Lobby cards come in two basic types. *Title cards* reproduce poster art, usually the same art appearing on the film's half-sheet. *Scene cards*, usually made in sets of eight, feature photos from the film; in the 1950s, these were generally black and white shots that were (crudely) tinted in color.

In addition to these posters, NSS made several larger sizes. **Three-sheets** (41 x 81 inches) and **six-sheets** (81 x 81 inches) are, as their names imply, respectively about three and six times the size of a one-sheet. These posters were too large to be printed in single pieces. Three-sheets generally come in two pieces, while six-sheets come in four. Even larger is the **24-sheet**, which is—you guessed it—twenty-four times larger than a one-sheet. These are billboard posters, the same ones you see along the interstate, and yes, people *do* collect them, and no, I don't have the *first idea* what they do with them. Paper the entire house, I suppose.

NSS also made relatively small numbers of 30 x **40 inch** and **40 x 60 inch** posters. These are printed on card stock and seem to be found rolled fairly often, but they are rare and frankly, I haven't seen enough of them to be able to generalize about them. The 40 x 60 of *Atragon*, for instance, is just a larger version of the one-sheet with superior printing, but the 30 x 40 of *Forbidden Planet* is a garishly colored redrawing of the one-sheet that looks like a bad black-light poster from the '60s.

Re-issues

NSS performed a singularly useful service for collectors in dating their posters. All NSS posters bear a simple dating system in fine print at the bottom of the poster; the notation "56/155" on the one-sheet from *Earth Versus the Flying Saucers*, for instance, means that it was the 155th title released by NSS in 1956.

Reissue posters of 1950s SF movies are relatively rare but they do exist and collectors should be wary of them. If a film was to be re-released, NSS sometimes would reprint the poster from the original plates, introducing a small "R" before the date in their code. In such cases, this "R" may be the *only way* to tell whether a poster is a reissue and not an original. The original, naturally, always commands a premium on the collectors' market.

Foreign posters

Foreign posters represent an interesting but problematic category for the collector. Many foreign posters for 1950s SF movies are extremely attractive, particularly French and Belgian posters; the French poster for *The War of the Worlds*, for example, is infinitely superior to its American counterpart. However, the thorny issue of *provenance*—in this case, establishing whether a given poster is an original issue—has thus far kept them from developing into a significant market for American collectors.

A great deal has been written about this issue in trade publications, much of it conflicting. However, what does seem to be agreed-upon is this: both French and Belgian posters were extensively reprinted in the 1970s. These reprints were intended as cheap art posters (dorm decor, I suppose) and not as counterfeits for unwary collectors. Unfortunately, some unscrupulous individuals have sold the reprints in the U.S. as originals, at high-dollar collector prices—and *there's no easy way to tell the reprints from the originals*.

The problem is that European posters of the 1950s weren't dated by their printers. The reprints are the same size as the originals, and appear to be struck from the original plates. The French reprints apparently are made on a slicker stock than that used in the 1950s, but it's a fairly subtle difference. With

Belgian posters, there's one reasonably sure way to tell an original; the Belgian authorities of that period required movie posters being displayed at theaters to bear a tax stamp that resembles a postage stamp. Not all originals have this stamp, but all posters bearing the stamp allegedly *are* originals. (On the other hand, there you are, with an ugly stamp on your poster.)

Beyond this data, all is confusion. Recently, a prominent poster dealer claimed in a collectors' publication that Belgian reprints all bear the words "printed in Belgium" in English, while originals bear a similar notice in French. A few weeks later, another dealer experienced in European posters promptly contradicted the first claim, saying he knew of a number of originals with the English notice.

I'm very fond of Belgian posters and display several in my collection, so I'm not trying to warn you away from foreign posters. But I would be hesitant to pay exorbitant prices for foreign material unless I was *extremely* sure it was original. And enough collectors seem to feel this way to keep prices on most foreign posters relatively low.

Where to find posters

Ha ha! You can't! They're all gone!

Just kidding, but it *is* getting harder.

Collector's guides for other pop-culture items tend to advise you to search your attic and visit local garage sales, or words to that effect, and I certainly wouldn't want to discourage you from doing so. Realistically, however, the scarcity of vintage movie posters makes it unlikely that you'll ever stumble on a "find" in this way, unless you locate a family of ushers and projectionists. (Note: Some weeks after I wrote this, a person I know found an original *The Thing* one-sheet for $10 at a garage sale! I swear! Miracles still happen, I guess.)

Die-hard poster fans search for old movie theaters, particularly those in out-of-the-way places, which may have failed to return posters. Still others have sniffed out defunct poster exchanges, companies that used to provide posters for second-run movie houses. However, I suspect that most of the remaining finds of this kind will be made by professional dealers who have the time, experience, and inclination to spend months on the road looking for posters. (I've known a few such individuals and believe me, they are *very good* at what they do.)

For those of us who aren't willing or able to spend our summer holidays playing poster detective, more conventional methods will have to suffice. Translation: We're going to pay collectors' prices.

Shops and conventions

Many comics and SF-related shops carry recent movie posters, but stores that deal in vintage movie paper are relatively scarce outside the country's better-heeled metropolitan areas, such as Los Angeles, San Francisco, and New York. However, many of these will sell through the mail. (See Appendix.)

Poster shows and conventions attract dealers and collectors from all over the nation; they're good places to meet other collectors and see a lot of different items. (You may also get the opportunity to do a bit of haggling.) Shows that specialize in vintage movie paper (as opposed to garden-variety comics and SF conventions) also tend to be concentrated in the Northeast and California. Your local comics or SF shop should be able to tell you whether any shows are scheduled for your area; if not, and if you've got the bug *bad enough*, you may find it worth your while to take a shopping vacation to a major East- or West-Coast show.

Collectors' publications

Probably the single most important source for beginning collectors of 1950s science fiction—especially if, like me, you live not on the coasts but somewhere in the Big Flyover—is *Movie Collector's World*, a biweekly trade journal featuring hundreds of ads from poster dealers and collectors who use its pages to buy, sell and trade among each other. *MCW* also features a directory of stores dealing in movie memorabilia, announcements for poster shows across the nation, ads for upcoming auctions, and so forth. The paper caters to collectors of all types of movie posters, but '50s SF is a prominent part of the mix. A similar publication, *The Big Reel*, carries some poster

ads as well as many ads for movies on videotape and in 16mm film. (See Appendix.)

Mail order

Mail order is reasonably safe (but so is sky-diving, say). Any sane collector would prefer to buy posters in person, where you can see the merchandise before buying, but the material is so scarce and so scattered around the country that unless you live in one of those major cities we've already mentioned, you very nearly *have* to order by mail. I've made dozens of poster deals through the mail over the last few years, and I've only had one genuinely unpleasant encounter. Even then, I finally got most of my money back, although it took several months.

Even so, it was a scary experience, and one that reminded me that mail order is unquestionably a bit of a gamble. If something goes wrong, you will be dismayed to learn how little interest the postal inspectors have in your $400 ripoff. And always remember the tiny print in *MCW*'s masthead: "The Publisher is not responsible for any transactions made as a result of any advertising carried in *MCW*." Note that it does not say "unless we're moved by your sad story."

It's still worth it, though, if you don't live in an area that gives you regular access to collectors' conventions. For one thing, as you develop connections among other collectors, you may start to turn up deals that don't appear in the trade journals or receive advance word on ads before they appear in print. You can strike up trades and hear about things that friends of friends have available. The larger your network of acquaintances in the hobby, the more likely you are to uncover that special item you're looking for.

Auctions

Vintage movie posters can also be purchased at auction, either in person or via phone bids. Some auctions are conducted entirely via mail and phone bids. For better or worse, auctions seem to be driving the market right now, in terms of pricing; more about that later. Auctions usually offer a good variety of classic 1950s science fiction titles, but be prepared to pay top dollar—or more. The Appendix lists several auction houses that sell movie posters; these companies should be able to provide you with information and catalogs concerning their next offerings.

Poster market trends

Since the mid-1980s, the science fiction poster market has quite literally exploded, both in the number of active collectors and the prices commanded by key titles. What was once a fairly relaxed hobby has now taken on something of the atmosphere of the Chicago commodities exchange (not that I'm bitter).

In retrospect, however, it's clear it was bound to happen, for several reasons.

First, public interest in science fiction of all sorts has risen *enormously* in the fifteen years since *Star Wars* forever changed the pop-culture landscape. There aren't any census figures on SF fans, but judging from the way the hobby has evolved in the last decade or so, it seems certain that the number of serious collectors has doubled or tripled. Those of us who remember the halcyon days of the late 1970s, when *The Beast From 20,000 Fathoms* one-sheets changed hands for $20 and a hearty handshake, are understandably upset about the jostling hordes of new collectors with whom we now have to compete. A more philosophical attitude is that our taste has been confirmed; our hobby has arrived—which is little enough comfort when you're confronting sticker shock over a thirty-five-year-old piece of paper.

Second, these crowds of collectors are competing for *truly rare* items. Movie posters, unlike comics, toys, baseball cards, and other high-dollar pop collectibles, were *never produced for the public in large quantities.* "Golden-Age" comic books, for instance, were produced in runs of up to a million per issue; by contrast, press runs for 1950s one-sheets *rarely exceeded 5,000 or so.* Other sizes were made in even smaller press runs.

Moreover, these posters were *not* sold to the public. On the contrary, theaters typically returned posters to the National Screen Service for credit against future posters; NSS, in turn, recycled these posters to other theaters, often until they fell apart

from constant handling. (Posters that weren't returned were supposed to be destroyed by the theaters, although this rule was about as strictly enforced as the do-not-remove notices on mattress tags.) Granted that comics, posters, and other collectibles all have fallen prey over the decades to neglect, greasy fingers, rough handling, and paper drives, vintage posters began from a *far smaller base* of copies in existence.

Finally, in the last few years, the science fiction poster market has become of interest to *speculators* who are aware of the above facts. I'm not using the word "speculator" in a pejorative sense (although many long-time collectors do); I simply mean that some persons pursuing and buying the finest SF posters are doing so in the expectation of making an eventual profit, not out of any particular love for the posters or the genre. At least part of the tremendous rise in the value of the top posters is due to such speculation. The major speculators have filled the pages of *Movie Collector's World* with increasingly hysterical-sounding advertisements boasting of the wheelbarrows full of money they'll spend on your posters (never as much as you would make by selling them on your own, by the way).

The speculators have arrived for one reason—they believe that, in view of their limited quantities, their historical and esthetic significance and their popularity, the best 1950s SF posters are *significantly undervalued.* The most expensive comic book sells for about $100,000; the most valuable baseball card also takes six figures. By contrast, as of mid-1992, *none* of the posters in this book sells for more than about $5,000—or about one-tenth of the price of a really crummy Andy Warhol lithograph, to look at it another way.

Auctions and the market

A related factor that affects pricing is the advent of major poster auctions. Auctions have been around for awhile, but the 1990 entry of the international auction house Christie's into the poster market in particular helped to attract the attention of wealthy speculators and collectors of typically hyperinflated 1980s art, such as those crummy Warhols I just mentioned.

To people with the ability and the desire to shed hundreds of thousands of dollars on decor, a few thousand for a cheery robot poster is no big deal, particularly not if they expect it to appreciate. (I should note that most posters included in major auctions tend to be classics of the 1920s through 1940s, but representative examples of the best 1950s SF posters are nearly always featured.) The result is that prices in auctions tend to be significantly higher than in other settings, such as collectible shows or collector-to-collector sales.

Of course, relatively few posters change hands in these auctions, and relatively few collectors participate in them. Nonetheless, auction prices are important, for a simple reason: they serve as a benchmark for the rest of the hobby. It's human nature to accept the highest price you've ever heard for an item as its true value, *if* you already happen to own that particular item.

In fall 1991, for instance, I knew of several *Invasion of the Saucer-Men* one-sheets for sale in the neighborhood of $1,000 to $1,200. In the December 1991 Christie's auction, however, a *Saucer-Men* one-sheet sold for about $2,000. For a few months, *MCW* and *The Big Reel* carried no paper for sale on this title; you could almost feel the market holding its collective breath. Then, in early 1992, I began seeing *Saucer-Men* one-sheets offered for sale once again—at its new "official" price of $2,000 or more.

To sum up in country-simple language, there are probably more persons searching for the best 1950s science fiction posters than there are copies of these posters in existence. That's the recipe for today's market, in which a poster selling for $600 in January may well go for $1,200 in July.

And whither poster prices? Don't I wish I knew. Will prices continue to soar until each bug-eyed monster commands the sort of money currently associated with Rembrandt etchings? Or will people one day decide that *The Day the Earth Stood Still* isn't worth as much as a Hyundai? A lot of long-time collectors (like me, for instance) have devoutly wished for such an event, in dreamier moments, but it smacks of wishful thinking. There has to be a plateau out there, somewhere, but there's little evidence that

we've found it yet. And most collectors will agree that, each time we've thought a piece has gone as high as it could possibly go, it's promptly gone higher.

Forbidden Planet is a good example. There was a slightly tattered specimen of the one-sheet priced at $450 in a Houston collectors' shop *for years* in the mid-1980s. My friends and I often chuckled over the dealer's optimism; what blockhead would pay *that much?* Many collectors were astonished when *Forbidden Planet* climbed into the vicinity of $600 six years ago; shocked when it broke $1,000, about four years ago; truly discombobulated as it hopped, skipped, and jumped to $3,000 to $4,000 by late 1991; and now, with reports of a 1992 auction price of $6,050, there's just *no words* for how collectors feel—*if* they don't have it yet.

The Appendix offers a brief and strictly subjective accounting of the most valuable 1950s science fiction movie posters, and estimates their *approximate* value ranges as of mid-1992. Please note that prices can be expected to continue ratcheting upwards, and some values given in this list may be slightly out of date by the time you purchase this book. Furthermore, we should remember that even today, there still are many beautiful '50s SF posters— a number of which are illustrated in this book— available for well under $100.

Condition

As with any delicate paper collectible, condition is an important consideration in evaluating a poster's value—or it damned well *should* be, any way. My single biggest complaint about practices within the movie poster hobby is the persistently sloppy grading or outright misrepresentation of condition practiced by all too many poster dealers. Of course, this is primarily a problem with mail orders, since in face-to-face encounters you're presumably able to inspect the wares before buying.

Movie paper collectors lack a single, uniform grading system to categorize poster condition, which is part of the problem. Modern-day comics collecting has become as frenetic and joyless as the trading of pork-bellies futures, but at least that hobby has a coherent and universally applied grading system. Instead, poster collectors primarily use two looser and more informal approaches to describe condition. The first is adapted from comics collecting, which in turn adapted *its* references from coin collecting. In this scheme, poster condition is graded *more or less* according to the following categories.

- **Mint** A poster that looks as if it were just printed. In the case of forty-year-old posters, mint condition is like true love or perfect virtue—an ideal rather than an everyday fact.

- **Near-mint (NM)** The real-world equivalent of mint. As good a specimen as you're likely to find; bright colors, no fading or browning, no tears, tape stains, ink stains, pinholes, fold damage, etc. Nearly as rare as mint. As unfolded ("rolled") one-sheets are virtually unknown,· folding alone should not eliminate a one-sheet from NM status. Rolled half-sheets, inserts, and window cards are more common, and here folding probably should be considered unacceptable.

- **Fine (FN)** Still a very nice specimen, with a bright, clean image and no *significant* fading, browning, tears, tape stains, ink stains, pinholes, or fold damage or wear. (Deciding what constitutes "significant" damage, of course, could be a source of arguments for years to come.)

- **Very good (VG)** A poster which is still brightly colored and presentable; it probably looks very nice in a frame, but has some undeniable problems of the types cited above.

- **Good (G)** A damaged but presentable poster. Probably a well-used and frequently folded specimen, with noticeable fading and browning.

- **Fair (F)** A worn poster with considerable damage; possibly a few chunks of the image are missing.

- **Poor (P)** A rag, but a possible candidate for restoration (see below) if it's an exceptionally rare or valuable piece.

Of course, these categories aren't carved on stone tablets, and some may find the way I've described them either too harsh or too lenient. Nonetheless, these are the sorts of reliable definitions you should expect—and *demand*—in mail-order transactions.

Another grading system that's become increasingly popular in recent years is used by Christie's in their annual auction. Under this scheme, posters can be:

- **Condition A—Excellent** Posters in fine or better condition as described above; minor restoration along folds and minor damage in borders is acceptable.

- **Condition B—Fine** Slight restoration allowable in areas other than fold lines, and some fading or minor marks are allowable in the image area. These posters would range from very good to fine as defined above.

- **Condition C—Good** Posters may show significant damage and may have been restored considerably; pieces of borders may be missing, Such posters would range from poor to good as defined above.

Note that the A-B-C system specifically allows for restoration, a topic discussed below. Note also that informal, comics-adapted grading actually can be more rigorous than the Christie's system. In fairness to Christie's, however, we should remember that many of the posters they sell are extremely old and rare, and slightly looser grading may be justified. Besides, the "good-very good-fine" system is not often used with any precision—to say the least. As a grizzled veteran of bunches of mail-order deals, I've learned that all too many folks feel that "fine" means "I seem to remember it looked pretty good the last time I unpacked it, in 1978," while "very good" means "It's not actually on fire at the moment."

You should *not* put up with this. It's more often the result of laziness than deliberate fraud, but it's still misrepresentation. If enough poster dealers have overgraded or misrepresented merchandise thrown back at their heads, we may discourage this sort of behavior.

Poster repair

Formal paper restoration is a skilled and exacting craft, and you should not attempt ambitious repair work on your posters unless you are very sure of your skills indeed. Nevertheless, there are a few simple techniques short of formal restoration that you can use to improve your poster's appearance.

Tears and parting along fold lines—common in posters that have been repeatedly unfolded and refolded—are easily fixed with thin strips of archival (acid-free) tape on the reverse side. *Do not* use transparent tape or any other household tape, which will ultimately discolor and destroy the paper. (Seasoned collectors know that tape damage is one of the most common defects seen in old posters.) Archival tapes may be purchased or ordered through the better art-supply or frame shops. Thin paper archival tapes are better for repair purposes than the heavy linen tapes often used in frame shops. One good brand is a German product called Filmoplast. Pin and thumbtack holes, another common flaw, often can be made negligible with archival tape; simply back the hole with a tiny square of tape and, using a toothpick or similar tool, gently push the frayed edges of the hole down onto the tape.

Pigment loss along fold lines or around pinholes can sometimes be covered up with *light* applications of colored pencil in a similar shade. This works particularly well if the missing color is dark and neutral. Professional restorers often use watercolors for such repairs, but this is a permanent, irreversible medium, and again, it's not recommended unless you're completely confident of your abilities. *Don't* use a ballpoint pen or laundry marker for touchups, the ink of which can spread through the paper, making a worse defect than the one you're trying to fix.

Restoration

As movie posters have risen in value, many collectors have become aware of the uses—and the limitations—of professional paper restoration. Proper restoration can add immeasurably to the life, attractiveness and value of your posters. Poor restoration, however, can have just the opposite effect.

The movie poster hobbiest eagerly embraced poster restoration a few years back. Many major cities are home to at least a few paper restorers, who typically perform most of their work for art galleries and museums, and who can be found in the Yellow Pages under "Art Restoration and Conservation." In addition, several restoration services specifically court the movie poster hobby through ads in *Movie Collector's World*. However, be aware that there's been something of a movement *against* restoration recently, judging from the number of trade journal ads requesting "unrestored posters *only*."

The unfortunate fact is that there has been a lot of lousy restoration work foisted on collectors, and horror stories abound of expensive, unnecessary procedures done at the restorer's discretion, year-long turnaround times and shoddy work by anonymous assistants. (In early 1992, I personally examined an extremely rare and expensive poster purchased at the 1991 Christie's auction, and surprisingly the restoration work was quite poor, with painted "fixes" that didn't match the color of the surrounding paper and were still tacky to the touch.)

In addition, it's possible to become too impressed with the work of a *good* restorer; keep in mind that an *unrestored* fine-condition specimen will always be worth more than a restored poster that *looks* like it's in fine condition. In other words, you're better off buying a poster in fine condition for $300 than buying the same poster in poorer condition for $100 and spending $200 on subsequent restoration work, even if the results look pretty much the same. Finally, note that paper restoration is not cheap. You can expect to pay anywhere from $30 to $80 an hour for such work. Restoration really is recommended only for posters of sufficient value to make the effort worthwhile.

Despite these caveats, I *have* had posters restored and have been very pleased with the results. Good poster restoration can help protect your posters and make major flaws disappear as if by magic. The major restoration techniques include:

- *Cleaning*. This means just what it says; restorers can wash old posters in special detergents that remove years of dust, stains, pencil marks, etc., without affecting the poster's paper or inks. Generally, posters are cleaned as a prelude to linen backing (see below).

- *Deacifidication*. Posters with acid damage (fading and browning) can be deacidified either by a liquid or a gas method. Deacidification neutralizes the naturally occurring acids that cause paper to turn brown with age. It won't reverse acid damage, but it can stabilize the poster, halting ongoing damage and greatly extending the poster's life.

- *Bleaching.* Browned, faded posters can be brightened considerably by chemical bleaches; in addition, bleaching is virtually the *only* way to remove stains from mildew and other water damage. However, bleaching is an extreme measure that should not be used lightly, as it can change the color values of the poster's inks. Note that a good restorationist can safely bleach a browning poster's borders—where this sort of damage usually is most apparent—without bleaching the image area itself.

- *Linen backing.* The term is a misnomer. Actually, the process involves bonding a poster to acid-free rice papers with an archival paste; the resulting package is *then* mounted on thick and sturdy linen. Linen backing may sound superficially similar to dry-mounting, but unlike dry-mounting, linen backing will protect a poster without causing it to discolor over time. In addition, a good linen mount can make even stubborn fold lines virtually disappear. Linen backing is most commonly used for larger posters (one-sheets and up). Smaller posters on sturdier stock, such as half-sheets and inserts, can backed with rice paper only, which is cheaper and still affords good protection.

- *In-painting.* In-painting is the most expensive, extreme and controversial restoration measure. In-painting, generally done with water colors, can range from simply "touching up" fold-wear damage to *actually painting in missing parts of an image* (hence the name). Collectors tend to be a lot more comfortable with the former than the latter, which requires a skilled and experienced hand. Colors and imagery must *precisely* match the missing portions, or the results will look worse than no repair at all. Extensive in-painting is most common for exceptionally old and rare posters, such as those from the silent era; very few posters from the 1950s merit this expensive and problematic procedure.

Poster storage

As with any other rare paper collectibles, your posters' primary enemies are light, heat, humidity, and rough handling. Naturally, the amount of protection you'll provide for each piece depends on how much you value it. Ideally, you'd like to see them all sealed in bulletproof, nitrogen-flooded cases, like the Magna Carta, but the national-deficit-sized prices charged at the neighborhood frame shops force most of us to be more judicious.

First a few very important don'ts.

Don't store posters folded. Even though most posters were folded during their original usage, there's no reason for you to compound the damage and wear caused by repeated folding and unfolding. Folded posters usually can be flattened nicely for display simply by placing them between sheets of a low-acid foam board and pressing the resulting stack with books or other weights for a week or so.

Don't store your posters between sheets of brown cardboard, at least not for very long. Acid damage—the browning and fading caused by acid migration from cardboard, newsprint, or other paper products with a high wood-pulp content—can take months or years to become apparent, but I've seen the results and it's not pretty.

Finally, *don't* dry-mount or laminate your posters, no matter how nice you think the results will be. Both of these processes are irreversible and will inevitably destroy your posters. Furthermore, most experienced collectors know this, and you will find that laminated and dry-mounted pieces command little value in the collectors' market.

At minimum, *do* keep your posters out of direct sunlight and away from moisture, either stored flat or in a large, sturdy packing tube. If you choose flat storage, you should stack the posters between sheets of some protective material; regular cardboard is obviously out of the question. Acid migration is considerably less serious from coated stocks and mat boards, but I wouldn't advise long-term storage in anything other than acid-free board. Standard foam boards are around 95 percent acid-free and reasonably inexpensive.

Plastic storage tubes are available at the better stocked blueprint and art-supply stores. If you use a cardboard tube, be sure to wrap a sheet of mylar around your posters to provide an acid stop before placing them in the tube. Mylar is available by the roll from blueprint as well as plastics companies. This wonderful stuff, which is available under various trade names, is tough, clear and, most importantly, *inert*. By inert, I mean that mylar does not break down over time in a way that can damage delicate paper. Vinyls and polypropylene—the substance used to make most inexpensive comics and movie poster bags—contain nasty by-products of the plastics-making process called *volatile plasticizers*. These substances degrade over time (and more quickly if exposed to sunlight), yellowing the plastic and eventually damaging whatever is stored within.

Display

If you wish to display your posters—and one assumes that, if you like these things, you will want to do so—framing is the most durable and protective method. It also can be pricey, as per my wisecrack above. You can reduce your costs by using the frame kits sold by art-supplies stores and various mail-order companies, and purchasing your own foam-board backing and glass separately.

Matting your pieces is expensive but provides additional protection, and is particularly important in humid climates. In damp environments, water vapor tends to become trapped between the glass and the artwork; without the air space provided by a mat, mildew can form on your posters, permanently staining them. Naturally, mats and any tape used in framing should be acid-free.

For one-sheets and larger posters, Plexiglas is preferable to regular glass because it is lighter and nearly unbreakable, although care must be taken not to scratch its surface. (You'll find that Plexiglas is considerably cheaper at glass and plastics companies than at frame shops.) Avoid hanging posters in areas exposed to direct sunlight. For your most valuable posters, you may wish to consider using "UV" Plexiglas, which is treated to block harmful ultraviolet radiation from sunlight and fluorescent lamps; it's about twice as expensive as regular Plexiglas.

Even with penny-pinching, it's nearly impossible to frame a one-sheet for less than $60 or so. If you can tolerate a less formal presentation, you might consider a low-cost method that provides acceptable protection and looks pretty decent on the wall: cut (or have cut) a piece of foam board to a size about two inches larger all the way around your poster; mount your poster on the board with a hinge of acid-free tape, and wrap poster and board in clear mylar, securing it at the back of the foam board with any strong tape (I find that strapping tape works well). This "wrapping" method also provides excellent protection for long-term storage.

Selected Filmography

Key to abbreviations: P = producer; D = director; S = screenplay; FX = special effects.
(Titles in **bold** indicate movies of above-average interest or merit not discussed in *Yesterday's Tomorrows*.)

➤ 1950

Destination Moon
P: George Pal.
D: Irving Pichel.
S: Robert A. Heinlein, Alford "Rip" van Ronkel and James O'Hanlon.
Production designer: Ernest Fegté.
FX supervisor: Lee Zavitz.
Animation director: John S. Abbott.
Astronomical art: Chesley Bonestell.
Starring John Archer (Jim Barnes), Warner Anderson (Dr. Charles Cargraves), Tom Powers (Gen. Thayer) and Dick Wesson (Joe Sweeney).

Rocketship X-M
P, D, S: Kurt Neumann.
FX: Jack Rabin and Irving Block.
Starring Lloyd Bridges (Floyd Graham), Osa Massen (Lisa Van Horne), John Emery (Dr. Karl Ekstrom), Noah Beery, Jr. (Bill Corrigan), Hugh O'Brian (Harry Chamberlain) and Morris Ankrum (Dr. Robert Fleming).

➤ 1951

The Day the Earth Stood Still
P: Julian Blaustein.
D: Robert Wise.
S: Edmund H. North.
FX: Fred Sersen, L.B. Abbott and Jimmy Gordon.
Matte and other effects: Ray Kellog and Emil Kosa.
Starring Michael Rennie (Klaatu), Patricia Neal (Helen Benson), Hugh Marlowe (Tom Stevens), Billy Gray (Bobby Benson) and Sam Jaffe (Dr. Barnhardt).

Flight to Mars
P: Walter Mirisch.
D: Lesley Selander.
S: Arthur Strawn.
FX: Irving Block and Jack Rabin (but credited to Jack Cosgrove).
Starring Cameron Mitchell (Steve Abbott), Marguerite Chapman (Alita), Arthur Franz (Dr. Jim Barker), Virginia Huston (Carol Stafford), John Litel (Dr. Lane) and Morris Ankrum (Ikron).

The Man From Planet X
P, S: Aubrey Wisberg and Jack Pollexfen.
D, production design: Edgar G. Ulmer.
FX: Andy Anderson and Howard Weeks.
Optical effects: Jack Rabin.
Starring Robert Clarke (John Lawrence), Margaret Field (Enid Elliot), Raymond Bond (Prof. Elliot) and William Schallert (Dr. Mears).

The Thing From Another World
P: Howard Hawks.
D: Christian Nyby.
Alleged "real" director: Howard Hawks.
S: Charles Lederer.
FX: Linwood Dunn.
Starring Kenneth Tobey (Capt. Patrick Hendry), Margaret Sheridan (Nikki Nicholson), Douglas Spencer (Ned "Scotty" Scott), Robert Cornthwaite (Prof. Carrington), Dewey Martin (Bob) and James Arness (the Thing).

When Worlds Collide
P: George Pal.
D: Rudolph Maté.
S: Sydney Boehm.
FX: Gordon Jennings and Harry Barndollar.
Technical advisor and production illustrator: Chesley Bonestell.
Starring Richard Derr (Dave Randall), Barbara Rush (Joyce Hendron), Larry Keating (Dr. Cole Hendron), Peter Hanson (Tony Drake) and John Hoyt (Sydney Stanton).

➤ 1952

Red Planet Mars
P: Anthony Veiller and Donald Hyde.
D: Harry Horner.
S: John L. Balderston and Anthony Veiller.
Starring Peter Graves (Chris Cronyn), Andrea King (Lynda Cronyn), Herbert Berghof (Franz Calder), Walter Sande (Admiral Carey) and Marvin Miller (Arjenian).

The Beast From 20,000 Fathoms
P: Jack Dietz.
D: Eugene Lourié.
S: Louis Morheim and Fred Freiberger.
FX: Ray Harryhausen.
Starring Paul Christian (Tom Nesbitt), Paula Raymond (Lee Hunter), Cecil Kellaway (Dr. Thurgood Elson) and Kenneth Tobey (Col. Jack Evans).

Cat-Women of the Moon
P, story, FX: Jack Rabin and Al Zimbalist.
D: Arthur Hilton.
S: Roy Hamilton.
Starring Sonny Tufts (Laird Grainger), Victor Jory (Kip Reisler), Marie Windsor (Helen Salinger), Carol Brewster (Alpha), Douglas Fowley (Walt Willis), Bill Phipps (Douglas Smith) and the ineffable "Hollywood Cover Girls" as the Cat-Women.

Invaders From Mars

P: Edward L. Alperson, Sr.
D, production design: William Cameron Menzies.
S: William Cameron Menzies, John Tucker Battle and Richard Blake.
FX: Jack Rabin and Irving Block.
Starring Jimmy Hunt (David Maclean), Arthur Franz (Dr. Stuart Kelston), Helena Carter (Dr. Pat Blake) Leif Erickson (George Maclean), Hillary Brooke (Mary Maclean) and Morris Ankrum (Col. Fielding).

It Came From Outer Space
P: William Alland.
D: Jack Arnold.
S: Ray Bradbury and Harry Essex.
FX: David Horsley.
Starring Richard Carlson (John Putnam), Barbara Rush (Ellen Fields), Charles Drake (Sheriff Matt Warren), Russell Johnson (George), Kathleen Hughes (Jane) and Joseph Sawyer (Frank Daylon).

Phantom From Space
P, D: W. Lee Wilder.
S: Bill Raynor and Myles Wilder.
FX: Alex Welden.
Photographic effects: Howard A. Anderson.
Starring Ted Cooper (Lt. Hazen), Rudolph Anders (Dr. Wyatt), Noreen Nash (Barbara Randall), Harry Landers (Lt. Bowers), James Seay (Maj. Andrews) and Dick Sands (the Phantom).

Project Moonbase
P: Jack Seaman.
D: Richard Talmadge.
S: Robert A. Heinlein and Jack Seaman.
FX: Jacques Fresco.
Starring Donna Martell (Col. Breiteis), Ross Ford (Maj. Moore), Larry Johns (Dr. Wernher) and Hayden Rorke (Gen. Greene).

Robot Monster
P, D: Phil Tucker.
S: Wyott Ordung.
FX (such as they are): Jack Rabin and David Commons.
Starring George Barrows (the "Ro-Man" and "the Great One"), Gregory Moffett (Johnny), George Nader (Roy), Claudia Barrett (Alice) and John Mylong (the Professor).

The War of the Worlds

P: George Pal.
D: Byron Haskin.
S: Barré Lyndon.
Special optical effects: Paul K. Lerpae, Aubrey Law and Jack Caldwell.
Mattes and production paintings: Chesley Bonestell, Jan Domela and Irmin Roberts.
Starring Gene Barry (Dr. Clayton Forrester), Ann Robinson (Sylvia Van Buren), Les Tremayne (Gen. Mann), Lewis Martin (Pastor Matthew Collins), Robert Cornthwaite (Dr. Pryor) and Sandro Giglio (Dr. Bilderbeck).

The Creature from the Black Lagoon
P: William Alland.
D: Jack Arnold.
S: Harry Essex and Arthur Ross.
Starring Richard Carlson (David Reed), Richard Denning (Mark Williams), Julia Adams (Kay Lawrence), Nestor Paiva (Lucas), Whit Bissell (Dr. Edwin Thompson), Ben Chapman (the Creature out of water) and Ricou Browning (the Creature in underwater scenes).

Target Earth
P: Herman Cohen.
D: Sherman A. Rose.
S: William Raynor.
FX: Dave Koehler.
Starring Richard Denning (Frank Brooks), Kathleen

Crowley (Nora King), Richard Reeves (Jim Wilson), Virginia Grey (Vicki Harris) and Robert Roark (Davis).

Them!
P: David Weisbart.
D: Gordon Douglas.
S: Ted Sherdeman.
Giant ants: Dick Smith.
Starring Edmund Gwenn (Dr. Harold Medford), James Whitmore (Sgt. Ben Peterson), James Arness (Robert Graham), Joan Weldon (Dr. Patricia Medford) and Onslow Stevens (Gen. O'Brien).

Tobor the Great
P: Richard Goldstone.
D: Lee Sholem.
S: Philip MacDonald.
FX: Howard and Theodore Lydecker.
Starring Billy Chapin ("Gadge" Robertson), Taylor Holmes (Dr. Nordstrom), Charles Drake (Dr. Ralph Harrison), Karin Booth (Janice Robertson) and Lew Smith (Tobor).

20,000 Leagues Under the Sea
P: Walt Disney.
D: Richard Fleischer.
S: Earl Felton.
FX: Ralph Hammeras.
Matte paintings: Peter Ellenshaw.
Starring James Mason (Capt. Nemo), Kirk Douglas (Ned Land), Peter Lorre (Conseil) and Paul Lukas (Prof. Pierre Arronax).

➤ 1955

The Conquest of Space
P: George Pal.
D: Byron Haskin.
S: George O'Hanlon.
FX: John P. Fulton, Irmin Roberts, Paul K. Lerpae, Ivyl Burks and Jan Domela.
Starring Walter Brooke (Col. Samuel T. Merritt), Eric Fleming (Capt. Barney Merritt), Mickey Shaughnessy (Sgt. Mahoney) and Phil Foster (the annoying Jackie Siegle).

Devil Girl From Mars
P: Edward J. Danziger and Harry Lee Danziger.
D: David MacDonald.
S: John C. Mather and James Eastwood.

FX: Jack Whitehead.
Starring Patricia Laffan (Nyah), Hugh McDermott (Michael Carter), Hazel Court (Ellen Prestwick) and Adrienne Corri (Doris).

It Came From Beneath the Sea
P: Charles H. Schneer.
D: Robert Gordon.
S: George Worthing Yates and Hal Smith.
FX: Ray Harryhausen.
Starring Kenneth Tobey (Pete Mathews), Faith Domergue (Lesley Joyce) and Donald Curtis (John Carter).

Revenge of the Creature
P, story: William Alland.
D: Jack Arnold.
S: Martin Berkeley.
Starring John Agar (Prof. Clete Ferguson), Lori Nelson (Helen Dobson), John Bromfield (Joe Hayes), Nestor Paiva (Lucas) and Ricou Browning (the Creature).

Tarantula
P: William Alland.
D: Jack Arnold.
S: Robert M. Fresco and Martin Berkeley.
FX: Clifford Stine and David S. Horsley.
Starring John Agar (Dr. Matt Hastings), Mara Corday ("Steve" Clayton), Leo G. Carroll (Prof. Gerald Deemer) and Nestor Paiva (Sheriff Jack Andrews).

This Island Earth
P: William Alland.
D: Joseph Newman (Jack Arnold is alleged to have directed the Metalunan sequences).
S: Franklin Coen and Edward G. O'Callaghan.
FX: Clifford Stine and David S. Horsley (and dozens more).
Starring Rex Reason (Cal Meacham), Jeff Morrow (Exeter), Faith Domergue (Ruth Adams), Lance Fuller (Brack), Russell Johnson (Steve Carlson) and Douglas Spencer (the Monitor).

➤ 1956

The Creature Walks Among Us
P: William Alland.
D: John Sherwood.
S: Arthur Ross.
Starring Jeff Morrow (Dr. William Barton), Rex

Reason (Dr. Thomas Morgan), Leigh Snowden (Marcia Barton), Ricou Browning (the Creature before transformation) and Don Megowan (the Creature after transformation).

Day the World Ended
P, D: Roger Corman.
S: Lou Rusoff.
Monster design: Paul Blaisdell.
Starring Richard Denning (Rick), Lori Nelson (Louise Maddison), Paul Birch (Maddision), Adele Jergens (Ruby), Touch (later Mike) Conners (Tony), Paul Dubov (Radek) and Paul Blaisdell (the Mutant).

Earth Versus the Flying Saucers
P: Charles H. Schneer.
D: Fred F. Sears.
S: George Worthing Yates and Bernard Gordon.
FX: Ray Harryhausen.
Starring Hugh Marlowe (Dr. Russell Marvin), Joan Taylor (Carol Hanley Marvin), Donald Curtis (Maj. Huglin) and Morris Ankrum (Gen. John Hanley).

Fire Maidens of Outer Space
P: George Fowler.
D, S: Cy Roth.
Starring Anthony Dexter (Luther Blair), Susan Shaw (Hestia), Owen Berry (Prasus) and Harry Fowler (Sydney Stanhope).

Forbidden Planet
P: Nicholas Nayfack.
D: Fred McLeod Wilcox.
S: Cyril Hume.
FX: A. Arnold Gillespie, Glen Robinson, A.D. Flowers and many more.
Starring Walter Pidgeon (Dr. Edward Morbius), Leslie Nielsen (Commander John J. Adams), Anne Francis (Altaira Morbius), Warren Stevens (Lt. "Doc" Ostrow), Jack Kelly (Lt. Jerry Farman), Richard Anderson (Chief Quinn), Earl Holliman (Cookie) and Robbie the Robot.

Godzilla, King of the Monsters
P: Tomoyuki Tanaka.
D: Inoshiro Honda (American footage by Terry Morse).
S: Takeo Murata and Inoshiro Honda.
FX: Eiji Tsuburaya *et al.*
Starring Raymond Burr (Steve Martin—American release only), Takashi Shimura (Dr. Yamano),

Momoko Kochi (Emiko), Akira Takarada (Ogata) and Haru Nakajima (Godzilla).

Invasion of the Body Snatchers
P: Walter Wanger.
D: Don Siegel.
S: Daniel Mainwaring and Sam Peckinpah (rewrites).
FX: Milt Rice.
Starring Kevin McCarthy (Dr. Miles Bennell), Dana Wynter (Becky Driscoll), King Donovan (Jack Belicec) and Carolyn Jones (Teddy Belicec).

It Conquered the World
P,D,: Roger Corman.
S: Charles B. Griffith (Lou Rusoff received screen credit).
FX: Paul Blaisdell.
Starring Peter Graves (Dr. Paul Nelson), Lee Van Cleef (Dr. Tom Anderson), Beverly Garland (Claire Anderson), Sally Fraser (Joan Nelson), Russ Bender (Gen. Pattick), Jonathan Haze (Pvt. Manuel Ortiz), Dick Miller (Sgt. Neill) and Paul Blaisdell (the Venusian monster).

The Mole People
P: William Alland.
D: Virgil Vogel.
S: Lazlo Gorog.
Special photography: Clifford Stine.
Mole People design: Jack Kevan and Millicent Patrick.
Starring John Agar (Dr. Roger Bentley), Cynthia Patrick (Adad), Hugh Beaumont (Dr. Jud Bellamin), Alan Napier (Elinu), Nestor Paiva (Etienne Lafarge) and Arthur D. Gilmour (Sharu).

Phantom From 10,000 Leagues
P and editing: Jack and Dan Milner.
D: Dan Milner.
S: Lou Rusoff.
FX: Jack Milner.
Starring Kent Taylor (Dr. Ted Stevens/"Ted Baxter"), Cathy Downs (Lois King), Michael Whalen (Prof. King), Philip Pine (George Thomas), Vivi Janiss (Ethel Hall) and Rodney Bell (Bill S. Grant.)

The She-Creature
P: Alex Gordon.
D: Edward L. Cahn.
S: Lou Rusoff.
FX: Paul Blaisdell.
Starring Chester Morris (Carlo Lombardi), Marla

English (Andrea), Lance Fuller (Dr. Tom Erickson), Tom Conway (Timothy Chappel) and Ron Randell (Lt. James).

World Without End
P: Richard Heermance.
D, S: Edward Bernds.
Starring Hugh Marlowe (John Borden), Nancy Gates (Garnet), Nelson Leigh (Dr. Gailbraithe), Booth Colman (Mories), Rod Taylor (Herbert Ellis) and Christopher Dark (Henry Jaffe).

➤ 1957

The Amazing Colossal Man
P, D, FX: Bert I. Gordon.
S: Mark Hanna and Bert I. Gordon.
Starring Glenn Langan (Col. Glenn Manning), Cathy Downs (Carol Forrest) and William Hudson (Dr. Paul Lindstrom).

Attack of the Crab Monsters
P, D: Roger Corman.
S: Charles B. Griffith.
Starring Richard Garland (Dale Drewer), Pamela Duncan (Martha Hunter), Russell Johnson (Hank Chapman), Leslie Bradley (Dr. Karl Weigand) and Mel Welles (Jules Deveroux).

Beginning of the End
P, D, FX: Bert I. Gordon.
S: Fred Freiberger and Lester Gorn.
Starring Peter Graves (Ed Wainwright), Peggie Castle (Audrey Aimes) and Morris Ankrum (Gen. Arthur Hanson).

The Black Scorpion
P: Frank Melford and Jack Dietz.
D: Edward Ludwig.
S: David Duncan and Robert Blees.
FX: Willis O'Brien and Pete Peterson.
Starring Richard Denning (Hank Scott), Mara Corday (Teresa), Carlos Rivas (Artur Ramos) and Mario Navarro (Juanito).

The Deadly Mantis
P: William Alland.
D: Nathan Juran.
S: Martin Berkeley.
Starring Craig Stevens (Col. Joe Parkman), William Hopper (Dr. Ned Jackson) and Alix Talton (Marge Blaine).

The Giant Claw
P: Sam Katzman.
D: Fred F. Sears.
S: Samuel Newman and Paul Gangelin.
Starring Jeff Morrow (Mitch MacAfee), Mara Corday (Sally Caldwell) and Morris Ankrum (Lt. Gen. Edward Lewis).

The Incredible Shrinking Man
P: Albert Zugsmith.
D: Jack Arnold.
S: Richard Matheson and Richard Alan Simmons.
Special photography: Clifford Stine and Tom McCrory.
Starring Grant Williams (Scott Carey), Randy Stuart (Louise Carey), Paul Langton (Charlie Carey), April Kent (Clarice), Raymond Bailey (Dr. Thomas Silver) and William Schallert (Dr. Arthur Bramson).

Invasion of the Saucer-Men
P: James H. Nicholson and Robert J. Gurney, Jr.
D: Edward L. Cahn.
S: Robert J. Gurney, Jr. and Al Martin.
FX: Howard A. Anderson and Alex Weldon.
Saucer-men and props: Paul Blaisdell.
Starring Steve Terrell (Johnny), Gloria Castillo (Joan), Lyn Osborn (Art) and Frank Gorshin (Joe).

The Invisible Boy
P: Nicholas Nayfack.
D: Herman Hoffman.
S: Cyril Hume.
FX: Jack Rabin, Irving Block and Louis DeWitt.
Starring Richard Eyer (Timmie Merrinoe), Philip Abbot (Dr. Merrinoe), Diane Brewster (Mary Merrinoe), Harold Stone (Gen. Swayne), Dennis McCarthy (Col. Macklin) and Robby the Robot.

I Was A Teenage Frankenstein
P: Herman Cohen.
D: Herbert L. Strock.
S: Aben Kandel (billed as "Kenneth Langtry").
Starring Whit Bissell (Professor Frankenstein), Gary Conway (the monster), Phyllis Coates (Margaret), Robert Burton (Dr. Carlton).

I Was a Teenage Werewolf
P: Herman Cohen.
D: Gene Fowler, Jr.
S: Aben Kandel (writing as "Ralph Thornton").
Starring Michael Landon (Tony Rivers), Yvonne Lime (Arlene) and Whit Bissell (Dr. Alfred Brandon).

Kronos
P, D: Kurt Neumann.
S: Lawrence Louis Goldman.
FX: Jack Rabin, Irving Block and Gene Warren.
Starring Jeff Morrow (Dr. Leslie Gaskell), Barbara Lawrence (Vera Hunter), John Emery (Dr. Hubbell Eliot) and George O'Hanlon (Dr. Arnold Culver).

The Land Unknown
P: William Alland.
D: Virgil Vogel.
S: Laslo Gorog.
FX: Clifford Stine, Fred Knoth, Orien Ernest, Jack Kevan and Roswell A. Hoffman.
Starring Jock Mahoney (Cmdr. Hal Roberts), Shawn Smith (Maggie Hathaway), Henry Brandon (Dr. Charles Hunter) and William Reynolds (Lt. Jack Carmen).

The Monolith Monsters
P: Howard Christie.
D: John Sherwood.
S: Norman Jolley and Robert M. Fresco.
FX: Clifford Stine.
Starring Grant Williams (Dave Miller), Lola Albright (Cathy Barrett), Les Tremayne (Martin Cochrane), Trevor Bardette (Prof. Arthur Flanders) and Linda Shelley (Ginny Simpson).

The Monster That Challenged the World
P: Jules V. Levy and Arthur Gardner.
D: Arnold Laven.
S: Patricia Fielder.
FX: Augie Lohman.
Starring Tim Holt (Lt. Cmdr. John Twillinger), Audrey Dalton (Gail MacKenzie) and Hans Conried (Jess Rogers).

The Night the World Exploded
P: Sam Katzman.
D: Fred F. Sears.
S: Jack Natteford and Luci Ward.
Starring Kathryn Grant (Laura Hutchinson), William Leslie (Dr. David Conway) and Tris Coffin (Dr. Ellis Morton).

Not of This Earth
P, D: Roger Corman.
S: Charles B. Griffith and Mark Hanna.
FX: Paul Blaisdell.
Starring Paul Birch (Paul Johnson), Beverly Garland (Nadine Storey), Morgan Jones (Harry Sherbourne), William Roerick (Dr. Frederick Rochelle), Jonathan Haze (Jeremy Perrin) and Dick Miller (Joe Piper, vacuum-cleaner salesman).

20 Million Miles to Earth
P: Charles H. Schneer.
D: Nathan Juran.
S: Bob Williams and Christopher Knopf.
FX: Ray Harryhausen.
Starring William Hopper (Col. Calder), Joan Taylor (Marisa), Frank Puglia (Dr. Leonardo), John Zaremba (Dr. Judson Uhl), Thomas Browne Henry (Gen. MacIntosh) and Bart Bradley (Pepe).

➤ 1958

The Astounding She Monster
P, D: Ronnie Ashcroft.
S: Frank Hall and (unbilled) Ronnie Ashcroft.
Starring Robert Clarke (Dick Cutler), Kenne Duncan (Nat Burdell), Marilyn Harvey (Margaret Chaffee), Jeanne Tatum (Esther Malone), Ewing Brown (Brad Conley) and Shirley Kilpatrick (the Alien).

Attack of the 50 Foot Woman
P: Bernard Woolner.
D: Nathan Juran (billed as "Nathan Hertz").
S: Mark Hanna.
Starring Allison Hayes (Nancy Fowler Archer), William Hudson (Harry Archer), Yvette Vickers (Honey Parker) and Ken Terrell (Jess Stout).

The Blob
P: Jack Harris.
D: Irvin S. Yeaworth, Jr.
S: Theodore Simonson and Kate Phillips.
FX: Barton Sloane.
Starring Steve McQueen (Steve Andrews), Aneta Corseaut (Jane Martin) and Earl Rowe (Dave).

The Brain Eaters
P: Edwin Nelson.
D: Bruno Ve Sota.
S: Gordon Urquhart.
Starring Edwin Nelson (Dr. Paul Kettering), Alan Frost (Glenn), Jack Hill (Sen. Walter K. Powers), Joanna Lee (Alice Summers) and Jody Fair (Elaine).

The Brain From Planet Arous
P, photography: Jacques Marquette.
D: Nathan Juran (billed as "Nathan Hertz").
S: Ray Buffum.
Starring John Agar (Steve March), Joyce Meadows (Sally Fallon), Thomas Browne Henry (John Fallon) and Robert Fuller (Dan). Brains voiced by Dale Tate.

The Colossus of New York
P: William Alland.
D: Eugene Lourié.
S: Thelma Schnee.
FX: John P. Fulton.
Staring John Baragrey (Dr. Henry Spensser), Otto Kruger (Dr. William Spensser), Charles Herbert (Billy Spensser), Mala Powers (Anne Spensser), Ross Martin (Dr. Jeremy Spensser) and Ed Wolff (the Colossus).

The Crawling Eye
P: Robert S. Baker and Monty Berman.
D: Quentin Lawrence.
S: Jimmy Sangster.
FX: Les Bowie.
Starring Forest Tucker (Alan Brooks), Janet Munro (Anne Pilgrim), Jennifer Jayne (Sarah Pilgrim), Laurence Payne (Philip Truscott) and Warren Mitchell (Professor Crevett.)

Fiend Without a Face
P: John Croydon.
D: Arthur Crabtree.
S: Herbert J. Leder.
Animation effects: Florenz von Nordhoff and K.L. Ruppel.
Starring Marshall Thompson (Maj. Jeff Cummings), Kim Parker (Barbara Griselle) and Kynaston Reeves (Prof. Walgate).

The Fly
P, D: Kurt Neumann.
S: James Clavell (yes, *that* James Clavell).
FX: L.B. Abbott.
Makeup: Dick Smith and Ben Nye.
Starring Al (David) Hedison (André Delambre), Patricia Owens (Hélène Delambre) and Vincent Price (François Delambre).

I Married a Monster From Outer Space
P, D: Gene Fowler, Jr.
S: Louis Vittes.
FX: John P. Fulton.

Starring Gloria Talbott (Marge Farrell), Tom Tryon (Bill Farrell), Chuck Wassill (Ted), Maxie Rosenbloom (Grady) and Ken Lynch (Dr. Wayne).

It! The Terror From Beyond Space
P: Robert E. Kent.
D: Edward L. Cahn.
S: Jerome Bixby.
Monster suit: Paul Blaisdell.
Starring Marshall Thompson (Col. Ed Carruthers), Shawn Smith (Ann Anderson), Kim Spalding (Col. James Van Heusen) and Ray "Crash" Corrigan (the Martian).

Monster on the Campus
P: Joseph Gershenson.
D: Jack Arnold.
S: David Duncan.
FX: Clifford Stine.
Starring Arthur Franz (Dr. Donald Blake), Joanna Moore (Madeline Howard) and Judson Pratt (Lt. Mike Stevens).

Queen of Outer Space
P: Ben Schwalb.
D: Edward Bernds.
S: Charles Beaumont (story by Ben Hecht).
Starring Zsa Zsa Gabor (Talleah), Eric Fleming (Capt. Neil Patterson), Laurie Mitchell (Queen Yllana) and Paul Birch (Professor Konrad).

Satan's Satellites
P: Franklin Adreon.
D: Fred C. Brannon.
S: Ronald Davidson.
FX: Howard and Theodore Lydecker.
Starring Judd Holdren (Larry Martin), Wilson Wood (Bob Wilson), Aline Towne (Sue Davis) and Lane Bradford (Marex).

The Space Children
P: William Alland.
D: Jack Arnold.
S: Bernard C. Schoenfeld.
FX: John P. Fulton.
Starring Adam Williams (Dave Brewster), Peggy Webber (Anne Brewster), Johnny Crawford (Ken Brewster), Michel Ray (Bud Brewster), Sandy Descher (Eadie Johnson), Jackie Coogan (Hank Johnson) and Russell Johnson (Joe Gamble).

Terror from the Year 5000
P, D, S: Robert L. Gurney, Jr.
Starring Ward Costello (Robert Hedges), Joyce Holden (Claire Erling), John Stratton (Victor), Frederic Downs (Professor Howard Erling) and Salome Jens (nurse/Future Woman).

War of the Colossal Beast
P, D, FX: Bert I. Gordon.
S: George Worthing Yates.
Starring Dean Parkin (Glenn Manning), Sally Fraser (Joyce Manning) and Roger Pace (Maj. Baird).

➤ 1959

The Cosmic Man
P: Robert A. Terry.
D: Herbert Greene.
S: Arthur C. Pierce.
FX: Charles Duncan.
Starring Bruce Bennett (Dr. Karl Sorenson), John Carradine (the Cosmic Man), Angela Greene (Kathy Grant), Paul Langton (Col. Mathews) and Scotty Morrow (Ken Grant).

4D Man
P: Jack Harris and Irwin S. Yeaworth, Jr.
D: Irwin S. Yeaworth, Jr.
S: Theodore Simonson and Cy Chermak.
FX: Barton Sloane.
Starring Robert Lansing (Scott Nelson), Lee Meriwether (Linda Davis), James Congdon (Tony Nelson), Robert Strauss (Roy Parker) and Edgar Stehli (Dr. Theodore W. Carson).

The Giant Behemoth
P: David Diamond.
D: Eugene Lourié.
S: Eugene Lourié and (unbilled) Daniel Hyatt.
FX: Jack Rabin, Irving Block and Louis DeWitt.
Stop-motion animation: Willis O'Brien and Pete Peterson.
Starring Gene Evans (Steven Karnes), André Morell (Prof. James Bickford) and Jack MacGowran (Dr. Sampson).

Journey to the Center of the Earth
P: Charles Brackett.
D: Henry Levin.
S: Walter Reisch and Charles Brackett.
FX: L.B. Abbott, James B. Gordon and Emil Kosa, Jr.

Starring James Mason (Prof. Oliver Lindenbrook), Pat Boone (Alec McEwen), Arlene Dahl (Carla Goetaborg), Thayer David (Count Saknussemm) and Peter Ronson (Hans Bjelker).

Plan 9 From Outer Space
P, D, S, editor: Edward D. Wood.
FX (ha!): Charles Duncan.
Starring Gregory Walcott (Jeff Trent) Mona McKinnon (Paula Trent), Dudley Manlove (Eros), Tor Johnson (Inspector Clay), Vampira (zombie woman) and Bela Lugosi (old man).

Teenagers From Outer Space
P, D, S, FX, virtually everything: Tom Graeff.
Starring Tom Graeff billed as "David Love" (Derek), Dawn Anderson (Betty Morgan), Harvey B. Dunn (Grandpa Morgan) and Bryan Grant (Thor).

The World the Flesh and the Devil
P: George Englund.
D, S: Ranald MacDougall.
Mattes: Lee LeBlanc and Matthew Yuricich.
Starring Harry Belafonte (Ralph Burton), Inger Stevens (Sarah Crandall) and Mel Ferrer (Benson Thacker).

➤ 1960

The Angry Red Planet
P: Sid Pink and Norman Maurer.
D: Ib Melchior.
S: Ib Melchior and Sid Pink.
FX: Herman Townsley, Herb Switzer, Howard Weeks and Jack Schwartz.
Starring Gerald Mohr (Col. Tom O'Bannion), Nora Hayden (Dr. Iris Ryan), Les Tremayne (Prof. Theodore Gettell) and Jack Kruschen (Sgt. Sam Jacobs).

The Atomic Submarine
P: Alex Gordon.
D: Spencer Gordon Bennet.
S: Orville H. Hampton.
FX: Jack Rabin, Irving Block and Louis DeWitt.
Starring Arthur Franz (Cmdr. Richard "Reef" Holloway), Brett Halsey (Carl Neilson), Dick Foran (Capt. Dan Wendover) and Tom Conway (Sir Ian Hunt).

Beyond the Time Barrier
P: Robert Clarke.
D: Edgar G. Ulmer.
S: Arthur C. Pierce.
FX: Roger George.
Photographic effects: Howard A. Anderson.
Production design: Ernst Fegté.
Starring Robert Clarke (Maj. Bill Allison), Darlene Tompkins (Trirene), Vladimir Sokoloff (the Supreme), Red Morgan (the Captain) and Arianne Arden (Markova).

The Time Machine
P, D: George Pal.
S: David Duncan.
FX: Project Unlimited (Wah Chang, Gene Warren and Tim Baar)
Stop-motion animation: David Pal and Don Sahlin.
Makeups: William Tuttle.
Starring Rod Taylor (George), Yvette Mimieux (Weena), Alan Young (David and James Filby) and Sebastian Cabot (Dr. Philip Hillyer).

12 to the Moon
P: Fred Gebhardt.
D: David Bradley.
S: DeWitt Bodeen.
FX: Howard A. Anderson.
Starring Ken Clark (Dr. John Anderson), Tom Conway (Feodor Orloff), Michi Kobi (Dr. Hideku Murata), Tony Dexter (Dr. Luis Vargas) and Richard Weber (Dr. David Ruskin).

Village of the Damned
P: Ronald Kinnoch.
D: Wolf Rilla.
S: Stirling Silliphant, Wolf Rilla and Ronald Kinnoch (billed as "George Barclay").
Starring George Sanders (Gordon Zellaby), Barbara Shelley (Anthea Zellaby), Martin Stephens (David Zellaby), Michael Gwynn (Alan Bernard) and Laurence Naismith (Mr. Willers).

The Wasp Woman
P, D: Roger Corman.
S: Leo Gordon.
Starring Susan Cabot (Janice Starlin), Fred Eisley (Bill Lane), Michael Mark (Eric Zinthrop) and Barboura Morris (Mary Dennison).

➤ 1961

Atlantis, the Lost Continent
P, D: George Pal.
S: Daniel Mainwaring.
FX: A. Arnold Gillespie and Lee LeBlanc.
Optical effects: Robert R. Hoag.
Matte paintings: Lee LeBlanc and Matthew Yuricich.
Starring Anthony Hall (Demetrios), Joyce Taylor (Princess Antillia), John Dall (Zaren), Edward Platt (Azor), Edgar Stehli (King Kronas) and Wolfe Barzell (Petros).

Gorgo
P: Wilfred Eades.
D: Eugene Lourié.
S: John Loring and Daniel Hyatt.
FX: Tom Howard.
Starring Bill Travers (Joe Ryan), William Sylvester (Sam Slade), Vincent Winter (Sean) and Martin Benson (Dorkin).

Journey to the Seventh Planet
P, D: Sidney Pink.
S: Ib Melchior and Sidney Pink.
FX: Bent Barfod (Danish effects); Jim Danforth, Wah Chang and Project Unlimited (American effects).
Starring John Agar (Capt. Don Graham), Carl Ottosen (Cmdr. Eric Nilsson), Ann Smyrner (Ingrid), Mimi Heinrich (Ursula) and Greta "Three-eyed Sloth" Thyssen (Greta).

Konga
P: Herman Cohen.
D: John Lemont.
S: Aben Kandel and Herman Cohen.
Starring Michael Gough (Dr. Charles Decker), Margo Johns (Margaret), Claire Gordon (Sandra Banks), Jess Conrad (Bob Kenton) and Austin Trevor (Dean Foster).

Mysterious Island
P: Charles H. Schneer.
D: Cy Endfield.
S: John Prebble, Daniel Ullman and Crane Wilbur.
FX: Ray Harryhausen.
Starring Michael Craig (Capt. Cyrus Harding), Joan Greenwood (Lady Mary Fairchild), Gary Merrill (Gideon Spilett), Herbert Lom (Capt. Nemo), Michael Callan (Herbert Brown), Percy Herbert (Sgt. Pencroft), Beth Rogan (Elena) and Dan Jackson (Neb).

The Phantom Planet
P: Fred Gebhardt.
D: William Marshall.
S: William Telaak, Fred De Gorter and Fred
    Gebhardt.
Director of photographic effects: Louis DeWitt.
Starring Dean Fredericks (Capt. Frank Chapman),
    Dolores Faith (Zetha), Coleen Grey (Liara),
    Tony Dexter (Herron) and Francis X. Bushman
    (Sesom).

➤ 1962

The Day the Earth Caught Fire
P, D, story: Val Guest.
S: Wolf Mankowitz and Val Guest.
FX: Les Bowie and Brian Johncock.
Starring Edward Judd (Peter Stenning), Janet Munro
    (Jeannie Craig) and Leo McKern (Bill Maguire).

First Spaceship on Venus
P: Newton P. Jacobs, Paul Schreibman and Edmund
    Goldman (American version).
D: Kurt Maetzig.
S (European version): Jan Fethke, Wolfgang
    Kohlhaase, Guenter Reisch, Guenter Ruecker,
    Alexander Stenbock-Fermor, Kurt Maetzig and
    J. Barckhausen. (Whew!)
FX: Ernst and Vera Kunstmann, Jan Olejniczak and
    Helmut Grewald.
Special photographic effects: Martin Sonnabend.
Starring Guenther Simon (Robert Brinkman), Yoko
    Tani (Sumiko Ogimura), Oldrick Lukes
    (Haringway), Kurt Rackelmann (Professor
    Sikarna) and Michal Postnikow (Durand).

Panic in Year Zero!
P: Arnold Houghland and Lou Rusoff.
D: Ray Milland.
S: Jay Simms and John Morton.
Starring Ray Milland (Harry Baldwin), Jean Hagan
    (Ann Baldwin), Frankie Avalon (Rick Baldwin)
    and Mary Mitchell (Karen Baldwin).

Reptilicus
P, D: Sidney Pink.
S: Sidney Pink and Ib Melchior.
Starring Carl Ottosen (Gen. Mark Grayson), Ann
    Smyrner (Lise Martens), Mimi Heinrich (Karen
    Martens) and Asbjorn Andersen (Prof. Otto
    Martens).

➤ 1963

X—the Man with the X-Ray Eyes
P, D: Roger Corman.
S: Ray Russell and Robert Dillon.
Staring Ray Milland (Dr. James Xavier), Diana Van
    Der Vlis (Dr. Diane Fairfax), Harold J. Stone (Dr.
    Sam Brant), John Hoyt (Dr. Willard Benson) and
    Don Rickles (Crane).

➤ 1964

Atragon (Kaitei Gunkan)
P: Yuko Tanaka.
D: Inoshiro Honda.
S: Shinichi Sekizawa.
FX: Eiji Tsuburaya.
Starring Yu Fukiji (Captain Shinguji) and Yoko
    Fujiyama (Shinguji's daughter).

First Men in the Moon
P: Charles H. Schneer.
D: Nathan Juran.
S: Nigel Kneale and Jan Read.
FX: Ray Harryhausen.
Starring Edward Judd (Arnold Bedford), Lionel
    Jeffries (Cavor) and Martha Hyer (Kate).

The Time Travellers
P: William Redlin.
D: Ib Melchior.
S: Ib Melchior.
FX: David Hewitt.
Starring Preston Foster (Dr. Erik von Steiner), Philip
    Carey (Steve Conners), Merry Anders (Carol
    White) and Stephen Franken (Danny McKee).

The Top Titles

This is an informed but opinionated list of the most desirable 1950s science fiction movie posters, with estimated value ranges as of September 1992. I fully respect your right to disagree violently. The market is accelerating quickly at present, and in time the values quoted here will probably be too low. However, the *relative* values among these titles generally should hold true regardless of how the market fluctuates.

Estimated values are quoted as fairly broad ranges because this reflects the reality of the market. The poster market is red-hot but anarchic. Prices don't march in lockstep to a single price guide, as do comics.

If you collect for any length of time, you learn that the price of any desirable item usually falls into one of several categories, which we might call the Steal price, the Fair price, the High-Fair price, and Too Much. Consider the ranges given here as straddling the first three categories; it's up to you to decide whether you're getting a good deal or not.

The value range quoted for each title, unless otherwise noted, is for a *one-sheet in fine condition* as described elsewhere in this book. As I've already hinted, my personal opinion is that one-sheets are only rarely the best posters available on 1950s science fiction titles. Furthermore, three- and six-sheets have become significantly more popular in the last few years, and now usually sell for more than one-sheets. Nonetheless, probably because it's the "standard" poster most of us remember from the theaters of our youth, the one-sheet remains the most popular poster size among collectors and serves as a useful benchmark.

With some specific exceptions noted below, other poster sizes can be valued roughly as follows:

Three-sheets and six-sheets:	120-200 percent of the one-sheet value
Inserts and half-sheets:	50-80 percent
Window cards:	30-40 percent
Title cards:	15-50 percent
Lobby scene cards:	10-40 percent

A note on condition: as I've indicated, overgrading is all too common in the poster field. Even so, as a general rule, I've found that condition is not quite as big a factor in pricing movie posters as with other collectibles, such as comics and ball cards. (In those fields, prices fall off sharply if the piece in question is not in fine or better condition.) I suspect that the poster market's greater tolerance for poorer condition is due both to the fact that posters in fine or better condition are truly rare, and that collectors have become increasingly aware that competent paper restoration can fix many problems. For this reason, many collectors don't consider minor stains and tears to be fatal flaws.

As a general rule of thumb, posters in very good condition might take 80 percent of the prices listed below; in good condition, 50 percent. In any lesser condition, the value is residual—perhaps 10 to 20 percent of the prices listed, unless the piece is a particularly rare title.

Forbidden Planet	$3,000-$5,000
The Creature from the Black Lagoon	$3,500-$5,000
The Day the Earth Stood Still	$3,000-$4,500
The Man From Planet X	$1,750-$2,500
Invasion of the Saucer-Men	$1,750-$2,500
Attack of the 50 Foot Woman	$1,500-$2,000
Invaders From Mars	$1,000-$1,500

(Note: This was a 1953 film, but a number of one-sheets exist that feature a 1955 date in one corner in addition to the 1953 date. No one seems to know whether these are original, misprinted one-sheets or an obscure re-issue struck from the original plate. In any case, one recently took about $1,000 in a Christie's auction.)

Tobor the Great	$800-$1,200
War of the Worlds	$800-$1,200
The Beast From 20,000 Fathoms	$800-$1,200
This Island Earth	$750-$1,200
Revenge of the Creature	$800-$1,000
When Worlds Collide	$750-$1,000
Robot Monster	$700-$1,000
Plan 9 From Outer Space	$700-$1,000

(Note: Prices for *Plan 9* and *Robot Monster* reflect their status as the two most celebrated awful science fiction movies ever made. By any objective standard, the artwork on these posters is amateurish and unexceptional, but There It Is. *Plan 9* material in particular is extremely rare and the price range quoted here may well be too low.)

Godzilla	$600-$1,000
Devil Girl From Mars	$600-$850

(Note: The British version of this one-sheet fetches up to $800 to $1,000, although personally I prefer the American version.)

The Wasp Woman	$600-$800
Tarantula	$500-$800
It Came From Outer Space	$400-$800
The Astounding She Monster	$400-$800
Attack of the Crab Monsters	$600-$750
The Thing From Another World	$600-$750

(Note: Many collectors prefer the *Thing* insert and half-sheet, which feature photos of the cast, to the one-sheet, which is rather plain. For this reason, the smaller pieces fetch about the same price as the one-sheet. All posters feature the same organic-looking lettering.)

Destination Moon	$500-$750
Them!	$400-$600

(A high-end sleeper; probably undervalued at this price.)

Queen of Outer Space	$400-$600
Invasion of the Body Snatchers	$400-$600
Cat-Women of the Moon	$400-$600
Earth Versus the Flying Saucers	$400-$600
It Came From Beneath the Sea	$400-$600
Not of This Earth	$400-$600
The Mole People	$350-$450
The Incredible Shrinking Man	$300-$400
Target Earth	$300-$400
Flight to Mars	$250-$400
It! The Terror From Beyond Space	$250-$350

Three Oddities

The B-style half-sheet from *War of the Worlds* is infinitely superior to any other piece from the film; it portrays the movie's "Martian war machines" laying waste to Los Angeles, while the other posters feature a dull painting of a menacing Martian hand. Popular legend has it that these posters were never released to theaters, but I'm reliably informed that this isn't the case. Still, the B-style half-sheet is extraordinarily rare, and easily sells for $4,000 to $6,000 in fine condition.

A similar situation exists with *Invasion of the Body Snatchers*. The superior B-style half-sheet, popularly called the "spotlight dance" (it shows the film's principals illuminated in sinister beams of light from the sky) typically sells for $800 to $1,000, substantially more than the one-sheet commands.

Last, and possibly rarest. Most posters from Ray Harryhausen's fine 1957 monster movie, *20 Million Miles to Earth*, feature some of the dullest artwork to appear on any SF poster of the era (basically, uninspired paintings of the monster's leg and back). However, an *extremely* rare alternate one-sheet was printed featuring a photo of the movie's monster fighting an elephant—the film's most famous sequence. This American-printed poster was used overseas and not, so far as I have been able to determine, in the U.S. It doesn't appear in the movie's pressbook, but a source that I trust has seen it. Due to the movie's popularity and the rarity of this item, it could be expected to sell for at least $1000 to $1,500.

Collectors' Resources

Publications

Movie Collector's World
P.O. Box 309
Fraser, Michigan 48026

The Big Reel
3130 U.S. 220
Madison, North Carolina 27025

Movie Poster Shops and Dealers

Cinemonde
1932 Polk Street
San Francisco, California 94109
(415) 776-9988 or 776-5270

Colony
1619 Broadway
New York, New York 10019
(212) 265-2050 or 265-1260

Gone Hollywood
172 Bella Vista Avenue
Belvedere Island, California 94920
(415) 435-1939

Hollywood Movie Posters
900 East Karen Avenue, Suite 215B
Las Vegas, Nevada 89109
(702) 735-8170

The Last Moving Picture Company
6307 Hollywood Boulevard
Hollywood, California 90028
(213) 467-0838

Motion Picture Arts Gallery
133 East 58th Street, 10th floor
New York, New York 10022
(212) 223-1009

The Paper Chase
4073 LaVista Road, Suite 363
Tucker, Georgia 30084
(800) 433-0025

Movie Poster Auctions

Camden House Auctioneers, Inc.
427 Cañon Drive
Beverly Hills, California 90210
(310) 246-1212

Christie's East
219 East 67th Street
New York, New York 10021
(212) 606-0400

Hollywood Poster Art
65 Hudson Street
Hackensack, New Jersey 07601
(201) 488-6333

Poster Mail Auction Co.
R. Neil Reynolds
P.O. Box 133
Waterford, Virginia 22190
(703) 882-3574

That's Entertainment, Inc.
222 Blue Hills Road
North Haven, Connecticut 06473
(203) 872-9207

Selected Bibliography

I would like acknowledge my indebtedness to and my *intense* admiration of Bill Warren's *Keep Watching the Skies!: American Science Fiction Movies of the Fifties* (Jefferson, North Carolina: McFarland and Company, Inc., 1982 and 1986). This two-volume, 1,300-page survey is simply the most detailed and entertaining survey of 1950s science fiction film ever written. Time and again I've had what I briefly fancied to be an original insight into SF film—only to find it ensconced somewhere in Warren's massive tome. When I think of the male-pattern baldness I've incurred in preparing *this* modest volume, I can only stand in complete awe of Warren's accomplishment.

Other Books on Science Fiction Film

Atkins, Thomas R., ed. *Science Fiction Films*. New York: Monarch Press, 1976.

Baxter, John. *Science Fiction in the Cinema*. New York: A.S. Barnes, 1970.

Biskind, Peter. *Seeing is Believing: How Hollywood Taught Us to Stop Worrying and Love the Fifties*. New York: Pantheon Books, 1983. (Chapters 3 and 4 concern SF film.)

Broderick, Mick. *Nuclear Movies*. Jefferson, North Carolina: McFarland and Company, Inc., 1991.

Brosnan, John. *Future Tense*. New York: St. Martin's Press, 1978.

Brosnan, John. *The Primal Screen: A History of Science Fiction Film*. London: Orbit Books, 1991.

Frank, Allen. *The Science Fiction and Fantasy Film Handbook*. Totowa, New Jersey: Barnes and Noble Books, 1982.

Harryhausen, Ray. *Film Fantasy Scrapbook*, second edition, revised. Cranbury, New Jersey: A.S. Barnes and Co., Inc., 1974.

Hickman, Gail Morgan. *The Films of George Pal*. Cranbury, New Jersey: A.S. Barnes and Co., Inc., 1977.

Kinnard, Roy. *Beasts and Behemoths: Prehistoric Creatures in the Movies*. Metuchen, New Jersey: The Scarecrow Press, Inc., 1988.

Lentz, III, Harris M. *Science Fiction, Horror and Fantasy Film and Television Credits*. Jefferson, North Carolina: McFarland and Company, Inc., 1983.

Morris, Gary. *Roger Corman*. Boston: Twayne Publishing, 1985.

Naha, Ed. *The Films of Roger Corman: Brilliance on a Budget*. New York: Arco Publishing, Inc., 1982.

Parish, James Robert, and Michael R. Pitts. *The Great Science Fiction Pictures*. Metuchen, New Jersey: The Scarecrow Press, Inc., 1977.

Pink, Sidney. *So You Want to Make Movies: My Life as an Independent Film Producer*. Sarasota, Florida: Pineapple Press, Inc., 1989.

Pitts, Michael R. *Horror Film Stars*, Second Edition. Jefferson, North Carolina: McFarland and Company, Inc., 1991.

Reemes, Dana M. *Directed by Jack Arnold*. Jefferson, North Carolina: McFarland and Company, Inc., 1988.

Rovin, Jeff. *From the Land Beyond Beyond*. New York: Berkley Windhover Books, 1977.

Weaver, Tom. *Interviews with B Science Fiction and Horror Movie Makers*. Jefferson, North Carolina: McFarland and Company, Inc., 1988.

Weaver, Tom. *Science Fiction Stars and Horror Heroes*. Jefferson, North Carolina: McFarland and Company, Inc., 1991.

Periodicals

Castle of Frankenstein. North Bergen, New Jersey: Gothic Castle Publishing, 1962-1975.

Cinefantastique. Oak Park, Illinois: Frederick S. Clarke, 1970-present.

Filmfax. Evanston, Illinois: Michael Stein, 1986-present.

Starlog. New York: O'Quinn Studios, 1976-present.

Other works

Belfrage, Cedric. *The American Inquisition 1945-1960: A Profile of the "McCarthy Era."* Indianapolis, Indiana: Bobbs-Merrill, 1973.

Gunn, James. *Alternate Worlds: The Illustrated History of Science Fiction*. Englewood Cliffs, New Jersey: A and W Visual Library, 1975.

Hegenberger, John. *Collector's Guide to Treasures from the Silver Screen*. Radnor, Pennsylvania.: Wallace-Homestead, 1991.

Hine, Thomas. *Populuxe*. New York: Alfred A. Knopf, Inc., 1987. (A fine and highly recommended consumer's-eye-view of 1950s social history.)

Horsley, Edith. *The 1950s*. The Mallard Press, 1990.

Moskowitz, Sam. *Seekers of Tomorrow: Masters of Modern Science Fiction*. Westport, Connecticut: Hyperion Press, Inc., 1974.

Rebello, Stephen, and Richard Allen. *Reel Art: Great Posters From the Golden Age of the Silver Screen*. New York: Abbeville Press, 1988. (Rebello's 1988 *Cinefantastique* article, "Selling Nightmares: Movie Poster Artists of the 1950s," is still the best scholarly work concerning 1950s SF poster artists.)

Index